AIDS
Ministry in the Midst of an Epidemic

AIDS Ministry in the Midst of an Epidemic

Wendell W. Hoffman

and

Stanley J. Grenz

BAKER BOOK HOUSE
Grand Rapids, Michigan 49516

Library of Congress Cataloging-in-Publication Data

Hoffman, Wendell W.
AIDS ministry in the midst of an epidemic.

1. AIDS (Disease)—Patients—Pastoral counseling of. 2. church work with the sick. 3. AIDS (Disease)—Religious aspects—Christianity. I. Grenz, Stanley, 1950–
BV4460.7.H64 1990 261.8'321969792 89-32312
ISBN 0-8010-4346-8

Printed in the United States of America

To our parents, the late Rev. Richard and Clara Grenz and the Rev. Walter and Phyllis Hoffman, who taught us early in life that ministry begins with the loving acceptance of others, no matter who they are or what their background may be.

Contents

Foreword

We live in a crisis-ridden world. Adam, it has been ironically suggested, probably made some such doleful comment to Eve after they were expelled from Eden and after Cain, their older son, killed his brother Abel. Crisis has been woven into the fabric of humanity's saga from its very beginning. Violence, famine, drought, pestilence, and natural disasters have plagued mortals throughout the millennia of history. Despite the astonishing achievements of science and technology in recent centuries, our planet is still blighted by hunger, poverty, and disease, to say nothing of injustice, oppression, and ghastly events like the Holocaust. Even in the so-called advanced countries, agonizingly complex problems cry out for solution. And new problems continue to develop, including the all too prevalent use of drugs and the accompanying devastating ramifications, especially the problem of AIDS. What sociological seer could have predicted that such a deadly epidemic was going to emerge, a problem that medically and morally would prove a veritable Pandora's box?

What ought to be the Christian response to this devastating disease which will, unless checked by some therapeutic breakthrough, bring excruciating death to multitudes of people? Ignorance, panic, and misinformation compound the difficulty for churches and clergy, ethicists and theologians, to formulate an answer which is pastorally effective, ethically sound, and biblically oriented.

How grateful I am, therefore, that two eminently qualified evangelicals have given us this most helpful guidebook for a distinctively Christian response to the AIDS issue! Drs. Grenz and Hoffman, each from the perspective of his own specialization, have provided the expert, balanced, objective data and insights which we need to disseminate the truth about AIDS as well as to minister in the name of the compassionate Christ to individuals afflicted with this lethal sickness. I can only hope that this tract for the times will be widely read and its wise counsel followed.

Vernon Grounds
President Emeritus
Denver Conservative Baptist Seminary

Preface

"Doctor, do you believe in heaven and hell?" This question—posed in late 1984 by a person recently diagnosed with AIDS to me, his physician—forms the genesis of this book. I had completed my infectious disease training six months earlier, and was serving as a staff consultant in that subspecialty at a large clinic in the greater Boston area. The number of AIDS cases was rapidly rising nationwide, and Massachusetts was certainly no exception.

This particular patient was homosexual in orientation and had sought advice out of his fear of being at risk for AIDS. His worst expectation was realized when he was told that his blood test was positive for the virus that causes AIDS—HIV. Shortly thereafter he developed purple spots on his face and neck, the most conspicuous of which occurred on the tip of his nose. A skin biopsy of one of these spots revealed the cancer known as Kaposi's sarcoma. This placed him in the AIDS category.

At first, the patient's spiritually oriented question regarding heaven and hell took me by surprise. But I soon realized that it arose out of a deep searching that had been prompted by the prospects of a "premature" death. In the past the man had had little connection with church or religion. In fact, he had recently engaged in a long conversation with his father in which they discussed why God had never seemed to play much of a role in their family life.

Through this and many subsequent similar experiences with other AIDS patients, their family members, and their friends, I developed an increasing burden to know how individual Christians and the church as a whole could engage in ministry in the midst of this epidemic. As the ideas for a book on the subject began to take shape, I turned to my friend and colleague, Stan Grenz, for the development of the theological issues raised by the AIDS epidemic.

Our conviction is that practical forms of ministry to AIDS patients must arise out of a theoretical basis and a motivation to become involved that is both theologically sound and medically informed. This book seeks to provide reasons for the church to intervene in the lives of persons affected by AIDS. When seen together, the dual factors ought to give rise to a loving, compassionate response by God's people.

The medical information presented herein comes from an extensive review of the literature, with primary citations indicated wherever possible. We have attempted to include the most important facts concerning AIDS to date, emphasizing a balanced interpretation of their significance. A major frustration lies in the fact that information regarding HIV and AIDS is appearing in rapid-fire order. This explosion quickly dates any book dealing with the subject. Nonetheless, the core concepts regarding the disease presented in these pages should provide the reader with a basis for incorporating and interpreting new information as it becomes available.

We are grateful to Baker Book House for its willingness to enter into this publication venture with an unknown infectious-disease physician and a young theological educator from the Midwest. We are indebted to Jackie Frier, Cindy Hewitt, Donna Fodness and Joy Huisman for the many hours of manuscript preparation. Thanks also to Jane Chu Thompson for her skillful contribution in providing the drawings that make up appendixes A-F.

Lastly, without the loving encouragement and patience of our wives and life partners, Holly Hoffman and Edna Grenz, this book would never have become a reality.

Wendell W. Hoffman, M.D.

Introduction

Identifying the Barriers to an AIDS Ministry

In August 1348, Italian trading ships from the East brought to the shores of Europe an ill-fated import—flea-infested rats, carrying what came to be known as the Black Death. During the next two years, as many as one-third of the population of Europe died from either bubonic or pneumonic plague. Most severely struck were the weakest age groups: young children and the aged. Rather than being a one-time occurrence, the plague returned repeatedly during the subsequent decades, eventually reducing the population by as much as 50 percent.[1]

The general response to this epidemic was less than adequate. There were those individuals, of course, who sought to minister to its victims, often at great personal risk. Yet, so widespread was the fear of this disease that one chronicler suggested that the dead were buried not out of a sense of pity, but out of the dread of contagion. The crisis led to the search for a scapegoat. Latent anti-Semitism broke into the open as a convenient candidate was found in the Jewish population. Jews were accused of poisoning wells and purposely contaminating food. So intense was this reaction that the pope finally interceded with an edict threatening excommunication to anyone guilty of burning a Jew.

The intensity of the Black Death and the reactions of people to it changed the course of medieval history. In fact, this plague is often viewed as standing at the end of one era and the beginning of another. In his classic treatment of the Middle Ages, historian Henri Daniel-Rops summarizes the impact of the calamity on the continent of Europe:

> The Black Death (1348–50) marks a turning-point in the history of Europe. It ended the wonderful surge of vitality which had brought society to its highest summits; henceforward Christendom was a broken reed. The great age of the Cathedral and the Crusade ended in putrefaction and in horror.[2]

Today's "Black Death"

In the 1980s, there began to spread throughout the world an epidemic that has the potential to become as devastating and consequential to our modern era as the Black Death that marked the end of the Middle Ages—Acquired Immunodeficiency Syndrome, commonly called AIDS. In March 1986, the World Health Organization predicted that between 50 and 100 million persons worldwide would be infected by the AIDS-causing virus. When coupled with a conservative estimate of a 30-percent death rate, this prediction has resulted in projections of 15 to 30 million deaths from the disease.[3] The parallel to the estimated 17 to 28 million casualties from the Black Death is sobering indeed!

One major difference makes the twentieth-century epidemic potentially even more destructive than its predecessor. The medieval plague preyed largely on young children and the aged, leaving the childbearing segment of the population relatively intact. AIDS, however, has the opposite tendency. While no age group is intrinsically shielded from the virus, the major risk categories to date are composed of persons in the prime childbearing ages. For this reason, AIDS not only poses a threat to the current population, but carries the potential to affect coming generations as well. It could possibly even usher in the end of our "modern" era. Citing T. S. Eliot's statement, "This is the way the world ends, not with a bang, but a whimper," Helen Singer Kaplan, director of the Human Sexuality Program of the New York Hospital-Cornell Medical Center, declares, "In this age of AIDS there is a real danger that the world as we know it might end not with a nuclear bang, but with the whimpers of dying AIDS patients."[4]

As in the case of its predecessor, today's "Black Death" has advanced unabated by what many critics see as a less-than-adequate response from most segments of society. This widespread hesitancy to take action may be understood partly by the early association of AIDS with homosexuality. The assumption that AIDS is a "gay disease" has remained difficult to dislodge from the public consciousness; yet, the disease has largely affected heterosexual persons in Africa, in Haiti is spreading more rapidly among such persons than among practicing homosexuals, and is now following this trend in the United States as well.[5] The link drawn between AIDS and homosexual practices has led to many wild "solutions" to the crisis. Although writing more narrowly, from a British perspective, Hancock and Carim draw together examples of such solutions from various corners of the globe:

> When the five-times former mayor of Houston, Louie Welsh, stated as the only point of his comeback campaign that his way to combat AIDS would be to "shoot the queers," he got 40 percent of the vote. . . . Nor have such suggestions been confined to politicians tub-thumping in their own professional interests. Dr. Paul

> Cameron, an American psychologist associated with an organization called the Institute for Investigation of Sexuality, has warned that the mass murder of homosexuals might be undertaken as a last resort in the attempt to stop the virus spreading. He told a Channel 9 television interviewer in Australia: "It may come to the stage where vigilantes will be taking machine-guns into gay bars. Homosexuals could become an endangered species." He said gays should be quarantined. "AIDS is like the dagger at the heart of human civilization. Homosexuals are now having to pay the price for their unsanitary sexual habits." A spokeswoman for Channel 9 said afterward that 50 percent of callers agreed with Cameron's views.[6]

Because of its perceived link to the homosexual community and "questionable" sexual practices, the AIDS disease has remained an embarrassment to persons in many segments of society, including government, media, public health, medicine, and education. Many observers find it not surprising, therefore, that social agencies were slow to mount a concerted effort to conquer AIDS, when AIDS first came to public attention.[7] This purportedly slow response and the perception that a lack of concern dominates society as a whole have given rise to feelings of abandonment among many homosexually oriented persons who are fearful of contracting the disease. William Hoffman, who attempted to gain the hearing of the nation through a play portraying the response of a person infected by AIDS, expresses succinctly these feelings:

> But during the polio epidemic, as during the Tylenol and Legionnaire's disease scares, the media and the government committed themselves wholeheartedly to the side of the victims. In the early eighties, with few exceptions, the main concern of people outside the gay community was reassuring themselves that it was happening only to "them," and not to "us." I felt isolated from society in a way I never had before.[8]

Like society as a whole, Christians have not always offered a healing response to the epidemic. Some have been apathetic, either refusing to acknowledge the grim reality of the presence of AIDS in society or maintaining that—whatever problems the disease may cause—it cannot or will not affect "us." Public statements by Christians have likewise been varied. Some have categorized the epidemic as a homosexual problem or as merely the just punishment for homosexual practices. Others have sensationalized the situation, blowing out of proportion projections of its rate of increase and disseminating inaccurate information concerning the means of its spread. Such halfhearted or even misguided responses to AIDS have unfortunately resulted in a loss of credibility for the church in other segments of society. In a report for *Christianity Today* in which he asks, "Is compassion waning in light of a so-called gay disease?" Randy Frame quotes Harold Ivan Smith of a ministry organization called Tear Catchers as declaring, "AIDS researchers are increasingly looking at evangelicals as idiots and bigots."[9]

An AIDS Ministry in the Face of Barriers

Accusations of Christian hostility, inactivity, and apathy in the midst of the AIDS crisis may, of course, be grossly overstated. It is generally uncontestable that the people of God repeatedly display care and concern for persons in need. Yet, in many ways, the AIDS epidemic has presented a dilemma. The situation calls for a response, but it offers no obvious indication as to the direction such a response should take. In sensing this quandary, the church has been not unlike society in general, wanting to do something but not knowing quite what to do.

For this reason, AIDS is an especially frustrating problem for Christians. They sense a call to minister in the midst of this epidemic, yet barriers often arise, hindering genuine Christian action. Why is this the case? And what hinders ministry in this crisis? Although the potential problems are diverse and complex, three major barriers readily creep into the church and undercut (or at least complicate) a constructive Christian response to the epidemic. Becoming aware of these potential barriers is a first step in dealing positively with the AIDS crisis itself and with those directly or indirectly affected by the disease.

AIDS as a "Sinner's Disease"

One barrier to ministry in the midst of the AIDS epidemic arises from data about the way the disease is carried and transmitted. Medical researchers have determined that the AIDS-causing virus is transmitted through bodily fluids: specifically, semen, vaginal secretions, and blood. This means that AIDS is generally spread among adults through either sexual intercourse with an infected person or various rites and practices surrounding the drug culture, including the sharing of I.V. needles.

Knowledge that the highest risk categories for contracting the virus include sexually promiscuous homosexual or bisexual males and drug abusers (i.e., "sinners") readily leads to certain harmful attitudes. For many Christians, this generalization forms a barrier against a constructive response to the AIDS crisis.

One counterproductive attitude that arises is *apathy.* If AIDS is perceived as a sinners' disease, Christians can be lulled into believing that because they themselves do not rank among such sinners, they are simply unaffected by the crisis. If they smugly maintain that neither their families nor their church will ever be touched by the "plague," they may grow disinterested in the crisis as a whole and in those suffering with AIDS.

This attitude is both incorrect and naive as well as injurious to the Christian's role in the world. Even though one could hope that Christian families and congregations are never touched directly by the AIDS virus, the epidemic nevertheless does affect all of us. Apart from the toll in human misery that AIDS will extract from our fellow citizens, the crisis will have an ultimate financial impact on our society that no one can predict.[10] The social-security system, the cost of health care, insurance premiums, economic productivity, for example, are all adversely affected by the AIDS crisis. In these measurable ways and in a host of other intangibles, the epidemic already touches everyone. And the impact will increase dramatically in coming years.

The apathy that readily results from viewing AIDS as a sinner's disease is damaging to the Christian task because it may be accompanied by a refusal among individual Christians to view persons in the high-risk groups as the proper focus of the church's mission. Recent decades have brought a shift in the makeup of the church in this country. The main constituency of many congregations has become "middle-class America." As a result the outreach thrust of the church often focuses on suburban populations and on "respectable" social groups.

In part this is a natural, human development. People feel most comfortable in the presence of those with whom they share similarities, just as they often feel uncomfortable with persons who differ radically from themselves. The same principle is sometimes operative in the church. When we gather as Christians for worship or fellowship, we usually simply prefer to meet "good, respectable people" like ourselves. And because congregations are interested in their own survival, visitation and outreach programs easily focus on prospects who can strengthen the congregation, people who can offer financial support or assume positions of responsibility in church programs. While such attitudes may be natural, they nevertheless perpetuate a distancing from those suffering from AIDS—persons perceived to be "sinners."

Another harmful attitude that arises from overgeneralization about AIDS victims is *judgmentalism*. The awareness that to date in the U.S. the epidemic has stricken primarily homosexually oriented men and drug abusers ("sinners") can lead to a self-righteous spirit that hinders a constructive response to the AIDS crisis. Some Christians maintain that people who contract AIDS are simply reaping the just punishment of their immoral actions. This attitude parallels a similar response to the poor and the otherwise less fortunate. These people, some argue, deserve the poverty they are living in, because they are lazy, wasteful, or bad money managers. This judgmental attitude toward those nameless "others" is readily transferred to persons with AIDS. For are they not merely receiving the just wages of their sinful lifestyles? some ask rhetorically.

Where this attitude reigns, Christians find themselves "justified" in avoiding involvement with (and ministry to) those in need. Even more devastating than serving as a rationale for inactivity, however, negative generalizations about "sinners with AIDS" raise suspicions about anyone who senses a compulsion to become involved with helping them. And it places the responsibility to change one's lifestyle solely and squarely on the shoulders of the carriers and victims of AIDS. These people, some Christians suggest, are required to engage in self-reformation, for only in this way can they become fit recipients of our ministry and of God's saving grace! Little do those who espouse this view realize that it actually reflects a theology of "works"—the attempt to gain justification by personal merit (so categorically rejected by Paul)—rather than a biblical theology of grace.

Knowledge that the highest-risk groups for contracting AIDS include certain "sinners" can lead to a third unfortunate attitude, an unhealthy mixture of *fear and hate* that likewise produces a barrier against a constructive response to the crisis. In some circles, "sinners," but especially practicing homosexuals, are all characterized as fiendish ogres whose insatiable appetites led them to prey on innocent victims. This characterization leads to a fear and a loathing of "those people," especially because they purportedly are constantly recruiting innocent youth and seducing children to become involved in their own evil lifestyles.

The attitude of angry fear toward persons with AIDS may be augmented because of the contagious and deadly nature of this disease. A valid concern, but one that is often sensationally presented, is that AIDS patients and carriers will eventually infect the wider community, as their deadly illness spreads beyond their own social groupings. Such predictions of mass infection are reflected in indications that the epidemic has indeed moved beyond the homosexual community. Those who have received transfusions of infected blood products, the spouses of bisexuals, and babies born to women with AIDS comprise but three groups of innocent victims already caught by the spread of this disease. Awareness of the growing ranks of AIDS casualties who have contracted the disease through no personal deviant lifestyle only fuels the flames of fear and hatred.

AIDS as a Sexually Transmitted Disease

This second barrier is closely related to the first. Ministry in the midst of the AIDS epidemic can become difficult because of the perceived relationship between the disease and sexuality. Indeed, the highest number of cases of AIDS contagion have occurred through sexual contact. As a result, AIDS is often classified with gonorrhea, syphilis, and herpes as a sexually transmitted disease. Some people conclude from this that AIDS is actually caused by certain immoral sexual acts.

In the past, the church's response to issues surrounding human sexuality has not always been adequate. In many Christian circles, sex remains an embarrassing topic. Although less widespread than in certain previous eras, a fundamental dualism in approaching the topic is often present. Some Christians view the sexual nature of human existence as somehow ignoble, or at least less "holy" than other, more "spiritual" aspects of life.

The inability to develop a positive sexual ethic may be paralleled by a quick and condemnatory response to sexual sins. However, such a response forms a stark contrast to the posture of the Bible, being more reflective of that of the Pharisees who brought to Jesus a woman caught in adultery, for example, than of Jesus' firm, yet noncondemnatory response to her (John 8:3–11). Nor are Christians always willing to follow Paul's lead in placing sexual offenses in the same context and on the same level with more "respectable" sins, such as greed, slander (gossip), or dishonesty in business dealings (cf. 1 Cor. 6:9–10). Although the importance of marital fidelity as a picture of Christ's relationship to the church (Eph. 5:25–33) adds an important dimension to sexual sins, it is unfortunate that many Christians find themselves reacting to matters of sexual impurity with a vengeance not found in their response to other transgressions.

A hesitancy to become involved with persons touched by the AIDS epidemic can be the outgrowth of an understandable desire on the part of Christians to avoid being perceived as condoning what they believe are sinful sexual practices. Most Christians continue to uphold the traditional Christian morality, which includes a strong stand against adultery and insists that sexual relations are legitimate only within the context of marriage. This is, of course, proper. But, in the minds of some, ministering to persons who suffer from diseases (such as AIDS) contracted through sexual activity outside of the marriage relation implies sympathy for, or an openness to, sexual practices that lie beyond the limits delineated by the traditional ethic, if not a rejection of that ethic as a whole. As a result, Christians may be tempted to refuse to become involved in the AIDS crisis, believing that thereby they are taking a strong stand against the breakdown in morality they see prevalent in our society.

The tendency toward avoidance, condemnation, and noninvolvement increases when the issue of homosexuality is introduced. AIDS forces us to come face-to-face with our attitude toward this sexual orientation. Because the largest percentage of AIDS cases has been among homosexual males, some Christians accept the theory that homosexual activity is an actual cause of the disease. The perceived connection between homosexuality and AIDS is an important factor in the reluctancy on the part of some Christians to engage in any form of ministry to persons with AIDS. This ministry, they believe, would constitute an acceptance of the lifestyle that in their understanding spreads or even causes the disease, a lifestyle that for many Christians is totally abhorrent and unnatural.

Ministering to AIDS patients demands that believers come to terms with the deeper issues of human sexuality and the place of homosexuality within our understanding of this dimension of human existence. The question of the place of homosexuality within Christian sexual ethics has always been problematic. This problem, however, has become acute in recent years. The rise of the gay-liberation movement and the strong reaction it has generated, especially (but not exclusively) among conservative Christians, have resulted in a strained relationship characterized by distrust. Because a deep chasm often separates the church and the homosexual community, the church's attitude toward homosexuality looms as one of the uncompleted tasks facing the people of God in the closing years of the twentieth century.

Ministry in the midst of the AIDS crisis requires that we come to grips with the Christian understanding of human sexuality. A first step in this direction can be taken as we look more objectively at the disease itself. As will be shown later, sex acts do not *cause* AIDS. Nor is sexual encounter the only way in which the AIDS virus can be contracted, even though to date the primary means of spreading the disease has been sexual activity. The disease must be mentally separated from human sexuality or perceived sexual aberrations. Only then can true ministry in the midst of the epidemic transpire. For this to occur, we must come to understand that ministry to persons with AIDS in no way constitutes sympathy or support for practices that Christian caregivers perceive to be immoral.

AIDS as a Terminal, Contagious Disease

A third barrier that readily arises within the church and hinders ministry in the midst of the AIDS epidemic is its status as a terminal disease. In one sense, AIDS is similar to any terminal disease. Such illnesses evoke a negative reaction that forms a barrier to ministry because they are a reminder of the mortality we all share. We will all one day die. Seeing AIDS victims or even hearing about the epidemic are strong reminders of human mortality.

As with any terminal disease, so also with AIDS—ministry may be hindered by the human tendency to avoid bonding with those who will soon be taken from us. Rather than facing the pain of separation that comes at death, many people simply refuse to become psychologically and emotionally involved with terminal patients. The certainty of a relatively quick death by persons in the advanced stages of the AIDS disease and the hopelessness the illness engenders compound the psychological reluctancy that caregivers sense.

Although AIDS is similar to any terminal disease in several respects, it is characterized by certain unique aspects that impede ministry to an even greater extent. Because AIDS sufferers are generally in the prime of life, the disease reminds us that terminal illness does not strike only the elderly. Sickness and death simply will not be quarantined to this one segment of society. On the contrary, a terminal disease can be contracted by the strong, by those who are in the best years of their lives.

The AIDS epidemic reminds us that life is fragile at all stages. In an attempt to shield ourselves from this grim reality, we readily build a barrier against ministering to its victims.

This barrier is strengthened by the reluctancy many persons sense to witness the ebbing of strength from the ranks of the strong. Watching a twenty- or thirty-year-old male being wasted away by an AIDS-related disease becomes a stark and often unwelcomed reminder of our own weakness, which lies just beneath the surface even when we appear to be strong.

The connection between AIDS and death leads us back to its connection with sin. More so than any other disease, AIDS has been seen as a sin-related ailment. Because it appears to lead inevitably to physical death, AIDS forms a vivid illustration of the biblical teaching that the wages of all sin is death. To stand face-to-face with an AIDS victim, therefore, means to be confronted with the death-producing aspects of our own actions as well. And the knowledge that AIDS is often spread through lifestyles that contradict God's design and therefore stand under divine condemnation cannot help but remind us that there are aspects of our own lifestyles that likewise are deserving of death. Paul's ominous statement carries an all-inclusive tone—"for all have sinned and fall short of the glory of God" (Rom. 3:23). Because AIDS is a potent reminder of the theological truth that we are all sinners deserving of death, ministry to persons with AIDS may become a difficult and burdensome task.

The Church's Response

Barriers that impede ministry in the midst of the AIDS epidemic readily arise. If this is true, how should the church respond to the current crisis? This question is made even more urgent by the seeming legitimacy of the attitudes and feelings that produce these barriers.

The concerns voiced above must not be minimized or overlooked. For example, the mixture of fear and hate many persons have toward the social groups that are the primary victims of the AIDS disease is understandable. There have indeed been situations where the innocent have been seduced to become involved in evil lifestyles. And it is undeniably true that "the guilty" have infected innocent persons with this deadly disease. The most heart-gripping of these are the cases of infants born with AIDS and who are now unloved and unwanted for this reason.

Likewise understandable is the human tendency to avoid reminders of our own mortality, weakness, and sin. We simply do not want to be confronted either with the fact that we will one day die or with the reality of our present weaknesses, whether physical or spiritual. Given the stark picture of the fragile nature of all human life and the reality of human mortality that results from sin, so vividly painted by the AIDS epidemic, reluctancy to minister in the midst of the epidemic is understandable.

A further compounding factor is equally important. Not only is AIDS a terminal disease; it is also contagious. All communicable illnesses, and especially the deadly ones, strike terrorizing fear in our hearts. This is especially the case with AIDS. The situation has been aggravated by the lack of solid information and the abundance of misinformation surrounding the disease since it first came to the public attention. The information gap is exacerbated by the newness of the virus and the seeming inability of medical researchers to come to a full understanding of the disease. This, coupled with recent pronouncements concerning new surprises about the conduct of the virus and its potential, leaves the public with the sense that the medical community is helpless in the face of the epidemic. What appears to be a continuous need to revise past medical statements heightens the loss of credibility faced by medical professionals. Assurances that the disease cannot be contracted by normal, casual contact are often dismissed by the public as premature or even an attempt to cover up the true, grimmer reality.

While AIDS is a communicable disease that must be treated with respect, there is no warrant for hysteria. The ironic fact is that persons in advanced stages of the illness may be more threatened by casual contact with others than being themselves a threat. Their weakened immune systems make them susceptible to various infectious diseases that are relatively common to the general population. In spite of the findings of the medical community, however, Christians may be reluctant to come into contact with persons with AIDS. This reluctancy is based on both real and imaginary fears of contracting the dreaded illness.

Even though these fears and the barriers they produce are understandable, Christ calls his people to overcome such hindrances. We are called to move beyond whatever apathy and judgmental spirit may haunt the hidden recesses of our hearts. These attitudes serve only to prevent ministry to persons we consider sinful, such as the sexually promiscuous and drug abusers.

To fulfill our calling to minister to the needy in the midst of the AIDS crisis, we must be able to separate the medical and the moral aspects of AIDS, which aspects so often are simply fused together. Such a separation can be made in spite of a proper Christian abhorrence for sin if we come to see that in ministering to AIDS victims we are not condoning what we believe is an immoral lifestyle. The AIDS disease is not intrinsically a moral question. The greatest moral issue facing the church in the midst of the AIDS epidemic is not the Christian view of homosexuality or drug abuse, as important as these are. Rather, the central issue is whether Christ's disciples will be obedient to the mandate of their Lord, a mandate that includes offering an informed and compassionate response to this problem. As Christians, we are called to overcome our natural fear and hate by means of supernatural, divine love. Christ calls us to view persons with AIDS as persons whom God loves and who stand in need of the healing touch of Christ.

Christians are called to overcome the fear of contagion as well. Even if AIDS were highly contagious (which medical evidence indicates is not the case), the Christian mandate would require that we risk our lives for the sake of ministering to the needs of others. Risk taking is but the outworking of obedience to Jesus' statement, "For whoever wants to save his life will lose it, but whoever loses his life for me and for the gospel will save it" (Mark 8:35).

As we move beyond prejudice and fear, we may find to our surprise people who have been divinely prepared to receive our ministry. Because they are confronted with a hopeless and terminal disease, many AIDS patients are deeply interested in religious questions, especially questions about death, the afterlife, and God. On the basis of their study of AIDS patients, researchers Shelp, Sutherland, and Mansell declare, "The people with AIDS or ARC reported here (and others known to the authors) almost without exception felt some need for God."[11] As we minister, we may discover a similar situation. Persons struggling with AIDS constitute a fertile soil, prepared by God's Spirit for the caring ministry and gospel message of God's people.

Ministry to these individuals, as all ministry to persons in need, however, is not merely a one-way street. Christians often discover that in the process of caring for others they have become "the ministered unto." So also in this epidemic, persons touched by AIDS likewise have a gift to offer to those Christians who reach out to them. For this reason, we are called not only to minister, but also to be open to accept the ministry that our caregiving to needy persons struggling with AIDS can bring.

An Overview

Although the barriers hindering ministry in the midst of the AIDS epidemic are real, they are not to be sidestepped or dismissed prematurely. Rather, they must be dealt with honestly. At the same time, the Christian community is called to move beyond such barriers to be the people of God in a world of hurt. The mandate that Christ has given to the church knows no human boundaries; it encompasses *all* who are in need, including persons touched with AIDS. For this reason, we are challenged through the AIDS crisis to turn our attention away from the barriers that so readily arise and toward the task of ministry in the midst of the AIDS epidemic.

A step in this direction can be taken as we become more fully informed concerning this disease. With this in view, the following chapters seek to provide basic information concerning AIDS—first from a medical and then from a theological perspective. Part One focuses on the medical dimension. This section seeks to provide a scientific overview of AIDS: its causes, how it is and is not contracted, and the current outlooks for diagnosis and treatment. The goal of these pages is to provide a basis for an informed response to the AIDS epidemic, albeit from the viewpoint of medical science.

In Part Two, the focus shifts to the theological dimension. These chapters attempt to develop a biblical and theological understanding of the AIDS crisis, thereby to lay a specifically Christian foundation for the call to ministry that lies at the heart of the volume as a whole. On this basis, a theological case is then presented for overcoming the barriers already surveyed above.

The two dimensions, however, coalesce. Medical science and Christian theology speak with one voice, calling the church to active ministry in the midst of the AIDS epidemic.

Part One

Medical Perspectives and Context

1

The History of AIDS

History records many infectious diseases that grew to epidemic proportions. The bubonic plague of medieval Europe (also called the Black Death), the cholera epidemics of the nineteenth century, the influenza scourge of 1918, the struggle against polio in the 1950s, all bring to mind past major threats to mankind. These particular epidemics demonstrated that potentially life-threatening infection could be spread from person to person in different ways. With the plague, it was via insects (fleas); with cholera and polio, it was through ingestion of contaminated water and food; with influenza, the disease was airborne. With each of these epidemics, people became infected more by passive exposure than by active acquisition. With the AIDS epidemic, however, acquisition of the virus that causes the disease is predominantly related to specific human behaviors.

An AIDS Chronology

The history of AIDS is unique in medical history for two primary reasons: (1) it is, for the most part, a sexually transmitted disease; and (2) it is uniformly fatal. Although such other sexually-transmitted diseases as syphilis and gonorrhea have resulted in death, never before has there been such a strong connection between sex and fatality as seen with AIDS. It is profoundly troublesome to recognize this link between an activity that is so deeply human and pleasurable and a consequence that is so ultimate and feared. If one adds to this the lack of a cure despite extensive efforts thus far, what you have is an historical account of man's struggle with his greatest problem: himself. There are therefore few events in recorded medical history that rival the AIDS epidemic. The story is as follows.

Year One of the AIDS Epidemic (June 1981–June 1982)

It was June 5, 1981, when a Centers for Disease Control Morbidity and Mortality Weekly Report *(MMWR)* reported on five patients who had an unusual form of pneumonia caused by a parasite called Pneumocystis carinii.[1] The five patients were all previously healthy homosexual men and were treated at three different hospitals in Los Angeles, California, during the period from October 1980 to May 1981. None of these patients knew each other, and they had no common contacts or knowledge of any sexual partners with similar types of illnesses. Two of the five reported having frequent homosexual contacts with previous partners and all five reported using inhalant drugs, with one reporting intravenous (I.V.) drug abuse. Three had profoundly decreased numbers of lymphocyte cells. Conclusions at that time included a possible association between homosexual lifestyle and the development of Pneumocystis pneumonia.

The identification of Pneumocystis pneumonia among homosexual men was followed up by a number of reports of other unusual diseases occurring in this population. On July 4, 1981, Kaposi's sarcoma, which had previously been an uncommonly reported skin malignancy in the United States, was diagnosed in twenty-six homosexual men in both New York City and in California.[2] This cancer was described during the preceding thirty months, whereas a review of various large New York City cancer registries revealed only a smattering of cases of Kaposi's sarcoma occurring in men under age fifty in the two prior decades.

As with Pneumocystis pneumonia, it was thought that the occurrence of Kaposi's sarcoma among young, previously healthy, homosexual men was highly unusual, and no previous association between Kaposi's and sexual preference had been noted. The apparent clustering of both Kaposi's sarcoma and Pneumocystis carinii pneumonia suggested a common underlying factor, as a number of these cases had demonstrated suppression of the immune system. A virus known as cytomegalovirus (CMV) was a suggested cause, given the very high prevalence of CMV in the homosexual population (greater than 90 percent). There was also the observation of a possible relationship between CMV and the occurrence of Kaposi's sarcoma among previous American and European patients. CMV was subsequently excluded as the cause of this new syndrome.

By August 1981, it was noted that in addition to Pneumocystis pneumonia and Kaposi's sarcoma a number of other so-called opportunistic diseases were being reported in homosexual men, including several fungal infections (i.e., candida, involving the gastrointestinal tract), a tuberculosis-like illness (Mycobacterium avium intracellulare), and other viral infections (herpes simplex).[3]

In December 1981, Pneumocystis carinii pneumonia

was first reported in heterosexual drug abusers as well as in increasing numbers of homosexuals. These patients, like those reported earlier, were found to have abnormalities in their cellular immunity with depressed numbers of lymphocytes.[4] At this same time, various other possible causative agents were being proposed, including inhalants containing amyl nitrite (also called "Poppers"). These substances were known to be used frequently within the homosexual community as sexual stimulants or as recreational drugs. Inhalants were also subsequently shown not to play a causative role.

By May 1982, an enlarging picture of illness affecting homosexual men and drug abusers was becoming apparent. The occurrence of persistent and generalized lymphadenopathy (enlarged lymph nodes) was being reported among homosexual men in Atlanta, New York City, and San Francisco.[5] Approximately 70 percent of these patients had other symptoms, including fatigue, fever, night sweats, and weight loss of at least five pounds. Although many of these individuals gave a history of other sexually-transmitted infections (such as gonorrhea, syphilis, and amebiasis), it was concluded that none of these infections adequately explained the occurrence of lymphadenopathy. Studies of the immune system of several of these patients revealed very low levels of a critically important participant in the cell-mediated immune system, the T-helper lymphocyte.

By the end of the first year of the epidemic, 355 cases of Kaposi's sarcoma and/or serious opportunistic infections (KSOI syndrome), especially Pneumocystis carinii pneumonia, had been reported in previously healthy persons.[6] At that time, five states accounted for 86 percent of the reported cases (California, Florida, New Jersey, New York, and Texas). A clear predominance of homosexual or bisexual men was being seen (79 percent). In the sample, 12 percent were heterosexual men and 4 percent were heterosexual women.

Year Two of the AIDS Epidemic (June 1982–June 1983)

During the second year, great strides were made on many fronts. The name *acquired immune deficiency syndrome* (AIDS) was introduced in September 1982 to describe this new disorder. The Centers for Disease Control (CDC) proposed their first definition of AIDS as a "disease at least moderately predictive of a defect in cell mediated immunity occurring in a person with no known cause for diminished resistance to that disease. Such diseases include Kaposi's sarcoma, Pneumocystis carinii pneumonia and serious opportunistic infections."[7]

It was admitted that this first case definition probably did not include the full spectrum of AIDS manifestations, which were correctly thought to range from total absence of symptoms to mild symptoms (fever, weight loss, lymphadenopathy) to the full-blown syndrome such as those with Kaposi's sarcoma and Pneumocystis pneumonia. It was recognized at this point that the case mortality was extremely high, with 41 percent of the overall patients having already died.

In addition to homosexual/bisexual men and drug abusers, AIDS was reported in a number of other groups, including reports in July 1982 of AIDS occurring in patients from Haiti as well as in those with hemophilia A.[8,9] Although not recognized immediately, it became apparent that the Haitian patients were affected, not because of their geographic origin *per se,* but rather because of sexually promiscuous behavior. The reports of Pneumocystis pneumonia in three patients with hemophilia A raised the possibility of a blood-borne infectious agent, as all three of these males were heterosexual and none had a history of intravenous drug abuse. Several more reports in December 1982 of AIDS occurring in hemophiliacs further substantiated this group of individuals as being at risk.[10]

The spectrum of the AIDS epidemic further widened with reports in December 1982 of unexplained cellular immune deficiency and opportunistic infections occurring in infants. One of these was a twenty-month-old child from the San Francisco area who developed problems after multiple blood transfusions that included a transfusion of platelets derived from the blood of a man subsequently found to have AIDS.[11] The features of this infant's illness resembled those among adults with AIDS. Physicians from New York City, New Jersey, and California reported other infants and young children with immune deficiencies. The majority of these children were found to be born to mothers who were at high risk for AIDS, such as those using intravenous drugs. It was thought that transmission of an "AIDS agent" from mother to child either in utero or shortly after birth could account for the early onset of immune deficiency.

By early 1983, over 1,200 cases of AIDS had been reported to the CDC in the United States. Clearly, however, the problem was not only limited to this country but was also being reported in other parts of the world. In late 1982, sixty-seven cases of AIDS had been reported in Europe.[12] Physicians in Brussels and Paris found AIDS-like illnesses among African patients who were residing in Europe and who had no known risk factors for AIDS. These individuals also had lowered T-helper lymphocyte abnormalities of the type seen in AIDS patients in the United States.

As the AIDS epidemic grew, research to find the causative agent for AIDS intensified. An infectious agent, specifically a virus, was thought to be most likely. Two groups of investigators emerged as the leaders in the discovery of the cause of AIDS. These groups were headed by Dr. Robert Gallo of the National Institutes of Health in Bethesda, Maryland, and Dr. Luc Montagnier of the Pasteur Institute in Paris, France.

In February 1983, at the Cold Spring Harbor workshop on AIDS, Gallo proposed that AIDS was probably caused by a retrovirus. By May 1983, Montagnier and co-workers published information in *Science* regarding the isolation of a retrovirus from an AIDS patient with lymphadenopathy.[13] The virus was identified from the patient's lymph nodes and was therefore named the lymphadenopathy associated virus (LAV). Gallo subsequently reported (in May 1984) the same type of virus from two AIDS patients. He named the virus HTLV-III because of its resemblance to two other viruses, HTLV-I and HTLV-II.[14,15] HTLV stood for Human T-cell Lymphotropic Virus, indicating the primary cell that the virus attacked. Types I and II had been previously associated with the development of leukemia in human beings. The U.S. Department of Health and Human Services officially assumed a double generic name for the virus, calling it HTLV-III/LAV in recognition of the contributions of both the American and French investigator groups.

By the end of the second year of the AIDS epidemic (June 1983), 1,641 cases had been reported in the United States. It was realized that the epidemic was doubling in size every six months.[16] These startling facts resulted in the first Public Health Service recommendations for the prevention of AIDS in March 1983 and included the following:

1. Sexual contact should be avoided with persons known or suspected to have AIDS. It was emphasized that members of high-risk groups should be aware that multiple sexual partners increase the probability of developing AIDS.
2. Members of groups at increased risk for AIDS should refrain from donating plasma and/or blood.
3. Studies should be developed to provide an effective screening mechanism for plasma and blood.
4. Physicians should use blood transfusions only when medically indicated and, when possible, the per-

son's own blood should be retransfused (i.e., autologous blood transfusions).

5. The development of safer blood products for use in the management of hemophiliac patients should be pursued.[17]

Year Three of the AIDS Epidemic (June 1983–June 1984)

The third year of the AIDS epidemic was highlighted by further confirmation of the causative role of the virus discovered by Montagnier. As noted above, Gallo not only also isolated the virus from AIDS patients, but perfected a technique by which the virus could be grown in the laboratory, as well as techniques for detecting the presence of antibodies to the virus in the bloodstream.[18,19]

Several other studies showed a high prevalence of antibody to HTLV-III/LAV among the already identified high-risk groups, such as homosexual men, I.V. drug users, and persons with hemophilia A.[20,21] These studies provided additional support to the theory that HTLV-III/LAV was the causative agent of AIDS. They further demonstrated that the presence of the virus within these high-risk populations was much more common that AIDS itself. It became increasingly apparent that those sick from the virus represented only a small proportion of the total number of people infected. By the end of the third year of the epidemic, a total of 4,918 patients meeting the surveillance definition for AIDS had been reported in the United States.[22]

Year Four of the AIDS Epidemic (June 1984–June 1985)

The fourth year of the AIDS epidemic opened with a third group of investigators headed by Dr. Jay Levy isolating the virus from San Francisco AIDS patients.[23] These investigators named the virus AIDS Related Virus (ARV). Until this time the virus had been isolated either from lymph nodes or from T-lymphocytes present in the bloodstream. In October 1984, however, the virus was cultured from the semen of two patients with AIDS, thereby confirming the potential for the sexual transmission of the virus.[24]

Further major developments in November and December (1984) included the characterization of the structure of the virus, as well as the specific receptor to which the virus binds on the T-helper lymphocyte.[25,26] In January 1985, the genetic sequence of the AIDS virus was established by four separate groups, including Montagnier's and Gallo's. These studies revealed that although the various viral isolates were quite similar, there was a significant genetic variation between them.[27]

January 1985 also brought the first public-health-service interagency recommendations for the screening of donated blood and plasma for the antibody to HTLV-III/LAV.[28] Tests used to detect antibody to HTLV-III/LAV were licensed and commercially available in the United States by March of that same year. The screening test designated for use was the ELISA test, which was found to be highly sensitive (very low incidence of false negatives) and specific (very low incidence of false positives). It was suggested that the ELISA test be applied to all blood or plasma and that positive tests be confirmed by a second procedure called the Western Blot test.

It was recommended that those persons found to be positive for the virus refrain from donating blood or other body fluids (i.e., sperm). The public-health-service recommendations were being applied virtually throughout the United States by mid-1985. In addition to the screening of blood and plasma, the recommendations were expanded to donors of organs, tissues, and semen intended for human use.

With the rapid worldwide dissemination of information on AIDS, it was decided that a global sharing of information was needed. The first international conference on Acquired Immunodeficiency Syndrome was held in Atlanta, Georgia, on April 15–17, 1985, and was co-sponsored by the U.S. Department of Health and Human Services and the World Health Organization (WHO). This meeting was attended by over three thousand participants from fifty countries.

The general mood of the conference was one of shock at the extent to which the epidemic was becoming clarified on a worldwide basis. The conference prompted specific WHO recommendations to member countries in all identified areas of the AIDS epidemic.[29] As the fourth year of the AIDS epidemic drew to a close, ten thousand patients (9,887 adults and 113 children) from the United States had been reported with AIDS.[30] This represented a doubling of the number of cases from the previous year.

Year Five of the AIDS Epidemic (June 1985–June 1986)

As greater understanding of AIDS developed, it became apparent that a revision of the original case definition would be required. In late June 1985, the CDC revised its original 1982 definition for AIDS.[31] This was necessary because of several factors. The original definition had been proposed prior to the identification of the causative agent for AIDS (HTLV-III/LAV). The ability to detect the presence of this virus made it possible to include additional serious conditions in the syndrome as well as to improve reporting of new cases. The case definition also gave physicians the ability to exclude AIDS as a diagnosis if the patient's blood was negative for serum antibody to HTLV-III/LAV.

As the case definition for AIDS was becoming refined, the isolation of HTLV-III/LAV from other body fluids was being reported. In August 1985, the virus was reported from the tears of an AIDS patient at the National Institutes of Health.[32] Previously, the virus had been isolated from blood, semen, and saliva.[33] Despite the positive cultures from a variety of body fluids of infected persons, it was noted that transmission of HTLV-III/LAV by casual contact had not been documented. The emphasis on transmission through sexual contact (both homosexual and heterosexual), sharing of contaminated needles, and exposure to infected blood products continued to be made.

Although the predominant group at risk for AIDS in the United States remained homosexual and bisexual men, it was becoming increasingly clear that the virus could be spread through heterosexual contact as well. In September 1985, the Centers for Disease Control reported that out of the 8,374 cases of AIDS that had been acquired by sexual contact to that point, 133 were heterosexual men and women who denied belonging to known AIDS risk groups (i.e., homosexual/bisexual, I.V. drug use, etc.).[34] These individuals reported sexual contact with a high-risk group member for AIDS or an AIDS patient of the opposite sex. The predominant high-risk activity within this group, which included 118 women and 15 men, included sexual contact with intravenous (I.V.) drug users.

At the same time, evidence was pointing to the role of female prostitutes in the transmission of HTLV-III/LAV. Of ninety-two prostitutes tested in Seattle, Washington, 5 percent had positive blood tests for the virus. In Miami, Florida, ten of twenty-five prostitutes (40 percent) attending an AIDS screening clinic were also positive. Eight of these ten women reported prior intravenous drug abuse. An additional study of Haitian men from Miami and New York City with AIDS showed that their major risk factor was a history of contacts with prostitutes, suggesting that heterosexual contact was the major method of transmission in these cases.[35] Other studies from developing countries such as Zaire and Rwanda indicated the role of female prostitutes in transmission of HTLV-III/LAV.[36, 37]

In contrast to the marked male predominance of

AIDS cases in the United States, the ratio of male/female AIDS in places like Zaire was reported to be approximately one to one. This suggested that African AIDS was predominantly a heterosexually transmitted disease. The CDC strongly urged that all sexually active persons take into account their risks of acquiring infection, when having sexual intercourse with members of known AIDS-risk groups or with people who were the sexual contacts of risk-group members. Additionally, it was emphasized that the higher the number of sexual partners, the greater the risk of contact with the virus. Safer sexual techniques, such as the regular use of condoms, were suggested, even though their efficacy in reducing risk had not yet been established.

In October 1985, significant behavioral changes were being documented in homosexual and bisexual men, the group at highest risk for AIDS.[38] A study interviewing some five hundred men from San Francisco was conducted, with interviews being held in August 1984 and then again in April 1985. The proportion of those reporting monogamous, celibate, or safer sexual activity (i.e., avoiding anal intercourse) increased from 69 percent (in 8/84) to 81 percent (in 4/85). These surveys suggested that many men were realizing the importance of modification of their sexual practices and that encouragement in this regard would be the major means available to reduce infection risks.

While risk reduction was being reported within the homosexual community, the risk of AIDS in the pediatric population was being clarified. By December 1, 1985, some 217 cases of AIDS occurrences in children under 13 years of age had been reported.[39] This represented one percent of the approximately 15,000 AIDS cases at that time. A startling 60 percent of these children were known to have died. Of the 217 children reported, 165 (76 percent) had as their only risk factor being born to a mother who belonged to a group who tested positive for HTLV-III/LAV. An additional 18 percent of these cases were secondary to blood transfusions and included those children with hemophilia. Approximately one-half of the mothers of pediatric AIDS cases in this report were intravenous drug users, and an additional 10 percent were sexual partners of either I.V. drug users or bisexual men.

With the major risk factor for pediatric AIDS identified as being born to a mother who was at risk for AIDS, it was thought that the virus was transmitted during pregnancy or during labor and delivery. Transmission rates of HTLV-III/LAV from mother to child ranged up to 65 percent, suggesting that large numbers of infants with AIDS could be expected in areas of the world with childbearing women in high-risk categories.

With the isolation of HTLV-III/LAV from the breast milk of infected women, the possibility of this additional mode of transmission was raised.[40] Indeed, the first case of probable breast-milk-mediated virus transmission to a child was reported about the same time. In this case, the mother had acquired HTLV-III/LAV from a postpartum blood transfusion and had breast-fed the child for six weeks.[41]

As a result of the increasing numbers of pediatric AIDS, recommendations for counseling and testing to women in childbearing ages were proposed by the CDC and the U.S. Public Health Service. Women in high-risk groups for the development of AIDS were especially targeted.[42]

In February 1986, a report surfaced that indicated apparent transmission of HTLV-III/LAV from a child to his mother. The child, who was chronically ill with an intestinal disorder, had acquired the virus through a blood transfusion.[43] The mother, in this case, had been quite closely involved in the child's care and frequently came into contact with the child's blood and other body fluids. She did not wear gloves nor did she wash her hands after they were covered with blood, feces, saliva, and nasal secretions. There was no needle-stick exposure to the child's blood, and therefore this case drew a great deal of attention, since the CDC was aware of only one other report in which viral transmission apparently occurred through a nonparenteral route (i.e., no needle-stick exposure, puncture wound, etc.).

It was emphasized that on rare occasions the virus could be transmitted through unprotected contact with potentially infectious body fluids, such as blood, and so on. It was stressed, however, that the above case was likely atypical, in that none of the family members of over 17,000 AIDS patients reported to the CDC at that time had AIDS unless they, too, had high-risk factors. Additionally, at least seven prospective studies were in process evaluating risk to family members of patients with AIDS. Of the 350 family members studied who lived with an AIDS patient over a long period of time, none developed antibody to HTLV-III/LAV.

Although the capacity of HTLV-III/LAV to cause immune suppression was well known by December 1985, another dimension of this virus's effect on the body was being defined. Several studies showed HTLV-III/LAV's ability to directly attack the central nervous system.[44] These reports conclusively demonstrated that the virus was indeed active within the central nervous system and most likely the cause of a number of neurological syndromes seen within AIDS patients. The most common of these syndromes was a form of dementia. The studies demonstrated isolation of HTLV-III/LAV from cerebrospinal fluid, brain, spinal cord, and peripheral nerve tissue of patients with AIDS who had various neurologic symptoms.

Although the neurological complications of AIDS had been described previously, further evidence was required to prove the causality of the virus in these various neurological syndromes.[45] The establishment of HTLV-III/LAV's ability to infect the central nervous system implied a *direct killing effect* of the virus in addition to the *indirectly lethal effect* via immune suppression.

Year Five of the AIDS epidemic came to a close with three major developments. As noted before, a number of names had been proposed for the AIDS virus, including Human T-cell Lymphotropic Virus-III (HTLV-III), Lymphadenopathy Associated Virus (LAV), and AIDS Associated Retrovirus (ARV). Some controversy surfaced between the two major research groups from the Pasteur Institute in Paris and the National Institutes of Health in the United States. The argument arose over who actually first discovered the virus. By scientific tradition, the discoverers of the causative agent of AIDS would be privileged to name it, as well as benefit from possible royalties from sales of AIDS testing kits worldwide.

In May 1986, the International Committee on the Taxonomy of Viruses attempted to resolve things by giving the HTLV-III/LAV/ARV virus a new name. The committee proposed to name the virus the "Human Immunodeficiency Virus" or HIV. Since that time, HIV has become the name used throughout the scientific literature, in the media, and by official organizations, such as the U.S. Public Health Service.

The second development surrounded the proposal of a new classification system for HIV-related infections.[46] This new classification was proposed by the CDC and will be further illustrated in chapter 4, "The Clinical Manifestations of AIDS." The classification system recognized the growing spectrum of HIV-related illness and offered a better means to group patients infected with HIV. (See Appendix H.)

The third development was the Second International Conference on AIDS, which took place in Paris, France (June 23–25, 1986). The conference covered all aspects of contemporary AIDS research. As the First International Conference on AIDS in Atlanta, Georgia, was characterized by a sense of shock, a mood of despair lay over the second conference in Paris. This was in response to the realization that millions of persons were being infected with HIV worldwide and what the resulting death toll could mean in the ensuing years. Additionally, although much had been learned about how the virus affected the body, little had surfaced in terms of hope for a cure. The complexity of vaccine development was just being recognized. The most optimistic of those investigators stated that a vaccine would probably not be ready for at least another five years.

Year Six of the AIDS Epidemic (June 1986–June 1987)

As the sixth year of the AIDS epidemic dawned, its causative agent, HIV, had a new name and a new classification. However, old fears of potential life loss came to light at a major conference held June 4–6, 1986. The public-health service convened a meeting at the Coolfont Conference Center in Berkley Springs, West Virginia. This now-famous Coolfont Conference and the report that followed was the first attempt to project the impact of HIV into the early 1990s. At Coolfont, eighty-five experts from a variety of fields in AIDS research met together with the main purpose to provide a framework for the development of steps to prevent and control AIDS.

Projections of the effect of the epidemic by 1991 were made, including an estimation that over 270,000 cases of AIDS would be diagnosed by the end of 1991. The report also included an estimation that, during 1991 alone, more than 145,000 cases of AIDS would require medical care, with 54,000 actual patients dying. This would bring the cumulative number of deaths due to AIDS in the United States to more than 179,000. These numbers were based on another projection of the Coolfont Conference: that an estimated 1 to 1.5 million Americans would be infected with HIV to that point. Some 20 percent to 30 percent of these were estimated to be developing AIDS by the end of 1991, resulting in the figure of 270,000 cumulative cases. The empirical model used to develop these numbers was thought to possibly underestimate the actual number by at least 20 percent.

In addition to the numbers of persons with AIDS projected, an estimate of the financial cost of treating persons with AIDS was made. This cost was based on the calculation of approximately $46,000 per AIDS patient per year. It was estimated that a figure of between 8 and 16 billion dollars would be spent in 1991. This represented 1.2 percent to 2.4 percent of the expected total United States personal health care expenditure (650 billion dollars).[47]

Following the Coolfont report, the sixth year of the AIDS epidemic also opened with news of a second virus causing AIDS. In July 1986, reports out of West Africa (Guinea-Bissau, Cape Verde Island)[48] indicated that a new retrovirus had been identified. This virus was named HIV-2 and was found to be related to but distinct enough from HIV-1 so as not to be detectible by the methods used to identify HIV-1 antibody in the bloodstream. As with HIV-1, HIV-2 was found to be associated with an AIDS-like illness with accompanying findings of immune suppression. The virus was reported among heterosexuals, with almost none of the patients admitting to homosexual or I.V. drug-using activity.

In September 1986, the gloomy perception regarding therapy for AIDS was somewhat brightened with the report of a successful trial of an anti-HIV drug known as AZT (3 azidothymidine).[49] The study, which had been started in February 1986, demonstrated that AZT (also known as Zidovudine and Retrovir) decreased the incidence of opportunistic infections in AIDS patients as well as decreasing their overall mortality. Because of the dramatic statistical difference between those who received AZT versus those who did not, the trial was stopped and the drug was made available to all those included in the trial who had taken placebo. This initiative prompted a very rapid approval and deployment process of AZT, so that by March 1987 the Food and Drug Administration licensed the medication for use by all physicians throughout the United States (see chapter 5).

The possibility of HIV being transmitted by insects had been a prior concern and again was raised as a result of a high rate of AIDS being reported in western Palm Beach County, Florida. Considerable national attention was focused on this area, as the cumulative AIDS incidence there was similar to that of the city of San Francisco. An extensive investigation was carried out by the Centers for Disease Control in September 1986. Their findings concluded that, like elsewhere in the country, the infection was being spread predominantly by sexual transmission as well as through the use of contaminated needles for injecting drugs intravenously. Certainly this was the strongest argument against mosquito transmission. Additional evidence included the lack of AIDS occurrences in other individuals who would have been as likely to be exposed to insects as the AIDS patients themselves (i.e., household members, children, and the elderly.)[50]

On October 22, 1986, the U.S. Department of Health and Human Services released the Surgeon General's report on AIDS.[51] This document was the first major attempt at widespread education in the society at large. The report detailed basic facts about AIDS as to its cause, modes of transmission, effect on the body, and ways to prevent acquisition. The report stressed especially that the only major weapon available in fighting AIDS was education. The report down-played mandatory testing of low-risk populations as well as the use of quarantining those infected, except in rare circumstances of irresponsible behavior.

In April 1987, a specific classification for HIV infection in children under thirteen years of age was proposed.[52] Prior to this, the classification systems had been developed predominantly to characterize HIV in adult patients. As in the adult population, the pediatric classification system was designed primarily for public-health purposes, which would include defining which groups of children were involved by HIV as well as monitoring its spread through this part of the population. The system will be discussed further in the section on pediatric AIDS (also refer to Appendix J).

As the end of the sixth year of the epidemic came to a close, approximately 35,000 cases of AIDS had been reported in the United States. At this point it was noted that the period of time required to double the number of cases of AIDS was approximately thirteen months. This length of time had considerably lengthened as compared to the doubling time of five months reported early on in the epidemic.

Year Seven of the AIDS Epidemic (June 1987–June 1988)

The seventh year of the AIDS epidemic was not so much characterized by new information regarding AIDS as it was by reports of recategorizing current data. In August 1987, the Centers for Disease Control published their newest revision of the case definition for AIDS.[53] The objectives of the revised definition were (1) to effectively track the more severe manifestations associated with HIV; (2) to simplify the reporting of AIDS cases; and (3) to expand the definition based on incorporation of new information regarding AIDS (see Appendix H). By the end of 1987, 46,000 cases of AIDS within the United States had been reported to the CDC.

In January 1988, the first case of AIDS caused by HIV-2 was reported within the United States.[54] This patient (a female) was a West African who had come to the United States in 1987. She did not give any history of sexual intercourse, sharing nonsterile needles, or donating blood while in the United States. All of the patient's family members and household contacts both in the United States as well as abroad were reported to be well. Her AIDS illness was thought to have been acquired in West Africa, since it began before arrival in the United States. Because of the reports of HIV-2 infection in West Africa,[55,56] the FDA had initiated a surveillance program for HIV-2 in the United States, beginning in January 1987. Of the 22,699 serum samples screened for HIV-2, virtually none had evidence for the presence of this virus. It was emphasized that HIV-2 could be expected to occasionally occur in the United States as it had in Europe, where a number of patients from West Africa had been reported with HIV-2–related AIDS. An ongoing surveillance program for HIV-2 would be continued. (See note #54.)

The continued efforts to educate the general public of the United States culminated in the distribution of the brochure "Understanding AIDS," which was mailed to every home and residential post-office box by the U.S. Postal Service between May 26 and June 30, 1988. The brochure was written at a seventh-grade level and carried a simple, direct, and understandable message of how AIDS is and is not transmitted. The brochure emphasized that rather than placing emphasis on whether one is identified with a "risk group" for AIDS, it was more important that people evaluate their behavior in terms of personal risk. Approximately 107 million English-language versions of the brochure were sent out. The CDC received tremendous public response, estimating 1.5 million new calls to its national AIDS-information line (AIDS Hotline).

The seventh year of the epidemic ended with the Report of the Presidential Commission on the Human Immunodeficiency Virus Epidemic.[57] This report was submitted to President Reagan on June 24, 1988, and culminated a year-long process of investigation by the advisory commission he had appointed. The report was formulated after more than forty hearings in which the commission listened to testimonies from approximately six hundred of the most knowledgeable persons regarding the AIDS epidemic. The commission was chaired by retired U.S. Navy Admiral James D. Watkins of California. Other members on the commission included Colleen Conway-Welch, Ph.D.; John J. Credon; Teresa L. Crenshaw, M.D.; Richard M. Devos; Christine M. Gebbie, R.N., M.N.; Burton James Lee, III, M.D.; Frank Lily, Ph.D.; John Cardinal O'Connor; Benny J. Primm, M.D.; Penny Pullen; Cory Servaas, M.D.; William D. Walsh, M.D.; and Polly L. Gault.

The commission's report included nearly six hundred recommendations, with an estimated cost implementation for 1990 alone at three billion dollars. Some of these recommendations included (1) the requirement that state boards of education include AIDS education for elementary-school students; (2) that states adopt laws to make the knowing transmission of HIV a crime; (3) that sex offenders be tested for HIV, with their status being taken into consideration at sentencing and parole hearings. Additional recommendations included (4) the compassionate treatment of HIV-infected workers, with those on the job with AIDS being allowed to continue working as long as possible; (5) that comprehensive antidiscrimination legislation be enacted at the federal level; (6) that health-care providers should have an obligation to provide care regardless of patients' HIV status; (7) that state and local health agencies be funded to develop HIV partner-notification programs; (8) that prisoner testing be voluntary rather than mandatory; and (9) that the refugee-testing policy be re-evaluated. Clearly, the most controversial recommendation was the antidiscrimination legislation, which was supported by only a slim majority of commission members. At the time of the report, over 64,000 cases of AIDS had been reported to the CDC.

While news of the Presidential Commission's report on AIDS was being circulated within the United States, new data was being introduced at the Fourth International Conference on AIDS held in Stockholm, Sweden (June 13–17, 1988). The prior figure of 1 to 1.5 million HIV-positive people in the United States was reconfirmed, with a new AIDS case being reported in the U.S. on the average of every fourteen minutes. Drug-abuse experts meeting at the conference seemed to share the opinion that sterile-needle and syringe-exchange programs should be implemented, even though definitive proof of their success was lacking at that time. Evidence from Britain and the Netherlands suggested that such programs did not encourage people to use I.V. drugs.

Additional information presented at the conference suggested that many, if not all, HIV-infected persons will progress to AIDS. Researchers from a Belgian biotechnology company, Innogenetics, announced that they had discovered a third HIV, which they called HIV-III. The virus had been isolated from a healthy pregnant woman in Cameroon who was manifesting early signs of AIDS. Other researchers in attendance at the conference were largely skeptical of whether or not this was a distinctly new AIDS virus, saying that it was not different enough from HIV-1 or HIV-2 to be considered a new virus. The information on vaccine development during this conference was somewhat disappointing, with the recognition that HIV is very adept at avoiding the immune system in general despite high levels of antibody being produced by a number of different vaccines.

In addition to the reports by the Presidential Commission on AIDS and those generated at the Fourth International Conference on AIDS, new projections of AIDS cases in the United States were revealed. At a meeting in Charlottesville, Virginia, in early June 1988, U.S. Public Health Service officials announced that some 450,000 reported cases of AIDS could be expected by the end of 1993, with 100,000 cases occurring in that year alone. These projections were the first major revision since the Coolfont Conference two years earlier. The meeting included a hundred and fifty senior health officials and was closed to the public and the media.[58]

Year Eight of the AIDS Epidemic (June 1988–June 1989)

The eighth year of the AIDS epidemic began with a revised estimate of the total number of cases of AIDS worldwide. As of July 1, a total of 100,410 cases of AIDS had been reported to the World Health Organization (WHO) from 138 countries.[59] The WHO estimated that due to a tendency toward under-reporting and delays in disease manifestation, there had likely been approximately 250,000 cases of AIDS worldwide to that point. Extrapolating from this data, it was suggested that five to ten million persons worldwide were infected with HIV.

As growing numbers of cases of AIDS were being projected throughout the world, further understanding of the potential for discrimination against people with AIDS was being clarified. In a paper in the *New England Journal of Medicine,* investigators sought to answer this question. Their approach included examining public attitudes toward those with AIDS or asymptomatic HIV infection. The study revealed that persons diagnosed as having HIV infection, if disclosed, would face considerable discriminatory attitudes and even hostility from yet a substantial number of Americans. It was found, as a result of fifty-three national and international opinion surveys between 1983 and 1988, that one in four to one in five people in the United States believed that those with AIDS should be excluded from the work, school, and community environments. This number rose to one in three in the South. The study concluded that public-health education might not be enough to prevent discrimination and that actual new legislation may be the only way of creating a climate of safety for people with HIV-related infection.[60]

A controversial program for attempting to control HIV infection in the I.V. drug-use population was started in New York City in October 1988 with the nation's first needle-exchange program. In this endeavor, addicts who had been turned away from drug-treatment programs were enrolled to receive sterile needles. It was anticipated that during the next nine months the city would expect to recruit approximately four hundred addicts to receive needles and counseling, as well as another two hundred addicts to receive only counseling. The drug-behavior and infection status of both groups would then be compared to see how well the addicts would comply with the program and whether or not needle exchange would reduce actual infection.[61]

Early November 1988 brought preliminary information regarding the extent of HIV infection among college students. Data from the Centers for Disease Control and the American College Health Association suggested that as many as three in a thousand students carry the virus. These figures created considerable concern, and officials projected that if this data held constant, college students could be considered a high-risk group.[62]

The eighth year of the AIDS epidemic was culminated by the Fifth International AIDS Conference, which was held in Montreal, Canada (June 4–9, 1989). The conference reported many progresses in the fight against AIDS but no major breakthroughs. This particular AIDS conference, as opposed to the prior four conferences, was especially dramatized by the renewed emphasis on the social issues surrounding the AIDS epidemic. The more than eleven thousand participants represented an integration of both the scientific and social aspects of AIDS. The conference drew great media attention because of the presence of large numbers of AIDS activists who came to Montreal with carefully orchestrated plans to turn attention to their various agendas. Many of the scientists attending the conference were upset by the attention given these social issues at the expense of sharing scientific information.

New figures presented at the Montreal conference from the World Health Organization continued to make it clear that AIDS would remain a worldwide health problem. More than 157,000 cases of AIDS had been reported from 149 countries as of the beginning of June 1989, but because of incomplete reporting, the WHO estimated that nearly 500,000 persons have the disease. As reported previously, five to ten million people were likely infected with HIV worldwide.

Reports regarding vaccine development in general were less pessimistic than those reported in Stockholm, Sweden, at the Fourth International Conference on AIDS. A prominent name in the history of vaccine development, Dr. Jonas Salk, surfaced at the Montreal meeting. Dr. Salk created a stir when he reported to the press about preliminary results of animal and human trials that used a killed-HIV-vaccine approach. Initial phase one clinical trials, using Dr. Salk's vaccine in nineteen HIV-infected persons with AIDS-related complex, showed that the vaccine appeared safe, but that these data were too preliminary to draw any conclusions about the protective effect of the vaccine. Despite these reports of progress, vaccine researchers pointed out that a fundamental question remains: What constitutes an immune response that will protect against HIV infection?[63,64]

Year Nine of the AIDS Epidemic (June 1989–Present)

In late August 1989, new clinical trials involving the use of AZT were released by U.S. health officials. The studies looked at the efficacy of AZT in patients who were infected with HIV but who had not yet developed symptoms of AIDS. The studies showed that not only was AZT successful in delaying progression to the more serious manifestations of HIV, but it also effectively did this at a much lower dose than had previously been studied. The new findings were expected to expand the number of people taking AZT to perhaps as many as 600,000. Until these studies, AZT had only been recommended for the approximately 40,000 people who had AIDS or advanced ARC. Questions surrounding this new information included who would pay for the greatly magnified cost of AZT—running in the range of $7,000 to $8,000 per year per patient.[65] Shortly after the reporting of these new findings, the manufacturer of AZT, Burroughs Wellcome Company, announced that it was lowering the cost of AZT to the consumer by 20 percent.

By the end of August 1989, a total of 105,990 AIDS patients had been reported from the United States as well as its affiliated territories (Guam, U.S. Pacific Islands, Puerto Rico, and U.S. Virgin Islands). This number included 1,780 children less than thirteen years of age. Death rates of 58.2 percent for adults and adolescents and 54.6 percent for children were also reported.[66]

AIDS Before AIDS

The above account catalogs the major events that have characterized the AIDS epidemic since its outbreak in 1981. Retrospectively, the first cases of the current epidemic were seen in the United States in 1978.[67,68] In fact, when the medical literature has been extensively searched from 1950 to the present, it is apparent that sporadic cases of AIDS were occurring for several decades prior to the current epidemic. One study identified nineteen such unrecognized cases of AIDS in the pre-AIDS era.[69] These patients were reported from nine separate countries, including the United States, Canada, West Germany, Belgium, Denmark, Uganda, Israel, Sweden, and the United Kingdom. The earliest patient with possible AIDS in the United States may have occurred in 1952.

The earliest documentation of HIV infection in the United States occurred in a fifteen-year-old black male who was admitted to the St. Louis (Missouri) City Hospital in 1968 for extensive swelling of the lower half of his body. The individual was sexually promiscuous but had no history of intravenous drug use, nor had he received any prior blood transfusions. Over a period of sixteen months, he progressively deteriorated and at the time of death was severely emaciated. An autopsy was performed, and it was found that the patient had extensive Kaposi's sarcoma. Because of the very unusual nature of this case at the time, the patient's serum and autopsy tissue specimens were frozen. The serum was recently tested, using present-day techniques to detect the presence of the antibody to HIV, and it was found to be positive.[70]

Evidence of HIV infection in Africa goes back to as early as 1959.[71] The explanation for why HIV appeared only sporadically around the world prior to the current epidemic is unknown. The possibility of a recent genetic change in the virus and/or sociocultural factors involving sexual practices or numbers of sexual partners have been suggested.

The history of AIDS is a dramatic story of the explosion of a truly new disease syndrome, which has been extremely rapid in progression, worldwide in scope, and devastating in consequence. The story will continue to grow as increasing numbers of persons are affected. We will next turn, however, to discuss further the cause of AIDS, the human immunodeficiency virus (HIV).

2

The Cause of AIDS

Diseases and their causes have fascinated and challenged physicians since the dawn of modern medicine, and the Acquired Immunodeficiency Syndrome has certainly been no exception. With the identification of a virus within the lymph nodes of AIDS patients in 1983, the entire approach to this new disease dramatically changed.

The Causative Role of HIV

Increasing evidence has firmly established that the human immunodeficiency virus (HIV) causes AIDS. The strongest evidence in this regard comes from many studies that document the requirement for infection with HIV to develop AIDS.[1,2] This has been shown in each high-risk population group that saw the introduction of the virus followed within several years by the development of the clinical symptoms of AIDS. The data shows that AIDS and HIV are linked not only in the same population groups, but also in specific locations as well as periods of time. In fact, those countries where the prevalence of HIV antibody is low have an accompanying very low incidence of AIDS. Other strong evidence that supports the causative role of HIV is its link to blood-transfusion–associated AIDS.[3] Additionally, those pregnant women who are HIV-antibody positive will transmit the virus approximately 50 percent of the time to their newborn children, with the overwhelming majority of these developing AIDS by six years of age.[4] Those children who do not develop HIV infection subsequently do not develop AIDS.

The causative role of HIV is further supported when interruption of the virus has prevented the further appearance of AIDS in susceptible individuals. This is best demonstrated again in the area of blood-transfusion AIDS in the United States, where—after AIDS-antibody detection policies were implemented in March, 1985—the transmission dropped in some areas from as high as one in a thousand infected units to approximately one in forty thousand nationwide.[5] The consistent association of HIV with AIDS as well as the virtual elimination of AIDS within certain groups by blocking HIV transmission are the two greatest pieces of evidence that prove the causality of HIV.[6]

Viruses can be generally divided into two major groups, those containing DNA (deoxyribonucleic acid) as their major genetic information and those that contain RNA (ribonucleic acid). Examples of DNA viruses include the herpes-group viruses, such as herpes simplex, varicella zoster (the causative agent for chicken pox and shingles), and the Epstein Barr virus, which is the major cause of infectious mononucleosis. Representatives from the RNA virus group include the famous polio virus and the viruses that cause measles, mumps, influenza, and the common cold. HIV is an RNA virus that belongs to a group known as the retroviruses. (See Appendix A, fig. 1.)

Viruses can be truly called parasites in the sense that they require an organism's cell to live and reproduce. As noted above, they exist as either DNA or RNA surrounded by a coat of protein. Typically, DNA viruses attach themselves to the outside of a host cell, releasing their DNA inside the cell, followed by the incorporation of the viral DNA into the host's DNA. Following this process, copies of viral DNA are made, as well as of the protein coat, thereby creating a new virus that can further invade other host cells. This process is known as viral replication. On the other hand, most RNA viruses, after entering the host cell, directly control their own replication without incorporation into the host cell DNA.

As a retrovirus, HIV behaves somewhat differently from either DNA or other RNA viruses. The term *retrovirus* describes a unique process of what are called "reverse writing viruses." In this regard, HIV enters the host cell as RNA and then, through the action of a special enzyme called reverse transcriptase, literally makes a DNA copy of itself. Then, like any other DNA virus, an incorporation into the host cell DNA is seen, followed by the conversion back to the RNA form and subsequent processing into a mature virus. This virus is then released from the cell and is capable of infecting new cells. (See Appendix A, fig 2.)

Retroviruses are further divided into two groups, the first of which contain members that are associated with the transformation of normal cells into malignant cells, the so-called transforming retroviruses. The second group, to which HIV belongs, are characterized as viruses that infect cells and—instead of transforming them into malignant cells—cause cell death directly. These "cytopathic retroviruses" have also been termed *lentiviruses* and have been known for many years to cause infection in a number of different animal species. Examples of lentiviruses include the visna virus, which causes both pulmonary and neurological disease in sheep; the equine infectious anemia virus (EIAV), which causes both fever and anemia in horses; and the caprine arthritis encephalitis virus (CAEV), which causes arthritis, pneumonia, and encephalitis in goats and sheep. All of these viruses, including HIV, cause a slow and progressively fatal disease in their hosts.[7]

Besides its similarity to the aforementioned viruses, HIV has also been shown to be related to retroviruses that have been isolated from various primates. In 1985, the Simian T-cell lymphotrophic virus type III (STLV-III) was found in the African green monkey whose range includes much of equatorial Africa. This virus was found to cause a form of AIDS in these animals (Simian AIDS).[8,9] On the basis of its similar genetic structure to STLV-III and other lentiviruses, it was hypothesized that HIV may have developed as a result of a mutation sometime in the past, with a subsequent "jumping of species" to infect man, although when and where this might have taken place is not clear. The strongest evidence for the origin of HIV seems to point to central Africa, since the earliest identifiable antibody to HIV worldwide has been identified from stored serum obtained in 1959 from Zaire.[10] Possibly the virus then began to spread to the rest of central Africa during the early 1970s and later spread to the Caribbean, the United States, and Europe by the mid- to late-1970s.[11]

The structure of HIV has been completely worked out, as has its genetic content. HIV has a dense cylindrical core that is surrounded by a lipid envelope. The genetic information is made up of eight genes, all of which regulate the production of important proteins required for the virus's function. The three most important genes are the gag, pol, and env genes, which code for the core proteins (P18, P24), the reverse transcriptase enzyme, and the envelope proteins (gP41, gP120) respectively. (See Appendix A, fig. 1.)

The hallmark of the immune deficiency seen in AIDS is a depletion of a particular type of lymphocyte. There are two basic types of lymphocytes, B-cells and T-cells. The B-lymphocyte provides the basis for what is termed the humoral immune system. B-lymphocytes protect the body through the production of antibodies against foreign invaders. T-cells, on the other hand, form the basis for what is termed the cellular immune system, which provides immunity through the participation by a number of important cells that directly engage foreign invaders.

It is the cellular immune system that is most profoundly affected in AIDS, and this can be easily understood since one of the principal conductors of this arm of the immune system, the T-helper lymphocyte, is progressively destroyed by HIV. HIV selectively attaches to, incorporates into, and kills the T-helper cell. It was the progressive depletion of T-helper cells that was recognized early on in the AIDS epidemic and continues to be one of the primary defects found in AIDS patients. The T-helper cell is vitally important because of the many "helping" functions it performs. The loss of this cell is so important that the entire immune system is affected, resulting in so-called *global immune defect.* With progressive loss of immune function, the patient becomes vulnerable to a wide variety of what are termed "opportunistic diseases." These diseases can be grouped into two categories, the first including various types of infection and the second including various malignancies.

Opportunistic infections are caused by representatives of all classes of known microorganisms (viruses, bacteria, parasites, and fungi). Many of these infections are actually a reactivation of a latent or incubating organism that is normally suppressed by an intact cellular immune system. An example of this would be the cytomegalovirus (CMV), which is present in up to 60 percent of the normal population. When CMV is reactivated, such as can occur in AIDS, it can cause inflammation in the lungs (pneumonia), eyes (blindness), liver (hepatitis), and bowel (colitis). The most common opportunistic infection affecting AIDS patients is Pneumocystis cariini, a parasite that causes pneumonia and that was the first opportunistic disease identified as the epidemic began.[12]

Since the cellular immune system also functions as the tumor surveillance system of the body, it is not surprising that the loss of cellular immunity could predispose to the development of malignancies. The most common cancer involving the AIDS patient is Kaposi's sarcoma. Historically, Kaposi's sarcoma was considered a very benign form of cancer occurring predominantly in elderly people in the United States. With the progressive loss of cellular immunity, such as in AIDS, this tumor becomes extraordinarily "malignant," with spread to many other sites other than the skin where it usually begins.

The above scenario of progressive immune depletion, with the resulting development of opportunistic diseases, forms the first or "indirect" way that HIV kills. The other way that HIV kills is through a direct effect on the central nervous system (see Appendix B). Neurologic abnormalities are quite common in AIDS and occur clinically in up to 60 percent of patients, with 80 to 90 percent being found to have neurologic abnormalities at the time of autopsy. HIV appears to be transmitted to the central nervous system via certain white blood cells known as monocytes and macrophages.

Monocytes have the ability to engulf HIV and, unlike the T-helper cells, are not killed by the virus. Indeed, the monocyte may function as a reservoir for incubating virus, allowing HIV to reproduce inside the cell and go for many years before causing any observable symptoms. As the infected monocyte enters the central nervous system, it appears to result in the loss (atrophy) of brain cells. This may be due to direct injury to the nerve cell by HIV itself or through the blocking of important hormone-like factors within the brain that are necessary for the survival of nerve cells. One of these hormonal-like factors, neuroleukin, has been shown to be blocked from its normal binding to nerve cells by HIV.[13]

Whether indirectly through immune suppression and subsequent opportunistic invasion or through direct invasion of the central nervous system, the human immunodeficiency virus has posed incredible challenges for the medical community. Besides the complexities of how the virus interacts with the body's immune and central nervous systems, it also has the ability to change its own genetic information. The genetic variability of HIV has been recognized for some time, with possibly up to a 40 percent difference between various isolates. Not only do HIV viruses from different AIDS patients differ genetically, but the virus may change considerably with time in the same patient.

These differences in genetic information result from mutational alterations and provide the greatest barrier to the development of a vaccine. The driving mechanism behind HIV's genetic variability may lie in the enzyme reverse transcriptase, which converts the RNA form of HIV to a DNA form. This enzyme appears to cause faulty gene transfer during viral replication inside the host cell.[14] Although HIV changes in the variation of genetic information, these changes do not enhance its ability to be propagated by means other than high-risk exposures such as sexual contact, blood exposure via infected needles, and so on.

HIV is a fragile virus outside of its parasitic environment and does not live long outside of the host cell. HIV is inactivated by a variety of physical and chemical agents, such as common household bleach, various alcohol preparations, Lysol, iodine preparations (Betadine), and heat.[15] Several studies have shown that the virus is capable of living for up to 7–10 days outside of the body. Since the amount of virus used in these studies was approximately 100,000 times that of what would exist in the bloodstream of an AIDS patient, conclusions regarding HIV's ability to live outside the body must be carefully made. Although it may be true that HIV may live for short periods of time on inanimate objects (e.g., table top, door knob, toilet seat, etc.), there is no evidence that it can be transmitted from such objects.

The human immunodeficiency virus has been isolated from blood, semen, bone marrow, tears, saliva, cervical secretions, beast milk, cerebrospinal fluid, brain tissue, lymph node tissue, urine, and feces. Although isolated from these many body fluids and tissues, HIV has been shown to be transmitted only by the following ways: (1) sexual contact; (2) sharing contaminated needles; (3) infected blood or blood products; (4) infected organ or tissue transplants; (5) mother to infant during pregnancy or possibly at the time of delivery; and (6) breast-feeding. There are only scattered reports of possible transmission of HIV through oral sex or biting (see Appendix C and D). HIV is not transmitted through the air or via water, food, inanimate objects or insect exposure.[16]

HIV-2

For three years, HIV was thought to be the single virus responsible for AIDS. However, in 1986, another virus was isolated from patients from West Africa.[17] This virus, now called HIV-2, is similar to HIV-1 in terms of its transmission and risk-group involvement. Although closely related to HIV-1, HIV-2 differs enough from HIV-1 that it cannot be reliably detected by the same antibody detection methods used to detect HIV-1. Although very few isolates of HIV-2 have been found, it appears that the new virus is most prevalent in Guinea-Bissau, Senegal, the Cape Verde Islands and Gambia.

Persons infected with HIV-2 have been reported in Western Europe, Canada, Brazil, and the United States. Virtually all these patients apparently became infected through heterosexual contact with infected West Africans. Although HIV-2 does cause an AIDS-like illness, it appears to be a less dangerous virus than its cousin, HIV-1. HIV-2 may be detected by using specific antibody detection methods similar to HIV.

Currently, HIV-2 seems to be rare in the United States, having been reported in a total of six cases as of the end of August 1989. All but one of these cases of HIV-2 infection were reported from the northeastern part of the U.S., and all appear to have become infected through heterosexual contact with persons in West African countries. Although there has been no evidence for the presence of this virus in the blood-banking system, the FDA has recommended that all donated blood specimens that are positive for HIV-1 be tested for HIV-2, using HIV-2–specific tests. Additionally, blood-collection agencies have been instructed to exclude donors who have recently emigrated from sub-Sahara Africa or who have had sexual contacts with West Africans. It should also be noted that none of the six HIV-2 infected persons from the United States was a blood donor.[18,19] The identification of HIV-2 raises the possibility of other yet-unidentified human immunodeficiency viruses.

Methods to Detect HIV

The ability to detect the human immunodeficiency virus on a widespread basis has existed since 1985, when the Food and Drug Administration licensed the first screening test to detect antibodies to HIV. As a result of these testing techniques, much information has been gained about the extent of the prevalence of the virus within various population groups, and strategies for intervention and prevention have been improved. The greatest application has been in the area of screening the blood supply, thereby ensuring its safety.

HIV testing can be divided into three major areas. The first involves direct culturing of the virus within various types of cells in the laboratory setting. The techniques for HIV culture, however, are somewhat cumbersome, expensive, and time-consuming.[20,21] Such testing is also somewhat poor at detecting the presence of the virus. HIV-culturing techniques are therefore used within research facilities.

A second area of HIV testing involves techniques that directly detect antigens (i.e., proteins) either on the surface of HIV or within the virus. These methods show definite promise and indeed some laboratories are offering direct antigen techniques at the present time (i.e., P24 antigen testing). They may well eventually become more widely utilized, since they potentially can detect the presence of the virus prior to antibody formation.

The third area of testing for HIV involves methods used to detect antibodies against HIV. Antibody testing is the current method of choice for detecting HIV within potentially susceptible individuals.[22]

Two types of antibody tests exist. The first category of tests are utilized as screening methods to detect HIV. The second category of tests are called confirmatory tests, which are applied when the screening tests for HIV are positive. Both the screening and confirmatory tests are highly accurate, and both must be positive for an individual to be labelled as having HIV within his or her system.

The screening method for HIV used worldwide is called the ELISA test. This is the test that is first utilized by a physician when testing patients for the presence of HIV. ELISA testing is also the method used within the blood-banking system to rule out potentially infected donor units. The ELISA test is both highly sensitive and specific. The ability of a test to identify those who are infected is termed *sensitivity,* which is the probability that a test result will be positive if infection is present. *Specificity* is the ability of a test to exclude those who are not infected. This is also expressed as a probability or percentage indicating that a test result will be negative if infection is not present. Taken together, the sensitivity and specificity of a test describes the ability of the test to separate infected and uninfected populations.[23]

The ELISA test is not only highly accurate, but also is rapid, economical, and may be used by laboratories within the community. If an individual is positive by the ELISA screening test, the specimen is usually repeated again, using the same method; if positive a second time, it is sent on for confirmatory testing.

There are a variety of HIV-antibody tests that are utilized to confirm the presence of HIV following the use of antibody screening techniques. The most common confirmatory test utilized is the Western Blot test. This is a method that detects antibodies to individual HIV proteins. It is a more specific test than the ELISA but is much more complex to perform, interpret, and standardize.[24] Because of these difficulties, only certain laboratories that function as referral centers offer the Western Blot test. A blood test positive by both ELISA and Western Blot is termed a true positive.

There are situations where persons may be positive by the ELISA screening method but negative by Western Blot analysis. These individuals are termed false positives and are not actually infected with HIV. Rarely will the Western Blot test give indeterminant results, and in these situations other methods are available to confirm the presence or absence of HIV.

One of these confirmatory tests is called the indirect immunofluorescence (IFA) test. The IFA is an effective confirmatory test and, if ever automated, may be the best single test available. An additional confirmatory test is the radioimmunoprecipitation assay (RIPA). RIPA is a research method that is labor intensive and requires the utmost skill of trained technologists. It is not utilized on a widespread basis. A new test that shows great promise as a confirmatory test is the polymerase chain reaction, which utilizes technology that can identify the actual DNA sequences of HIV within blood specimens submitted. The polymerase chain reaction test is only available in a very few laboratories.

It should be emphasized that the process of developing tests used to detect the presence of HIV will be a very dynamic one, undergoing constant reevaluation while trying to apply the very best tests available.

Moving from a discussion of HIV itself, we will now look at those populations at risk and not at risk for AIDS.

3

The Epidemiology of AIDS

Epidemiology—the science of the study of disease occurrence within population groups—serves to identify factors that place persons or populations at risk for the development of a particular disease. In the case of AIDS, certain groups of people have been found to be at high risk, with others outside of these groups considered to be at negligible or no risk. This data has been borne out over time and is true worldwide wherever AIDS has been found. It is the intent of this chapter to explore who is at risk and *not* at risk for AIDS.

Global Patterns

It is critical to emphasize that AIDS is not just one country's problem, but rather has international implications and has taken on a global perspective. As of July 1, 1989, 149 countries had reported at least one AIDS case to the World Health Organization (WHO). Although the human immunodeficiency virus (HIV) appears to act in a similar fashion throughout the world in terms of the way it attacks the body, yet clearly there are geographic differences in how populations are affected as well as variations in how the disease manifests. Three global patterns of AIDS have been identified worldwide (see Appendix E).

Pattern 1 is that which characterizes North America and some areas in South America, Western Europe, Australia, and New Zealand. The major affected groups in Pattern 1 are homosexual and bisexual men and intravenous drug users. Heterosexual transmission thus far has been somewhat limited but is on the increase. Another characteristic of Pattern 1 is that transmission of HIV from contaminated blood or blood products would be considered relatively a thing of the past, as widespread testing for HIV is now practiced in the blood-banking system. Pattern 1 seems to reflect the fact that HIV was introduced into these areas in the mid to late 1970s or perhaps into the early 1980s.

Pattern 2, on the other hand, has a distribution including Africa, the Caribbean, and some additional areas of South America. In Pattern 2, heterosexuals are the main group involved, with up to twenty-five percent of the young adult population in certain urban areas being affected. Homosexual transmission and I.V. drug use are not major factors in the spread of HIV in this pattern. Transfusion of HIV-infected blood products, however, still remains a potentially major health problem. Because of the high prevalence of infected child-bearing women (i.e., 5 percent–15 percent in certain areas), the number of pediatric AIDS can be anticipated to be correspondingly high. Pattern 2 most likely reflects an introduction of the virus into these areas in the early to mid-1970s (somewhat earlier than Pattern 1).

Pattern 3 would include essentially the rest of the world and specifically Asia, the Middle East, Eastern

Europe, and so on. In these areas, there continues to remain a very low prevalence of HIV; relative to Patterns 1 and 2, AIDS does not appear to be a significant problem at present. Pattern 3 would be characterized by the introduction of HIV sometime in the early to mid-1980s.

The implication of these patterns from a historical perspective has been commented on in chapter 1. The available data suggests that HIV may have started to spread within urban areas of central Africa during the late 1970s, with subsequent spread to other parts of the world such as the United States and Western Europe thereafter. The World Health Organization has estimated that approximately 500,000 cases of AIDS occurred globally by mid-1989, with 5 to 10 million people being infected with HIV. The actual number of AIDS cases reported is much lower than the estimated number because of widespread underreporting (estimated 20 percent rate of underreporting or only eighty of a hundred cases will be reported).

Of those cases that have been reported worldwide, about 70 percent have been reported from the United States. Reporting of AIDS cases from the continent of Africa has no doubt been incomplete and in general delayed. It is important to understand the epidemiological differences between the United States and Africa as examples of Patterns 1 and 2 respectively. Much of the rest of this chapter will be devoted to these two geographic areas of involvement.

AIDS in the United States

Since 1981 and up until the date of this writing, just over 100,000 cases of AIDS have been reported from the United States, with over half of these persons having already died. AIDS is a disease predominantly involving young adults, with approximately 50 percent of cases occurring between ages 30 and 39, and 90 percent occurring between 20 and 50 years of age. AIDS has exerted a substantial impact on young-adult mortality; in 1987, AIDS deaths accounted for 11 percent of all deaths in men 25 to 34 years of age and 9 percent of all deaths in men aged 35 to 44. For women these proportions were 3 percent and 1 percent respectively.

Although white Caucasians have been the largest group reported with AIDS to date, the virus is rapidly spreading through the black and Hispanic communities. Comparing rates per 100,000 population, blacks are 3.2 times more likely, and Hispanics 2.8 times more likely, than whites to have AIDS. Most authorities estimate that soon these segments of the population will eclipse white Caucasians in terms of overall numbers affected. Correspondingly, AIDS is rapidly becoming a disease of the lower socioeconomic groups.

Clearly, the largest group affected in the U.S. thus far consists of homosexual or bisexual men without a history of intravenous drug use (61 percent). An additional 7 percent have been homosexual or bisexual I.V. drug users. The second biggest risk-factor group represents those heterosexual men and women with a history of I.V. drug use: 21 percent of the total cases. In addition, 1 percent of adults with AIDS have acquired it because of receiving blood factor products for the treatment of hemophilia. Another 2 percent of the cases in this country have been associated with other blood transfusions, with exposure occurring prior to the screening for HIV that began in 1985. Finally, 5 percent of the cases have been attributed to heterosexual transmission alone, the male-to-female ratio in this group being approximately one to one. Overall, the male-to-female ratio in the U.S. is at least four to one.

In the remaining three percent of adults with AIDS, the means of acquiring HIV is not known. When this group has been studied further with standardized questionnaires, approximately 40 percent give a history of another sexually transmitted disease and one-third give a history of prostitute contact. Therefore, most authorities point out that although a small category of individuals does exist where HIV exposure risk is unknown, it appears that most of these probably have had high-risk exposure. A breakdown of each of the HIV risk categories in the U.S. adult population is useful (see Appendix F).

AIDS in Homosexual and Bisexual Men

In the United States, most sexual transmission of HIV early on occurred between homosexual men, and this clearly was the first population involved.[1] There is little doubt that the degree of sexual promiscuity in this population promoted the rapid spread of HIV in the late 1970s and early 1980s. An example of this was highlighted in a recent book, *And the Band Played On: People, Politics, and the AIDS Epidemic* by Randy Schilts, who reported the multiple homosexual encounters of an airline steward from Montreal, Quebec, Canada.[2] This individual may have spread HIV to at least 40 of the first 248 cases reported in the United States by April 1982.

Although the mean annual number of sexual partners of homosexual and bisexual men is less than ten, a small subpopulation within the homosexual community reported very high numbers of different sexual partners per year, some reporting as many as a thousand different contacts. Because of the rapid spread of HIV within the homosexual community, the prevalence of this virus has risen to a very high level in certain areas such as San Francisco and New York City, where an estimated 70 percent of homosexual men are infected with the virus.[3] On a nationwide level, the proportion of individuals infected in the homosexual community has been estimated to be around 15 percent. If this is true, then possibly 900,000 to 1,000,000 homosexual and bisexual men may be currently infected in the U.S.

The risk of infection within the homosexual community clearly increases with the number of sexual partners and the frequency with which receptive anal intercourse is practiced.[4] Anal intercourse causes considerable trauma to the lining of the rectum, with subsequent bleeding and exposure of blood to infected semen.

Other risk factors for the development of HIV infection include a history of gonorrhea or hepatitis. Additionally, sores in the genital and anal area caused by such infections as genital herpes, chancroid, gonorrhea, syphilis, and Chlamydia may predispose to increasing the effectiveness of HIV's entrance into the body.[5] Also, uncircumcised men appear to be at greater risk. It should be noted that the rate of new infection among homosexuals has fallen tremendously because of significant behavioral changes within this group.[6]

Female-to-female transmission of HIV has been reported in several cases.[7] The risk factors here appear to be related to traumatic sexual practices. Overall, the frequency of female-to-female transmission appears to be extremely low.

AIDS in Intravenous Drug Users

As noted, I.V. drug users constitute the second-largest risk group for AIDS in the United States. It has been estimated that there are approximately 1.2 million intravenous drug users in the U.S., and as many as half of these in some areas are known to be infected with HIV. This is the case in New York City, which has approximately 200,000 intravenous drug users, with 100,000 of these being HIV positive.[8] The nationwide prevalence of HIV in I.V. drug-abusing individuals is estimated to be in the 20 percent range, although prevalence rates vary considerably from one geographic area to another.[9]

Several factors appear to be responsible for the rapid spread of HIV in I.V. drug users, the first being the marked increased incidence of intravenous drug abuse in general.[10,11] Supplies of heroin and cocaine, for instance, markedly increased in the New York City area during the late 1970s and early 1980s, which is the period of time when HIV may have been predominantly introduced into this country.

Another factor is the frequent sharing of needles that contain blood contaminated with HIV. The use of "shooting galleries" provides a context for frequent needle sharing and has been shown to be a risk factor for acquiring HIV.[12,13] "Shooting galleries" are places where used drug paraphernalia can be rented (typically for a dollar or two in New York). Also, many I.V. drug users borrow injection equipment kept by a drug dealer who provides it to customers.

In one study, drug users who used needles at "shooting galleries," particularly later in the AIDS epidemic, were at the highest risk for HIV infection. Additional risk factors for HIV infection in intravenous drug users includes (1) frequency of injection, which appears to be significantly higher for cocaine than for heroin; (2) sharing needles with strangers or acquaintances who are at high risk for HIV infection; (3) the higher prevalence of HIV antibody in blacks and Hispanics (which may be explained in part by higher exposure to "shooting galleries" as well as sharing needles with strangers and high risk acquaintances).[14]

It is important to point out how quickly HIV can spread among a local group of I.V. drug users. This has been demonstrated in several studies, with examples taken from Manhattan (New York City) showing a 40 percent prevalence of HIV among I.V. drug users within three years following the identification of the first HIV-positive individual.[15] In other places, such as Edinburgh, Scotland, the prevalence of HIV rose to approximately 50 percent in only two years after initial introduction of HIV into the community.[16]

Once HIV does become established within a local group, the potential for heterosexual transmission from that group is greatly heightened. This has been strongly demonstrated, again in New York City, where approximately 87 percent of heterosexually acquired HIV has resulted from sexual contact between an I.V. drug user and one who does not utilize drugs.[17] Other studies indicate that approximately 40 percent of the regular partners of intravenous drug users with AIDS have become infected with HIV.[18] Authorities have continued to recommend aggressive efforts at preventing heterosexual transmission from intravenous drug users to individuals who do not inject drugs themselves.

The overall risk-reduction efforts to prevent HIV infection among intravenous drug users will be critical to the control of the AIDS epidemic in the United States. It is debatable whether prevention of HIV infection in this group is actually possible. Clearly, merely providing information about AIDS to I.V. drug users will not be enough to stop HIV transmission. This is demonstrated by the fact that studies in New York City suggest that, as early as 1984, almost the entire intravenous drug user population in that city had knowledge of AIDS and that it could be spread through the sharing of contaminated drug paraphernalia.[19,20] Although behavioral changes were seen in approximately 50 percent of this group, the annual seroconversion rate (the rate of individuals turning from HIV-antibody negative to HIV-antibody positive) continued at about 7 percent (see Note #20).

Many strategies have been proposed, some quite controversial, such as teaching methods for sterilization of drug injection equipment (e.g., using bleach) or by legally providing sterile equipment. Although evaluation of drug-abuse treatment is beyond the scope of this text, it is clear that a multiplicity of methods and programs must be pursued. Clearly, intravenous drug users are a varied population with complex drug habits and sexual behaviors that may vary according to socioeconomic status, race, and ethnic background.[21,22,23] An open-mindedness about being innovative must be encouraged, as drug abuse has become one of the most critical issues of our time and for the U.S. society in particular.

AIDS in the Heterosexual Population

To date, 5 percent of the total number of AIDS cases in the U.S. have apparently been acquired heterosexually. The heterosexual transmission of HIV has been a very controversial subject and has received a tremendous amount of coverage in the media. Heterosexual transmission does occur, and this is evidenced by the AIDS epidemic in Africa and Haiti, where the disease is predominantly involving heterosexual groups. HIV has been isolated from semen and cervical secretions[24,25] and appears to be sufficiently transmitted to either partner by heterosexual vaginal intercourse. In the United States, the proportion of AIDS patients who have acquired their disease via heterosexual transmission is definitely on the rise. In 1985, 1.7 percent of adult cases of AIDS were acquired through heterosexual activity, compared with the present 5 percent figure. This trend is anticipated to increase with time.

Clearly, although the higher the number of heterosexual contacts, the higher the probability of transmission, there are well-documented cases of possible transmission after one or two sexual encounters.[26] A female who has unprotected penile vaginal intercourse with a male HIV carrier is exposed to a 1 in 500 chance of becoming infected after a single encounter.[27] The odds of contracting HIV from someone whose HIV status is unknown but who does not belong to any known high-risk group is 1 in 5,000,000 without using a condom and 1 in 50,000,000 with a condom. Anal intercourse appears to double the risk over vaginal intercourse alone.[28]

In male-to-female transmission, several high-risk groups of men have been identified, including hemophiliacs, intravenous drug users, bisexual men, and men who have acquired HIV through transfusion of other blood products. The rates of HIV infection to females having sexual contact with these various high-risk groups vary between 21 percent and 42 percent.[29,30,31,32]

In female-to-male transmission, prostitution is a major risk factor. Prostitutes provide a reservoir for HIV wherever they have been studied worldwide.[33] The connection of prostitution with intravenous drug use has been mentioned before, with data indicating that as many as 30 percent to 50 percent of women admitted to drug-abuse treatment programs have been involved in prostitution. As will be seen, African prostitutes also have a high incidence of HIV infection, although these individuals usually do not use intravenous drugs.

The possible modes of transmission of HIV during heterosexual activities include vaginal and anal intercourse, which are clearly the highest risk activities. The role of oral sex is somewhat less certain and is likely an improbable or highly infrequent mode of transmission by itself (i.e., apart from vaginal and/or anal intercourse). Kissing does not appear to spread HIV, and there are no well-documented cases in this regard. It is theoretically possible that a risk may exist from what is termed "deep kissing," where the virus could be transmitted through small breaks in the lining of the mouth or if there were mouth sores present.

The above comments pertaining to heterosexually acquired HIV infection have dealt with those individuals with exposure to known high-risk groups. There has been additional considerable concern about what the prevalence and subsequent transmission of HIV might be among heterosexuals if there are no other known risks in either partner. This data has been very difficult to come by, and only limited small studies exist. For example, certain selected segments of the general population have been studied in this regard, including military recruits and blood donors. It has been estimated from these studies that the actual prevalence of HIV infection for military applicants is 0.15 percent (i.e., 1.5

per 1,000) and for first-time blood donors 0.04 percent (i.e., 4 per 10,000).[34] Additional studies have been done in heterosexuals attending sexually transmitted disease (STD) clinics who did not use intravenous drugs. Totals from nine surveys involving STD clinics in six major cities were reported in December 1987. The prevalence of HIV ranged from 0 percent to 1.2 percent among heterosexual individuals without other identified risk factors. In surveys of homosexual patients at these same STD clinics, on the other hand, the HIV prevalence was much higher, ranging from 12 percent to 55 percent.[35]

It would therefore appear that HIV is not running rampant through the heterosexual population apart from exposure to high-risk individuals. This fact has been challenged by the new Masters and Johnson textbook, *On Sex and Human Loving* which came out in 1988.[36] The Masters and Johnson study clearly indicated a much higher prevalence of HIV in the heterosexual population (on the order of 5 percent to 7 percent). Although the book has been criticized because of how the studies were conducted, for example, the data presented cannot be completely ignored. Because of the known potential for heterosexual transmission, the likely overall low HIV prevalence in heterosexuals should not lead to complacency. With a very high incidence of sexual intercourse in high-school and college-aged populations, efforts must be directed toward strongly educating these people about the known potential for transmission of HIV and subsequently AIDS. This is illustrated by several recent studies that suggest that 1 out of every 500 (0.2 percent) college-age students may be infected with HIV.[37,38]

AIDS in Hemophiliac Blood-Transfusion Recipients

Hemophilia A and hemophilia B are inherited disorders of blood-clotting–factor deficiency. In the case of hemophilia A, there is Factor 8 deficiency and in hemophilia B, Factor 9 is deficient. These patients require clotting-factor concentrates that are produced from many donated units of blood. Such individuals were highlighted early in the epidemic as being at risk for AIDS. Reports of AIDS occurrences in hemophiliacs provided persuasive evidence that AIDS was almost certainly caused by a small particle, such as a virus, which could be passed on through the medium of blood products.[39] Indeed, prior to the screening of blood and plasma instituted in 1985, many individuals with these coagulation abnormalities were exposed to HIV.

Nationwide, there has been estimated to be approximately 15,500 people with either hemophilia A or B. Of these individuals, approximately 70 percent of those with hemophilia A and 35 percent with hemophilia B are HIV positive.[40] Hemophiliacs make up 1 percent of the AIDS population in the U.S. Currently, all clotting-factor concentrates are produced from donors screened for HIV antibody. The clotting-factor concentrates are also heat-treated, which inactivates any virus that might not have been detected in the screening process. Therefore, acquisition of HIV through clotting-factor concentrates should for the most part be a thing of the past.

AIDS in Other Blood-Transfusion Recipients

Transfusion-associated AIDS, apart from the hemophiliacs, has accounted for approximately 2 percent of adult patients with AIDS and 11 percent of children with AIDS. Individuals receiving blood transfusions between 1978 and 1985 would be considered at increased risk. The CDC has estimated that as many as 12,000 people living in the United States acquired a transfusion-associated HIV infection during this time period.[41] Most of these patients have received transfusions in the setting of various surgical procedures. The natural history of transfusion-associated AIDS has suggested that (1) over 95 percent of patients exposed to HIV through blood transfusions have become infected, and (2) AIDS might be expected to develop in approximately 50 percent of these individuals within seven years.[42]

As noted above, current screening techniques have greatly diminished the problem of transfusion-associated AIDS. The blood supply, however, can never be guaranteed 100 percent safe, since it is possible for a blood donor to be negative for HIV antibody while donating the unit of blood but actually be carrying the virus. Persons who become infected with HIV usually do not have detectable antibody for two or three months after initial contact with the virus. By six months, approximately 95 percent of those infected will test antibody positive, using current screening techniques. A few percent may never become antibody positive or will turn positive only after several years. Although uncommon, this problem of antibody negativity but virus positivity has been the subject of some concern in terms of HIV-infected units slipping through blood-bank screening programs. A number of studies have estimated the potential risks for acquiring HIV from an HIV-negative donor unit, showing approximate risks of 1 in 150,000 to 1 in 250,000.[43,44] Improved techniques for finding the virus in the bloodstream prior to the appearance of antibody are being developed.

AIDS in Children

As of September 1, 1989, 1,780 children (younger than thirteen years of age) had been diagnosed with AIDS. The risk groups for children have been mentioned before. Approximately 80 percent of children who have AIDS have acquired it via transmission from an infected mother. Another 11 percent have acquired it via blood transfusion, as noted above, with an additional 6 percent having acquired HIV as a result of having either hemophilia A or B. There are several case reports of HIV transmission through breast-feeding, and this would remain a plausible, although very infrequent, risk factor. In 3 percent of pediatric cases, the mode of HIV acquisition is unknown.[45] (See Appendix F.)

HIV Infection in the General Population

Attempts at estimating the prevalence of HIV in the general population of the United States have been difficult. Several groups have been tested and evaluated to try to estimate the overall prevalence. These include blood donors, military applicants, job-corps entrants, patients at sentinel hospitals, and some women of reproductive age. The overall prevalence among first-time blood donors and military recruits has been previously mentioned. Of the job-corps entrants tested (25,000 individuals), 0.33 percent (3 per 1,000) were HIV positive. At designated institutions (sentinel hospitals), patients from all age groups being treated for physical conditions not related to HIV were found to have an HIV prevalence of 0.32 percent (3 per 1,000). The testing of childbearing women in Massachusetts showed a prevalence of 0.21 percent (2 per 1,000).[46]

HIV Infection in Other Settings

Prisoners and health-care workers represent groups that have not yet been mentioned. The prevalence of HIV antibody among prisoners is higher than in the general population, likely reflecting an increased incidence of intravenous drug use and/or homosexual activity in prison. Many prisons have tested large numbers of individuals, and the rate of HIV positivity has ranged from 0.1 percent to 17.1 percent.[47]

The risk of acquiring HIV in a health-care setting appears to be very low, with the risk following needlestick exposure to be estimated at less than 1 percent. As of April 22, 1988, a total of fifteen patients worldwide had been reported to have acquired HIV in a health-care setting, with no other apparent risk outside of their employment. Eleven of these cases were reported from the United States, and most of these followed needlestick exposure. An additional seven health-care workers with no other identified risk factors reportedly have acquired HIV infection, but the documentation in these cases was not as reliable.[48]

Taken all together, the number of individuals infected with HIV in the United States has been estimated to be between 1 and 1.5 million. These figures correspond to a 0.4 percent to 0.6 percent infection rate in the U.S. population of 245 million. It is estimated that possibly as many as 2.5 million individuals will be infected by 1991, with between 250,000 and 300,000 cases of AIDS having been diagnosed. A cumulative death toll of 150,000 is expected, including some 54,000 deaths in that year alone. The annual number of new cases is projected to increase by 10,000 per year—from 39,000 in 1988 to 80,000 in 1992. Projections beyond this are difficult, but the number of people possibly infected by HIV may rise to 3.3. million by 1994. To extend this even further, by 2025, estimates of possibly up to 25 million people have been offered. The awesome potential death toll is obvious.

The Issue of Casual Contact

The previously described routes of transmission clearly account for the overwhelming majority of HIV infection in the United States. There still is great concern over the possibility of acquiring HIV through other means, such as "casual contact." It is critical at this point to emphasize that a rational response in this area must be based on objective information and not on theoretical possibilities. One cannot guarantee that HIV on rare occasions could not be transmitted by an alternative route not already mentioned. However, one does not or should not live on the basis of rare theoretical possibilities but rather on the basis of consistent, reproducible, and verifiable evidence. Since AIDS presents great potential for hysteria, it is crucial to act on fact rather than on feeling.

Although HIV has been recovered from saliva, the isolation rate is extremely low (on the order of 1 percent). There has been no convincing evidence that HIV may be transmitted through bites, although one case from West

Germany did suggest that a bite was the route of HIV transmission between two young siblings.[49]

Extensive studies have been done, focusing on family members of children and adults who have been infected with HIV. In all of these "household contact studies," none of the family members contracted HIV except if sexual contact was experienced or in the situation where children were born to infected mothers.[50,51] The risk of transmission in other social settings, such as in the community, the work place, the school, or the church, would be expected to be even lower than the household risk. (See Appendix C and D.)

There is currently no evidence that HIV can be transmitted by insects or via drinking water, food, inanimate objects (e.g., doorknobs, toilet seats), swimming pools, hot tubs, and so on. Additionally, the virus is not contracted via aerosolization and therefore cannot be "breathed in."

As can be seen from the above information, the transmission of HIV requires exposure to certain high-risk settings. *If the high-risk exposure is avoided, the risks for acquiring HIV and AIDS become extraordinarily small. Since the virus is not casually acquired, AIDS patients can be safely incorporated into a variety of different social contexts.*

AIDS in Africa

Just as the United States is the main example of Pattern 1 HIV transmission, so the continent of Africa is the prime example of Pattern 2. Soon after the reporting of AIDS cases in the United States, cases of the disease were seen in Africans residing in Europe,[52] and by March 1986, 157 cases of AIDS were reported among Africans living in eight different European countries.[53] Most of these individuals came from central African countries (e.g., 63 percent from Zaire).

What was very interesting early on was that the male-to-female ratio of these African cases was much different from that of their European or American counterparts. A male-to-female ratio of nearly one to one was seen early on, and 90 percent of these cases had no identifiable risk factors, such as homosexuality or intravenous drug use.[54] Other studies confirmed the equal distribution of AIDS among African men and women from such places as Kinshasa, Zaire.[55] More recent evidence suggests that in several central African countries an actual female predominance may exist, with more than a twofold greater risk for women.[56] Outbreaks of AIDS among men and women in Africa have been linked predominantly to heterosexual contact, and additional studies from Rwanda have shown that a significant number of female patients with AIDS were prostitutes (43 percent).[57]

Although it is difficult to assess precisely where the first AIDS cases occurred in Africa, it is apparent that HIV infection probably occurred earlier in Africa than in such other areas of the world as the United States, Europe, and Haiti. As noted before, the earliest evidence for the presence of HIV in the world was found by testing stored serum collected from Kinshasa (Zaire) in 1959.[58] Other stored sera from both East and West Africa in the 1960s and early 1970s have also shown a high prevalence of weakly HIV-positive specimens. Although this limited evidence points to the presence of HIV within central Africa prior to anywhere else, it should be noted that no firm conclusions can be drawn as to the origin of AIDS. In fact, actual AIDS-like cases in Africa began to appear at approximately the same time as in the United States. In Africa, AIDS was manifesting as an epidemic of a chronic wasting illness known as "slim disease," occurring in Kinshasa in the late 1970s as well as Uganda in the 1980s.[59] Both Kaposi's sarcoma and opportunistic infections were also showing a marked rise between 1978 and 1984, similar to that seen in the United States during this period.

Current data would suggest that central Africa is the most severely affected by HIV infection, although other areas of Africa are showing increasing numbers of cases of the disease. Countries reporting the presence of HIV have included (in alphabetical order): Botswana, Burundi, Central African Republic, Cameroon, Congo, Gabon, Gambia, Kenya, Malawi, Rwanda, Senegal, South Africa, Tanzania, Transkei, Uganda, Zaire, Zambia, and Zimbabwe. The actual prevalence of HIV has been variable, depending on the population selected. Studies have shown that among female prostitutes—depending on the geographic location as well as economic status—anywhere from 27 percent to 88 percent of these individuals are HIV positive.[60,61] The overall prevalence rate in certain African countries suggests that as many as 5 percent of the total population may be infected. If this is true, a staggering death toll can be anticipated by the year 2000.

The mean age of AIDS patients in Africa follows that seen in the United States (young and middle-aged individuals). Women with AIDS are more likely to be unmarried than their male counterparts, and at least a third of the married AIDS patients had at least one previous marriage.

As noted previously, it is apparent from numerous studies that neither homosexuality nor I.V. drug use seems to play a significant role in HIV transmission in Africa. Clearly, available data suggests that heterosexual transmission, blood transfusions, mother-to-child transmission during pregnancy, and possibly frequent exposure to unsterilized needles (apart from I.V. drug use) accounts for the spread of HIV in Africa.

Specific risk factors associated with HIV infection in African heterosexuals include (1) the number of sexual partners; (2) sexual contact with prostitutes; (3) being a prostitute; and (4) being a sexual partner of an infected person. As with AIDS patients in the U.S., HIV positivity has also been associated with other sexually transmitted diseases (STD's) such as chancroid, syphilis, and gonorrhea. Corresponding and additional factors that appear to enhance susceptibility to HIV during sexual transmission include the presence of ulcerative lesions on the genitalia (caused by other STD's), the uncircumcised state, and oral contraceptives. Because of the high incidence of HIV within childbearing-aged women in Africa, a significant number of newborn children are being infected with HIV.

Transmission of HIV via exposure to infected blood-donor units appears to be an ongoing problem in Africa, due to the fact that screening of donors is not performed for either hepatitis B or HIV in many areas. This, coupled with the high prevalence rate among blood donors in certain areas such as Uganda, Rwanda, and Zaire (8 percent to 18 percent), suggests that transfusion risk may still be quite high. Exposure to unsterilized needles or other instruments that would be used to pierce the skin for ritual purposes (i.e., scarification, tattooing, etc.) would also have the potential to transmit HIV.

As demonstrated in Pattern 1 areas, HIV does not appear to be more readily transmitted by casual contact in Africa. There is no direct evidence for insect transmission of HIV in Africa, as has also been the case in the United States.[62]

In addition to HIV, a second AIDS virus has been isolated, that being HIV-2, which was identified in 1985 in Senegal prostitutes.[63] The virus has been predominantly isolated from West African countries, and information suggests that—like HIV-1—HIV-2 infects populations in a similar manner, with heterosexual activity being the most predominant mode.

Clearly, the studies of AIDS in Africa have greatly helped in the overall understanding of the worldwide AIDS epidemic. To summarize, HIV in Africa is predominantly a heterosexually transmitted disease, with the main risk factor being the degree of sexual promiscuity rather than sexual orientation (as in the United States).

We will next turn our attention to what happens to the individual person infected with HIV, as consideration is given to the clinical aspects of AIDS.

4

The Clinical Manifestations of AIDS

The previous three chapters have focused on the historical developments in the AIDS epidemic, the causative agent of AIDS, as well as how the disease is transmitted and which population groups are affected. It is the intent of this chapter to present the current understanding of the wide clinical manifestations of the human immunodeficiency virus (HIV).

As already noted, the term *AIDS* was developed to describe a new disorder affecting previously healthy young adults who were reported with unusual infections as well as a rare form of skin cancer called Kaposi's sarcoma.[1,2,3] These conditions had been previously described only in patients who had immune suppression from other causes, including chemotherapeutic cancer drugs or underlying diseases that suppress the cellular immunity, such as various malignancies (i.e. leukemias and lymphomas). In addition, almost all of the initial patients described came from certain groups of people whose habits or lifestyles seemed to be placing them at risk for this disease (homosexual men and I.V. drug users).

The initial definition for AIDS was proposed by the Centers for Disease Control prior to the discovery of HIV and included patients with any of a number of opportunistic infections, such as Pneumocystis cariini pneumonia or with the malignancy known as Kaposi's sarcoma.[4] Two exclusionary provisions were included at first: (1) that AIDS could be diagnosed only if other causes for immune deficiency were ruled out; and (2) in the case of Kaposi's sarcoma, the patient had to be less than sixty years of age (since Kaposi's was known to affect predominantly elderly people in the non-AIDS population). With the identification of HIV as the cause of AIDS and with increasing numbers of people being tested positive for the virus, it became obvious that the definition for AIDS was inadequate and would require revision. (See Appendix G.)

HIV testing allowed the inclusion of additional opportunistic diseases to the AIDS group of disorders, therefore broadening the overall picture of AIDS itself. Additionally, there was a growing number of individuals being identified from the same high-risk groups as AIDS patients who were HIV positive but who had less severe manifestations (known as AIDS-related complex or ARC). These manifestations included such things as generalized lymph node enlargement (lymphadenopathy), weight loss, fever, night sweats, weakness, fatigue, and diarrhea. It was also noted that many of these individuals with "lesser manifestations" had the same lowering of their T-helper lymphocyte counts and that some went on to develop full-blown AIDS.[5]

In addition to AIDS and ARC patients, other groups of people who were HIV positive, from the same high-risk groups, felt completely healthy and had no untoward symptoms. With time, an entire spectrum of illness was seen, ranging from total lack of symptoms to very severe life-threatening disease. The common thread in all of this was the presence of HIV. Therefore, although "AIDS" has become the byword of this epidemic, what should be emphasized is *HIV-related disease,* of which AIDS is the most severe manifestation.

Classification of HIV-Associated Disease

As information regarding HIV grew, the terms used to describe the various stages of this virus, such as AIDS and ARC (AIDS-related complex), became somewhat confusing in the medical literature as they were being applied to different conditions by various research groups. The term *AIDS* was most often used to describe those patients with the most severe forms of the disease, particularly opportunistic infections and tumors. ARC, on the other hand, was typically applied to people who had "constitutional" symptoms such as fever, night sweats, weight loss, and less severe infections, including Candida infections of the mouth (thrush) and shingles. It became apparent that a more uniform classification was needed.

In 1986, two classifications were developed, the first by the Centers for Disease Control, which divided patients with HIV into four main groups, as well as a number of subgroups.[6] While this has proven to be a useful scheme of classification, it does not utilize the familiar terms, AIDS and ARC, which has bothered some clinicians. The other classification system was developed by the Walter Reed Army Institute of Research.[7] This system divides HIV-infected patients into one of six different stages, each describing a more severe clinical or laboratory effect of the virus. The major advantage of the Walter Reed classification is that it can be used to follow the progression of the effect of the virus on the body, as well as make it simpler to select groups of patients for study. The reader may refer to Appendix H to study the CDC classification system for HIV. For the purpose of this text and in view of the familiarity of the usual terms, the clinical manifestations of HIV will be described in four separate categories or stages: (1) acute HIV infection; (2) asymptomatic HIV infection and lymphadenopathy; (3) AIDS-related complex (ARC); and (4) AIDS. It should be noted that these stages cannot be thought of as being absolutely distinct from each other, since there is considerable overlap from one stage to the next. Also, the progression to AIDS (Stage 4) does not necessarily proceed from 1 to 4, as Stages 1, 2, and 3 may variably appear or never be apparent to the patient or physician.

1. Acute HIV Infection

Shortly following infection with HIV, many individuals (one- to two-thirds) will develop an acute mononucleosis-like illness that is usually sudden in onset and lasts from several days to a few weeks. Symptoms include fever, muscle and joint aching, enlarged lymph nodes, sore throat, headache and skin rash.[8,9,10] In addition, several more serious symptoms have been described, including a form of meningitis and encephalitis, which may result in mental status changes, seizures, and so on.

During this acute illness, patients often do not test positive for HIV antibody, and it is typically only after the resolution of their symptoms that HIV becomes detectable. Methods for directly detecting HIV instead of the antibody have been developed and are now being made increasingly available to clinicians caring for AIDS patients. These methods may show the presence of HIV even though the antibody may be absent.

Acute HIV infection, as noted, occurs within the first several weeks after contact with the virus and is usually completely self-limited, meaning that all manifestations resolve and the patient feels well again. Following the resolution of the illness, the patient then usually enters a phase known as asymptomatic (without symptoms) infection. Acute HIV infection corresponds to group one in the CDC classification system.

2. *Asymptomatic HIV Infection and Generalized Lymphadenopathy*

This early stage of HIV infection comprises groups two and three from the CDC classification system and describes those individuals who are HIV infected and either have no clinical manifestations of illness attributable to HIV or have generalized lymphadenopathy as the main clinical finding.

The asymptomatic HIV-positive population no doubt makes up the largest group of infected individuals. During this early stage of HIV infection, the patient feels well and in general has normal numbers of T-helper lymphocytes. Although HIV is dormant in the sense of not causing symptoms, it must be emphasized that the virus can definitely be transmitted at this stage through sexual contact, the sharing of contaminated needles, and so on. This stage, also called the "incubation period," lasts for a number of years (median of 9.8 years) before any symptoms attributable to HIV appear (i.e., ARC or AIDS).[11] Several studies corroborate that approximately 45 percent to 50 percent of those infected with HIV will progress to AIDS within ten years. The risk of progression to AIDS after HIV infection continues to increase with time, and most authorities believe that the natural course of HIV includes the eventual development of AIDS in all those infected.

The presence of lymphadenopathy in those with AIDS was noted early in the epidemic.[12] Indeed, the incidence of lymphadenopathy in patients with HIV infection is quite high, ranging up to approximately 70 percent.[13] In some cases, enlarged lymph nodes may be noted by the patients themselves, whereas in others it is first found during physical examination.

The "lymphadenopathy syndrome" (group three in the CDC classification) is defined by one centimeter in size lymph nodes at two different sites (other than the groin areas) that are present for at least three months. Additionally, it must be shown that the enlarged lymph nodes are not attributable to other causes and are not associated with other symptoms.

In a sense, the lymphadenopathy syndrome is closely associated with asymptomatic HIV infection, since the enlargement of these lymph nodes is painless and, as noted above, the patient may be completely unaware of this finding. The cause of lymphadenopathy is related to the immune system's reactive response to HIV and therefore represents a benign process in and of itself. Occasionally, tumors can involve the lymph system in AIDS (Kaposi's sarcoma and lymphoma), but typically the lymph nodes are much larger in these situations. Biopsies of continually enlarging lymph nodes are usually performed and help distinguish between benign and malignant causes of lymphadenopathy.

3. AIDS-Related Complex (ARC)

As knowledge of AIDS grew, it was apparent that many individuals developed signs and symptoms less severe than those found in AIDS patients but which seemed to predict the eventual development of full-blown AIDS. A number of terms were used to describe this stage of HIV infection such as "pre-AIDS" or "lesser AIDS." The term most commonly used is "AIDS-related complex" (ARC), which represents a middle stage of HIV infection. Patients in the ARC category have a number of common general symptoms, including fever for at least three months, night sweats, fatigue, diarrhea, weight loss, and lymphadenopathy.[14,15,16] A number of infections also occur in this group, including Candida infection of the oral cavity (thrush) and shingles (caused by herpes zoster).

It is clear that several of these clinical findings in

ARC patients predict progression to full-blown AIDS. Both thrush and certain forms of shingles have been strongly associated with progression to AIDS.[17] Also, those individuals who have reported fever, weight loss, and diarrhea have an increased risk to progress to AIDS.[18,19]

In ARC patients, as well as those in the asymptomatic/lymphadenopathy stage, a number of characteristic immune and blood-test abnormalities can be seen, including decreased numbers of T-helper lymphocyte cells, increased amounts of blood protein (serum globulins), and a condition known as anergy, which describes a decrease in the cellular immune system's ability to respond to common antigens as measured by skin testing. Other blood abnormalities may develop, such as a lowered total white-blood-cell count (leukopenia), lowered red-blood-cell count (anemia), and lowered platelet count (thrombocytopenia).

Some of these blood-test abnormalities that predict progression to AIDS include (1) low total numbers of T-helper cells[20] (i.e., counts lower than 400 cells per cubic millimeter of blood); (2) lowered blood counts (leukopenia, anemia, and thrombocytopenia)[21]; (3) elevated serum $Beta_2$ microglobulin (a blood protein); and (4) the appearance of HIV core antigen (P24 antigen).[22,23] The appearance of P24 antigen in the patient's serum is associated with a selective loss of antibody to the P24 antigen (while antibodies to other parts of the virus do not decline). The P24 antigen indicates that there is a rise in HIV activity, probably as a result of increasing impairment of the immune system's ability to control the infection.

4. AIDS

The last stage of HIV infection is the full-blown syndrome of AIDS itself. The number of HIV-infected persons who go on to develop AIDS is not completely known, since HIV has a long incubation period and therefore may not manifest with symptoms for many years after initial infection. As noted, the current information suggests that 45 percent to 50 percent of those individuals infected with HIV will develop AIDS within ten years. Since the risk of progressing to the AIDS stage definitely increases with time, theoretically every person infected with HIV may at some point develop AIDS, be it at three, five, ten, or fifteen years after infection. Some investigators feel that there may be a small proportion infected with HIV who will become truly "immune" to the virus and never develop symptomatic disease. This remains to be established.

It should be noted here that AIDS is not a single disease *per se,* but actually many different diseases that all share a common underlying cause, that of the human immunodeficiency virus. The definition for AIDS has changed as knowledge has increased. On August 14, 1987, the Centers for Disease Control (CDC) proposed its latest revision of the case definition for AIDS.[24] This represented an expansion of the prior definition and has resulted in better reporting of AIDS cases.

The revised definition is divided into three different sections dependent on the presence of HIV antibody (see Appendix G). The first section applies to those patients for whom HIV testing has not been performed or has given inconclusive results; the second refers to those for whom HIV testing is done and is positive. The third section includes those patients for whom laboratory tests were actually negative for HIV antibody. In all three areas, there is included a list of opportunistic diseases or, as the CDC has called them, "indicator diseases," which designate whether or not the diagnosis of AIDS can be applied. It is the presence of these opportunistic diseases that *indicate* the terminal-stage effects of HIV, both on the immune system as well as on the central nervous system (see chapter 2 on how HIV affects the body).

As noted above, the CDC's definition for AIDS

revolves around the presence or absence of HIV antibody. Those patients without laboratory evidence for HIV may be diagnosed as having AIDS if they have any one of the indicator diseases listed in section 1B (see Appendix G) *and* another cause of immune deficiency (i.e., besides HIV) is not present. Other causes of immunodeficiency that would disqualify the diagnosis of AIDS in this section would include (1) the taking of medications that would suppress the immune system, such as steroids or chemotherapeutic agents; (2) a number of malignancies that likewise can affect the immune system, including such disorders as Hodgkin's or non-Hodgkin's lymphoma, lymphocytic leukemia, and other cancers of the lymph system; (3) the presence of various congenital immune deficiency syndromes. (See section 1A.)

When HIV antibody is present by testing, the list of indicator diseases increases in addition to those listed in the first section. (See section 1B, 2A, and 2B in Appendix G.)

The last category in the definition of AIDS would include those patients who have negative HIV-antibody tests but are still diagnosed with AIDS because of the exclusion of other causes of immune deficiency and the presence of one or more of those indicator diseases listed in the first section as well as a T-helper cell count of less than 400 per cubic millimeter.

Once the patient has been diagnosed with one of the indicator diseases and therefore with AIDS, the survival prospects diminish considerably, with a mortality rate of approximately 80 percent at three years. The actual case-fatality ratio approaches 100 percent within five years after the diagnosis of AIDS. As of September 1, 1989, a total of 60,684 deaths had occurred in the U.S. from the adult/adolescent AIDS population (58.2 percent) and 971 deaths in the pediatric AIDS population (54.6 percent). Although AIDS mortality is certainly frightening, it should be emphasized that the life expectancy of AIDS patients has been definitely improving. This improved outlook is the result of earlier identification and management of HIV-related infection as well as the use of anti-HIV drugs such as AZT (see chapter 5).

The complexity of AIDS is appreciated when it is recognized that often times more than one indicator disease occurs in the same patient. Indeed, it is somewhat unusual for an AIDS patient to only have one opportunistic disease during his or her lifetime.

Indicator Diseases

At this point a discussion of the indicator diseases is in order, and these will be broken into four categories: (1) opportunistic infections; (2) AIDS-related malignancies; (3) HIV encephalopathy (HIV in the central nervous system); and (4) HIV wasting syndrome. Following that, a section on pediatric AIDS will be presented to highlight some of the differences between pediatric and adult AIDS cases.

Opportunistic Infections

An "opportunist" may be defined as one who takes advantage of a certain situation. An "opportunistic infection" is one that would not ordinarily occur with an intact immune system and therefore takes advantage of the lack of normal defense mechanisms that would protect the individual. Opportunistic infections are clearly the major cause of illness and death in HIV-infected patients, being responsible for 90 percent of the fatalities that occur in AIDS.

Although HIV-infected patients have an increased susceptibility to the more common infections in the community such as influenza, they are at greatest risk from organisms that typically only affect patients with disorders associated with immune suppression. AIDS is characterized by a marked deficiency in cell-mediated immunity, which is directly related to the loss of the T-helper lymphocyte cell. As the T-helper cell count progressively falls (especially below 400 per cubic millimeter), the risk for the occurrence of these opportunistic infections rises dramatically.

The clinical presentation of many of these infections is indolent and subtle. Often several infections may occur at the same time, and there is a high incidence of relapse. For the most part, effective therapy is available and, if started early, a high percentage will respond. Unfortunately, with such a high relapse rate, treatment must be continued for the lifetime of the individual. The characteristic opportunistic infections in HIV patients arise from the four major groups of organisms, those being parasites, fungi, bacteria, and viruses. Appendix I gives a listing of the clinical manifestations in HIV-infected patients. Since it is beyond the scope of this text to give an exhaustive discussion of each infection, the more common organisms will be highlighted.

Parasitic Infections. Clearly the most commonly recognized opportunistic infection in AIDS is caused by an organism called Pneumocystis cariini. Pneumocystis was the first manifestation of AIDS reported in the United States and heralded the beginning of the epidemic.[25] (See chapter 1.)

Pneumocystis cariini is a protozoan of mammals that is widespread throughout the world. Although it is poorly understood how humans acquire the organism, infection likely occurs early in life via the respiratory route. An affinity for the lungs is characteristic, and it remains in a dormant stage until significant depression of the immune system occurs, at which time it may reactivate and cause pneumonia. Pneumocystis pneumonia affects at least 80 percent of AIDS patients and is the initial AIDS-defining indicator disease in approximately 65 percent of HIV-infected persons.

Pneumocystis usually exhibits a number of signs and symptoms, including fever, shortness of breath, cough, and loss of exercise tolerance. It typically is subtle in its onset and indolent in its progression, with patients sometimes having symptoms for weeks and even months prior to the diagnosis being made.

The diagnosis of Pneumocystis is established through the use of a chest X-ray, and typically both lungs are involved. A firm diagnosis is made through the special staining of pulmonary secretions (such as sputum), where the organisms appear as numerous tiny cysts. Other times, more invasive techniques are used, such as examining the bronchial tree (through a bronchoscope) to obtain deeper specimens for examination. Although the physician can strongly suspect Pneumocystis on the basis of clinical presentation as well as the chest X-ray appearance, identification of the characteristic cysts from pulmonary secretions is necessary for a firm diagnosis.

Several medications are available to treat Pneumocystis, but two have clearly predominated. Both Trimethoprim/Sulfamethoxazole (trade names Bactrim or Septra) and Pentamidine are equally effective therapeutic agents for Pneumocystis pneumonia. However, both of these medications may have serious adverse side effects, and when a patient is intolerant of one, switching to the other is necessary. There are situations in which the infection does not respond to one agent but will respond to the other. Typically, therapy by either medication is continued for three weeks, after which lower-dose preventative therapy (prophylaxis) may be used because of the 10 percent-to-40 percent relapse rate within three months.

Three other protozoan parasites cause infections in AIDS patients, these being Cryptosporidium, Isospora belli, and Toxoplasma gondii. Both Cryptosporidium and Isospora cause chronic diarrhea in AIDS patients. Cryptosporidiosis is a persistent and debilitating diarrhea that has been reported in approximately 4 percent of AIDS patients in the United States.[26] Severe watery diarrhea, sometimes occurring ten to twelve times per day, may occur and last for long periods of time. The organism is identified in stool specimens, again through the use of special staining techniques. The therapy for Cryptosporidia has been frustratingly poor, with only one drug showing some promise: Spiramycin. This medication is not available routinely in the United States and must be obtained through special request. Isospora, on the other hand, is effectively treated by one of the same drugs used to treat Pneumocystis, that being Trimethoprim/Sulfamethoxazole.

Toxoplasma gondii is an organism whose definitive host is the cat, from which man acquires the infection. A large percentage of healthy adults have been infected with Toxoplasma, which (like Pneumocystis) goes into a dormant stage, only relapsing when the immune system becomes suppressed. Toxoplasma reactivates in the brain of AIDS patients, causing a form of localized encephalitis. Toxoplasmosis occurs in approximately 3 percent of AIDS patients, and its symptoms include paralysis, seizures, headaches, and stiff neck.[27]

The diagnosis of Toxoplasmosis is typically suggested through the use of computerized axial tomography scanning (CAT scanning) of the brain. The definitive diagnosis is made by brain biopsy, although often times this is not done because of the potential complications of this procedure. Therapy for Toxoplasmosis is often empirically started on the basis of the CAT scan. Two medications are used predominantly in the treatment of Toxoplasmosis: Pyrimethamine and a sulfa drug (Sulfadiazine). Approximately 80 percent of patients will respond with improvement of their symptoms within several weeks after beginning this therapy. Because of the high incidence of relapse following the recommended four-to-six week treatment course, ongoing therapy is usually maintained for the life of the individual.

Fungal Infections. Several fungal organisms cause infections in AIDS patients, those being Cryptococcus neoformans,[28] Candida albicans,[29] Histoplasma capsulatum,[30] and Coccidioides immitis.[31]

Cryptococcus neoformans is a fungus that causes meningitis, presenting most commonly as headache and fever. The diagnosis is made through performing special studies on cerebrospinal fluid (CSF) obtained via spinal tap. Treatment of Cryptococcal meningitis includes Amphoteracin B intravenously in combination with an oral medication, Flucytosine, both given for a total of six weeks. As before, because of the high relapse rate, ongoing suppressive therapy, usually with Amphoteracin B, is required for life. A new oral medication, Fluconazole, has shown considerable promise against cryptococcus and may be a major form of therapy in the future.

Candida infections of the mouth and throat are very common initial manifestations of HIV infection. Candida infection becomes an indicator disease of AIDS when it progresses beyond the throat into the esophagus, causing inflammation (esophagitis) and painful swallowing. Typically, Candida responds readily to orally administered medications, such as Nystatin, Clotrimazole, or Ketoconazole. Amphoteracin B is an intravenous medication that is occasionally necessary for those who do not respond to the oral forms of therapy.

Histoplasmosis and Coccidiomycosis are both yeasts that can cause disseminated fungal infection in AIDS patients. Histoplasma is predominantly found (endemic) in the central and southern United States, whereas Coccidioides is endemic in the southwestern United States, especially southern California and Arizona. Both may cause pneumonia and then spread beyond the lungs to such other organ systems as liver, spleen, lymph node, bone marrow, and central nervous system. To be brought under control, both of these yeasts require aggressive therapy in the form of Amphoteracin B, which typically takes several months to complete. Once again, the relapse rate is high and some form of ongoing suppressive therapy is required.

Bacterial Infections. The most important opportunistic bacterial pathogens in AIDS come from the Mycobacteria and Salmonella families. Mycobacterium tuberculosis is the cause of tuberculosis and is a frequent invader in HIV-infected patients.[32] Although for years the incidence of tuberculosis in the United States had been showing a downward trend, because of HIV and AIDS there has been a definite resurgence of TB around the world. Tuberculosis may appear as various forms of pneumonia in the HIV-infected patient, but it also can spread beyond the lungs to involve virtually any organ system. The treatment of tuberculosis is usually quite successful, with prompt response to classically used anti-TB drugs (Isoniazid, Rifampin, and Ethambutol).[33]

There are several related tuberculous-like organisms from the Mycobacterium family that also cause significant infection in AIDS patients. The most common of these is Mycobacterium avium intracellulare, which can be isolated from 40 percent to 60 percent of AIDS patients.[34] As in tuberculosis itself, Mycobacterium avium intracellulari causes systemic disease, with fever, weight loss, lymphadenopathy, and diarrhea. The organism can be isolated from a variety of sites, including blood, stool, urine, bone marrow, lymph nodes, and pulmonary secretions. It is a common cause of bone-marrow suppression (anemia) in the AIDS patient. Unlike tuberculosis, there are few effective treatment regimens for Mycobacterium avium because of its high degree of resistance to most anti-TB medications.

Salmonella bacteria typically cause diarrhea in the non-AIDS population. With HIV infection, however, Salmonellosis becomes a much more serious infection, with the bacteria spreading beyond the gastrointestinal tract and causing infection of the bloodstream.[35] The organism is usually sensitive to such commonly used antibiotics as Ampicillin, Trimethoprim/Sulfamethoxazole, and Chloramphenicol. A prompt response to one of these antibiotics is usually seen. Following treatment, chronic suppressive antibiotic therapy is usually required because of the high incidence of relapse.

Viral Infections. Several viral infections occur in AIDS patients as a result of immune suppression. The main representatives here come from the herpes-group virus family and include cytomegalovirus (CMV), herpes simplex, herpes zoster, and the Epstein Barr virus (EBV). It is characteristic of all members of the herpes-group family to persist in a so-called dormant phase—with herpes simplex and herpes zoster being stored in nerve endings, CMV in certain white blood cells, and EBV possibly in cells located in the mouth, throat, and salivary glands. With loss of normal immune control, each of these viruses can reactivate and cause inflammation in various parts of the body.

Cytomegalovirus is very common in the general population, occurring in some 45 percent to 80 percent of individuals, depending on the geographic location tested. Since CMV is transmitted sexually or by blood contact, those who are at risk for HIV are also likely to be infected with CMV.[36] Indeed, this is the case in the homosexual community, where over 90 percent have been exposed to the virus. CMV can reactivate and cause inflammation, primarily in the eyes, gastrointestinal tract, and lungs. When the eyes are affected, a form of progressive blindness occurs as a result of inflammation of the retina (chorioretinitis). Loss of sight is a particularly devastating complication in AIDS, given the multitude of other problems that AIDS patients usually encounter.

CMV may cause inflammation of the gastrointestinal tract, causing diarrhea, bleeding, and even bowel perforation. It may also cause pneumonia in HIV-infected patients, which is often life-threatening. CMV has also been reported to cause cerebral disease (encephalitis) and liver inflammation (hepatitis).

A recently FDA-approved and -released medication called Ganciclovir has been used in the treatment of the various manifestations of CMV in the AIDS patient. This medication has been successful in producing resolution of inflammation in many patients, but not all. The patient is usually treated for at least ten to fourteen days and thereafter several times per week for the rest of his or her life to prevent relapse.

Herpes simplex is a frequent cause of ulcerative disease, affecting the skin and mucous membranes of HIV-infected patients. Most commonly, the virus is seen in homosexual males who are HIV-infected, causing inflammation of the colon (colitis) as well as ulcerations in tissue surrounding the anus. This form of inflammation is associated with severe pain and weeping of affected tissues. Herpes simplex may also affect the mouth and lips, as well as cause encephalitis, meningitis, and esophagitis. It is treated with a drug called Acyclovir, which may be given either orally or intravenously and which is quite effective in ameliorating symptoms. Usually patients must be maintained on a chronic suppressive regimen to prevent relapse.

Herpes zoster is the causative agent of chicken pox and shingles. Shingles actually appears to be an early marker for the immune suppression associated with HIV infection and is usually included in the ARC category of patients. In one study, nearly 50 percent of patients who were HIV infected and who had shingles went on to develop AIDS.[37] It should be noted, however, that shingles can occasionally occur in otherwise healthy people who are HIV negative and therefore is not specific for AIDS-related disease.

Shingles usually involves one localized area of skin, but the virus can disseminate to other parts of the body, including involvement of the entire skin surface, as well as to the deeper organs such as the brain and liver. Acyclovir is again the drug of choice for the treatment of herpes-zoster–related infection and is quite effective, especially in the high-dose intravenous form.

The Epstein Barr virus (EBV) is the last member of the herpes-group family that affects HIV-infected patients, and this can be isolated from the throat of the great majority of AIDS patients (90 percent). EBV causes a lesion of the tongue known as oral hairy leukoplakia, which—although not causing significant discomfort—is bothersome to the patient. This virus has also been associated with a form of pneumonia in children with AIDS, called lymphocytic interstitial pneumonitis. EBV can cause certain types of malignancies of the lymph system in both adults and children with HIV infection (i.e., Burkitt-like lymphomas). There is no effective therapy for EBV infection.

AIDS-Related Malignancies

The other major group of "indicator diseases," besides the above-noted opportunistic infections that qualify HIV-infected patients as having AIDS, are the AIDS-related malignancies. These seem to develop because of the lack of a normal tumor-surveillance system, which is provided by an intact immune system. These malignancies include Kaposi's sarcoma, lymphomas, and several miscellaneous cancers.

Clearly, the most common malignancy involving AIDS patients is Kaposi's sarcoma, which up until the time of the AIDS epidemic was a rare and unusual tumor that most often occurred in elderly men of either Italian or Eastern European Jewish ancestry. It had also been reported to involve several other distinct populations such as young, black African men as well as patients receiving different forms of immune-suppressive therapy. The finding of Kaposi's sarcoma in previously healthy, young homosexual men in the United States became a major red flag pointing to an underlying acquired immune deficiency.[38,39] (See also chapter 1.)

Kaposi's sarcoma appears to arise out of the abnormal growth of cells that line blood vessels. It has been suggested that the profound loss of cell-mediated immunity, as well as the presence of certain tumor growth factors emitted by HIV-infected cells, sets up the situation for the development of Kaposi's.

Kaposi's sarcoma usually presents with skin lesions of various sizes and colors. Characteristically, these lesions are brownish red to purple in color and do not typically cause any pain. In addition to the skin, Kaposi's may involve the mucous membranes, such as the lining of the mouth. The cancer often spreads to involve the gastrointestinal tract, lung, liver, spleen, and even the brain. This fulminant "malignant" form of Kaposi's is contrasted to Kaposi's sarcoma, which occurs in the non-AIDS population as a very indolent and often times benign cancer.[40]

Therapy for Kaposi's sarcoma is somewhat limited. Localized skin lesions may be surgically removed or treated with radiation therapy. The more aggressive disseminated form of Kaposi's is treated at times with chemotherapeutic cancer agents that have variable response rates. Recently, the substance alpha-interferon (Roferon) has been shown to be effective in the treatment of Kaposi's. Roferon has received licensing from the FDA and is now on the market for general physician use.

The survival of patients with Kaposi's depends on the extent of the tumor. Localized disease (i.e., skin only) brings a life expectancy of up to two years, compared to a median survival of fifteen months with the disseminated form. If the patient has an opportunistic infection and Kaposi's sarcoma together, the median survival is very poor (seven months). Approximately 20 percent of AIDS patients will develop Kaposi's sarcoma. This percentage appears to be dropping from early in the epidemic, without a clear-cut explanation.

The other major group of malignancies occurring in HIV-infected patients are tumors of the lymph system, called lymphomas. Although reported in the AIDS population in June 1982,[41] lymphoma was not considered an indicator disease of AIDS until June 1985, at which time the definition of AIDS was expanded to include those persons who had high-grade lymphomas and were HIV positive.[42] The majority of these malignancies have occurred in the homosexual male population.

AIDS-related lymphoma is a very aggressive malignancy, often presenting with disease outside of the lymph tissue. The most common site in this situation is the brain, followed by the gastrointestinal tract, bone marrow, and liver. Typical symptoms include fever, drenching night sweats, weight loss, headaches, seizures, and paralysis. Therapy for AIDS-related lymphoma revolves around various chemotherapeutic regimens that have not shown significant success rates; indeed, the median survival of patients with this malignancy has been less than one year.[43,44]

Other cancers that have been associated with HIV infection include cancer of the anus and rectum (squamous cell carcinoma). These cancers have predominantly been reported in homosexual men who have practiced receptive anal intercourse and have had anal warts. Anal warts are caused by a papilloma virus, and many experts feel that this virus in the setting of HIV-induced immune suppression may be the cause of these anal cancers.[45] Other miscellaneous cancers have been reported in HIV-positive individuals, including cancer of the tongue, testicular cancer, and an ordinarily very benign cancer of the skin (basal cell carcinoma) that was reported to have spread widely in an HIV-infected homosexual male.[46] Since a clear link between these miscellaneous cancers and HIV has not been established, additional information is needed.

HIV in the Central Nervous System (AIDS Dementia Complex)

It has already been pointed out that both opportunistic infections and malignancies can affect the central nervous system (CNS). The ability of HIV to *directly* attack the CNS itself provides the context for the third group of indicator diseases that qualify patients for the diagnosis of AIDS.[47]

There is growing evidence that HIV probably infects the central nervous system very early on in most cases.[48] The patient may remain completely asymptomatic or develop encephalitis or meningitis as part of the mononucleosis syndrome described earlier under "Acute HIV Infection." These early central-nervous-system manifestations are usually self-limiting and resolve within several weeks. The virus may then enter an asymptomatic phase in the CNS or cause a chronic form of meningitis, which is manifested by stiff neck and headache.

In the latter stages of HIV infection, patients may develop the AIDS dementia complex, which by itself is an indicator disease for AIDS. AIDS dementia complex is actually a form of chronic encephalitis and is the most common and serious direct CNS manifestation of HIV. Although the AIDS dementia complex can be the initial manifestation of AIDS, it more characteristically appears after patients have developed major opportunistic infections or cancers.[49,50,51]

The clinical features of the AIDS dementia complex are similar to other dementing illnesses, such as Alzheimer's disease, but with a more rapid progression. The earliest symptoms include decreased concentration, memory loss, and mental slowness. Behavioral changes are also characteristic, with apathy, withdrawal, and agitation being seen. Motor skills are diminished, resulting in unsteady gait, loss of coordination, leg weakness, and so on. As the disease progresses, confusion and disorientation develop and the patient becomes unaware of his or her problem. Increasing leg weakness and gait disturbance, as well as loss of bladder and bowel control, are common. In the end-stage situation, the individual is bedridden and in a vegetative state.

The diagnosis of AIDS dementia complex is made on the basis of the overall clinical picture (detailed above) as well as by utilizing radiological techniques and examining the cerebral spinal fluid (CSF). The most common X-ray technique used is the CAT scan, which consistently shows a finding of brain atrophy in these cases. Examination of the CSF usually shows mildly elevated protein and slight elevation of certain inflammatory white blood cells. The treatment of AIDS dementia complex is limited at the present time, although there is some data that suggest that the antiviral drug Retrovir (AZT) may result in stabilization and even improvement of brain function.[52]

In addition to meningitis and the AIDS dementia complex, HIV also causes a number of other neurological syndromes. The virus involves peripheral nerves, causing neuropathy that may result in very painful sensations of the extremities as well as loss of sensory input and motor weakness. Additionally, HIV may involve the spinal cord, causing disturbances in muscle movement and coordination. This condition is called vacuolar myelopathy. As well as infecting peripheral nerves and the spinal cord, HIV infection is associated with an inflammatory illness of muscles called polymyositis, which manifests as progressive weakness, especially of the proximal extremity muscles.

Progressive multifocal leukoencephalopathy (PML) is a disease of the brain that is seen in HIV-infected patients. PML is caused by another virus from the papova virus family (called "JC virus") and is a progressive disorder. It may involve all aspects of brain function, resulting in multiple problems: paralysis, speech difficulties, imbalance, and so on. There is no treatment for PML and it is rapidly fatal.

Additional HIV-related central-nervous-system disorders include the occurrence of strokes and intracerebral bleeding. These entities are poorly understood as to cause.

HIV Wasting Syndrome

The HIV wasting syndrome has been recognized as AIDS in which gastrointestinal manifestations represent the dominant clinical picture. This would be analogous to the AIDS dementia complex, in which the central nervous system manifestations are predominant. The Africans called this syndrome "slim disease," originally describing in 1985 a condition of progressive weight loss and diarrhea in patients who were HIV positive.[53] The majority of these individuals were bedridden with nonbloody diarrhea, loss of appetite, and weight loss of at least ten kilograms.

Patients with the HIV wasting syndrome have no other identifiable cause to account for their gastrointestinal symptoms. These individuals appear to exhibit malabsorption, whereby nutrients are not absorbed through the normal mechanisms in the gastrointestinal tract. Treatment of the wasting syndrome may require placing the patient on intravenous feedings to provide calories, protein, and other nutrients.

Pediatric AIDS

Cases of children with AIDS were reported early on in the epidemic, and it became apparent that this subset of innocent victims would form a very tragic story within the overall AIDS population.[54,55] Transmission of HIV in children differs considerably from their adult counterparts. Some 80 percent of HIV-infected children acquire the virus by being born to a mother who is at risk for AIDS or who already has ARC or AIDS.[56] Often the mother has no symptoms but is HIV positive. Many of these women have a history of intravenous drug abuse or sexual contact with an intravenous drug user. The large proportion of such women are black or Hispanic, poor, and living in urban surroundings.[57,58]

The rate at which the virus is transmitted from mother to child has not been completely defined, but it appears to be approximately 50 percent.[59,60,61] Transmission occurs either during pregnancy via placental transfer or at the time of birth, with the infant's exposure to potentially infected maternal blood or birth-canal secretions. Since most such children are infected during pregnancy, approximately 50 percent are diagnosed during the first year of life and over 80 percent are diagnosed by three years of age.

Other ways in which HIV is transmitted in children include exposure to blood-product transfusion, accounting for some 11 percent of reported pediatric AIDS. An additional 6 percent of children with AIDS acquire HIV during the treatment of hemophilia and other blood-clotting disorders. (See Appendix F.)

As of September 1, 1989, 1,780 cases of AIDS had been reported in children under thirteen years of age in the U.S. Most public-health-service estimates state that the number of pediatric AIDS cases will exceed 3,000 by 1991. This will represent approximately 1 percent of the total number of AIDS cases in the U.S. at that time.

Just as in adults, a broad spectrum of clinical manifestations occurs in HIV-infected children, ranging from those without symptoms to those who are extremely ill. In general, the time from HIV infection to the onset of symptoms or AIDS itself appears to be shorter in children than in adults, with the shortest period of time occurring in those infants who have been infected during pregnancy.[62] Some general and nonspecific clinical findings include lymphadenopathy, enlargement of the liver and spleen, low birth weight, failure to thrive, weight loss, diarrhea, oral candidiasis (thrush), and fever. In addition to these nonspecific findings, HIV-infected children develop the same types of opportunistic infections as adults. The most common of these is Pneumocystis cariini pneumonia, which occurs in approximately half of pediatric AIDS cases.[63] (See classification of Pediatric HIV infections in Appendix J.)

Malignancies are in general a less common manifestation of AIDS in children than in the adult population.

For example, Kaposi's sarcoma is only being reported in approximately 4 percent of children with AIDS.[64] Malignant lymphomas are also quite uncommon in pediatric AIDS.

Like the adult cases, children can develop various manifestations of central-nervous-system infection. The most common manifestation in this regard is a form of brain deterioration (encephalopathy) that appears as a loss of motor skills and intellectual function. Other symptoms include paralysis, changes in muscle tone, difficulty with coordination, and sometimes even seizures.[65] This would be equivalent to the AIDS dementia complex seen in adults.

A very common manifestation of HIV infection in children is severe bacterial infection. Children with AIDS have an increased incidence of such infection, which appears in the form of bloodstream infection, pneumonia, meningitis, abscess, and cellulitis (bacterial infection of the skin). A wide variety of bacteria is responsible, including the more common bacteria that occur in the pediatric population in general, as well as some rare bacterial organisms. Treatment includes hospitalization for antibiotic therapy.[66]

Possibly the most characteristic feature of pediatric HIV infection is a form of pneumonia called lymphocytic interstitial pneumonitis (LIP). This entity occurs in just over 50 percent of children with AIDS but is quite rare in adults with AIDS.[67] The cause of LIP is not clear, but it may be a direct manifestation of HIV itself. The Epstein Barr virus also has been implicated as the cause. LIP is a chronic progressive form of inflammation of the lungs, causing cough and shortness of breath. There is no established therapy for LIP; although certain drugs have been tried (such as corticosteroids), the benefits of such therapy are not clear at the present time.[68]

There are a number of other syndromes that occur in children who are infected with HIV, and these in general are less well understood. Inflammation of the liver (hepatitis), kidneys (nephritis), heart (carditis), and the salivary glands (parotitis) have all been reported. Additionally, there has been described a congenital malformation syndrome, which includes such features as small head size, prominent box-like forehead, and various ocular and nasal deformities.[69] As in adults, children may manifest a number of bloodstream abnormalities, including low white-blood-cell count (leukopenia), low-red-cell count (anemia), and low platelet count (thrombocytopenia).

The mortality rate of pediatric AIDS is extremely high, with over 54.6 percent of children with AIDS having died (as of September 1, 1989). Those diagnosed with AIDS prior to one year of age have a shorter-term prognosis. In general, therapies are directed against the various opportunistic infections that occur. Application of antiviral drugs such as Retrovir (AZT) is currently underway, but this has not been as extensively evaluated as in the adult population. The issue of children with AIDS in the school is a very emotional one and will be discussed in chapter 6.

5

The Treatment of AIDS

The word *treatment* means different things to different people and in the area of AIDS could be applied in various ways. A wise physician once said, "I cannot cure every person who walks into my office, but I can help every person who comes to me in need." Treating AIDS patients is to a large extent helping them cope with the multifaceted nature of their disease. Although AIDS in many respects resembles other terminal illnesses, such as certain forms of cancer, it presents a unique challenge to the physician and other caregivers who participate.

AIDS is not just a physically devastating disease, but is also psychologically, socially, financially, and spiritually overwhelming. Therefore, to "treat" a person with AIDS one must have a profound sense of both the entire person and those who are close to him or her. Because the problems are multifaceted, the approach must be multidisciplinary, involving every aspect of the health-care delivery team as well as drawing on family, community, and church resources for support.

Many individuals from a variety of different fields are bringing their very best expertise, compassion, and care to AIDS patients and their loved ones. When viewed in this light, treatment holds great promise insofar as it meets devastated people at their deepest point of need. For the purposes of this text, however, treatment considerations will be limited here to the discussion of current medications, therapies, and the area of vaccine development.

According to the Pharmaceutical Manufacturer's Association, the number of companies developing AIDS therapies and diagnostic approaches is growing at a rapid rate.[1,2] As of September 1989, fifty-five companies were developing or co-developing different products, which represented an increase of fifteen companies over just two years earlier. There were sixty-seven medicines and vaccines in development, an increase of fourteen from the year before. These types of data show that there has been a concerted effort by the pharmaceutical industry to respond to the AIDS crisis. Indeed, Dr. Gerald A. Mossinghoff, president of the Pharmaceutical Manufacturer's Association, has stated that "never before have our companies mobilized more rapidly and so strongly against a disease."

Despite the number of companies involved and the number of products being developed, the immediate outlook for making a significant impact on HIV and AIDS appears to be guardedly optimistic at best. Indeed, there has been only one medication approved by the FDA for use in the direct suppression of HIV, and it by no means is a cure. Therapy for AIDS can be broken into three sections, the first being those medications used to treat the indicator diseases of AIDS and ARC, including both opportunistic infections and malignancies. Second are those therapies that act directly to combat or inhibit HIV itself. Third is the area of vaccines.

Indicator-Disease Therapies

Medications used in the treatment of opportunistic infections and malignancies have been touched on in chapter 4. As noted, a variety of different medicines are used with varying success in the treatment of the opportunistic diseases seen with AIDS. In the area of opportunistic infections, many of these therapies are quite successful, at least in producing a brief "cure" of the infection, driving it into a more dormant state. Examples of this would include the treatment of Pneumocystis cariini pneumonia, Toxoplasmosis of the brain, Cryptococcal meningitis, the various manifestations of Cytomegalovirus, and so on. Unfortunately, these therapies must be continued after the initial treatment phase because of the very high relapse rate of virtually all opportunistic infections. The patient is often therefore committed to multiple drugs for his or her lifetime.

Some of the same things hold true for AIDS-related malignancies, although the success in treating these devastating cancers has been very limited. Cancer chemotherapeutic agents themselves have considerable toxicities that limit their usefulness in the already-immunocompromised AIDS patient. New protocols are being developed all the time in the treatment of AIDS-related cancers and infections, but clearly a more ultimate hope for a cure will come from anti-HIV therapies or through vaccine development.

Anti-HIV Therapies

Therapies against the human immunodeficiency virus itself fall into three categories. The first are those drugs that act directly against the virus; second are those therapies that enhance the immune response to HIV (i.e., immune modulators). Third are the substances known as cytokines, which are naturally occurring proteins that regulate or modify the growth of specific cells that are critical within the immune response. At latest count there were approximately twenty antiviral drugs in different stages of development, along with eleven immune modulators and thirteen cytokines. Medications such as these require appropriate study so as to go through the accepted approval process that guarantees scientifically verifiable reliability. There are many bogus and anecdotal therapies being marketed that have no scientific basis for use. These can bring AIDS patients a great deal of false hope as well as possible physical side effects. It is critical that in the rapid effort to develop a "cure," scientifically sound principles be rigidly followed.

In the United States' system of drug development, which is without a doubt the most rigorous in the world, a drug must go through a number of steps before approval. In sanctioning AZT (also called Zidovudine or Retrovir), the Food and Drug Administration (FDA) set an all-time record in passing it through these stages. This demonstrates that potential and promising therapies can be rapidly advanced if necessary. AZT is currently the only approved anti-HIV drug available for general physician use.

The drug-approval process begins with laboratory evidence that suggests that a drug might be active against HIV. In the case of AZT, this was reported initially in February 1985 at the National Cancer Institute.[3] The drug was found to almost completely inhibit HIV viral replication in the laboratory.

Once an investigated new drug has been demonstrated to show potential in the laboratory, the sponsor may apply for human testing in the form of clinical trials. The FDA requires three phases before application may be made for new-drug approval. Phase 1 usually lasts approximately a year and includes studies that evaluate the safety profile of the drug. In the case of AZT, it was found that the drug was well absorbed when given by mouth, but that because of its short half-life, it would have to be dosed every three or four hours.[4] Additionally, AZT was found to have excellent penetration into the central nervous system (CNS), something that is not true of every drug but was thought to be very important here because of the known propensity of HIV to attack the CNS. The principal toxicity of AZT was found to be suppression of the bone marrow, with anemia (decreased red-blood-cell count) and leukopenia (decreased white-blood-cell count) being most frequently observed.

The second phase in the drug-approval process consists of studies designed to assess a potential drug's effectiveness. Phase 2 clinical testing may require up to two years to complete. In February 1986, 282 patients were entered into a Phase 2 multicenter trial to evaluate the effectiveness of AZT.[5] These patients included 160 with AIDS who had had at least one episode of Pneumocystis pneumonia and another 122 who had AIDS-related complex manifesting as either significant weight loss or Candida infection of the mouth. The trial was double-blinded, meaning that neither the physician nor the patient knew whether or not the latter was receiving AZT or placebo. By September 1986, twenty deaths were reported in the trial. Only one death occurred among the group members who were taking AZT, while nineteen deaths occurred among the patients who were receiving placebo. In addition, it was discovered that significantly fewer opportunistic infections had occurred in the AZT-treated subjects. There was also some evidence to suggest that the immune system was enhanced by AZT.

Because of the dramatic difference between the two groups, it was decided to stop the Phase 2 AZT study early and to treat with AZT all patients who had been receiving placebo. On March 20, 1987, the Food and Drug Administration approved AZT for use in patients who had AIDS manifesting as Pneumocystis pneumonia or those with AIDS-related complex who had T-helper cell counts of less than 200 per cubic millimeter.

As noted above, the approval of AZT for widespread use in HIV-related illness broke all previous records in terms of going from the laboratory and progressing through the various approval phases. In fact, the requirement for Phase 3 testing (prior to release of the drug) was dropped. Typically, Phase 3 trials involve testing larger numbers of volunteer patients (usually 1,000 to 3,000) at various institutions, such as hospitals and clinics. The purpose for Phase 3 trials is to confirm earlier efficacy studies as well as further evaluate potential adverse reactions. Phase 3 testing usually lasts approximately three years, with the final approval process taking an additional two or three years before FDA sanctioning.

In August 1989, the results of two Phase-3-like trials involving AZT were announced. Protocol 019 was a trial that involved the use of AZT in HIV-infected persons who had no symptoms (i.e., early in the course of HIV infection). This study involved three different groups of patients, with one group taking high-dose AZT (1,500 mg per day), the second group taking low-dose AZT (500 mg per day), and the third group taking a placebo. AZT was found to be effective in those patients who had T-helper cell counts less than 500, in terms of progressing to AIDS or severe ARC. Additionally, it was found that treatment in the high-dose AZT group was no more effective than in the low-dose group. On the basis of these results, the study was halted, and all those individuals taking placebo and who had T-helper cell counts of less than 500 were given AZT at the lower dose.

A second study, Protocol 016, studied the effects of AZT in HIV-infected persons who had early AIDS-related complex. This study involved 713 HIV-infected patients who had symptoms qualifying them for the early ARC stage. Participants in this study received either placebo or AZT at a dose of 1,200 mg daily. Once again, the results indicated a highly significant difference in the development of advanced ARC or AIDS between the treatment and placebo groups. Again the clear-cut benefit was observed in those with T-helper cell counts of less than 500. On the basis of these two Phase 3 studies, the knowledge regarding AZT's beneficial effect has been significantly advanced, showing that therapy may possibly be extended to those persons in the earlier stages of HIV infection. It has been estimated that the use of AZT may now extend up to approximately 600,000 persons in the United States with earlier manifestations of HIV. This would represent a significant increase from the approximate 40,000 patients who were taking the medication prior to the above study results.[6]

In addition to the observed benefits of decreased opportunistic infections, increased survival, and enhancement of immune status, AZT has been shown to cause substantial clinical improvement in neurological dysfunction.[7,8] This has been shown particularly in those patients with AIDS dementia complex. The beneficial effects of AZT on the neurological system are most likely related to its excellent penetration into the CNS. In contrast to the improvement in HIV-related neurological disease, AZT does not appear to have substantial effect on AIDS-related malignancies, such as Kaposi's sarcoma.

The original recommended dose for AZT was 200 mg taken orally every four hours (i.e., 1,200 mg per day). On the basis of the above-mentioned Phase 3 like trial (Protocol 019), it is anticipated that most patients on AZT will be managed on a lower dose (i.e., 100 mg orally, five times daily while awake). The benefits of the lower dose will be realized in terms of decreased toxicity, as only 3 percent of the persons taking the medication at this dose experienced side effects. Patients on AZT are followed at least every two weeks to measure complete blood counts, assessing potential bone marrow toxicity. Other side effects that occur much less frequently (less than 5 percent) have included gastrointestinal disturbances, headaches, nervousness, as well as muscle and joint aches (myalgias and arthralgias).

AZT is additionally being evaluated in several other patient groups. The drug is being looked at in HIV-infected pregnant women, as well as health-care workers who have sustained needle-stick punctures from patients who are HIV infected. The study of AZT is also being expanded into children and infants with HIV infection, where it is being shown to have a beneficial effect.[9] In late October, 1989, AZT was made available in syrup form on a limited basis to physicians caring for HIV-positive children who meet certain criteria, including either the presence of symptoms indicative of HIV or a low level of T-helper lymphocytes.

The initial beneficial effect of AZT in increased survival rates has been borne out with continued therapy over time. At eighteen months of therapy, although some individuals with AIDS who are on AZT do have disease progression, the survival rate has remained significantly increased at approximately 70 percent.[10] This is compared to the overall 30 percent-to-40 percent survival rate that would be estimated for those patients not taking the drug.

One concern in the use of AZT has been the observed development of HIV resistance to this medication. The mechanism responsible for this is not clear. It remains to be seen as to what extent the phenomenon of resistance will affect the use of AZT.

Although AZT is the only FDA-approved anti-HIV medication, a number of other antiviral drugs are in the development and testing process. These various agents are divided according to their site of action in the HIV reproduction cycle. AZT, for example, acts by inhibiting the critical enzyme called reverse transcriptase, which allows the RNA form of the virus to be converted into a DNA form. Other reverse transcriptase inhibitors include suramin, HPA-23, foscarnet, rifabutin, ddA, ddC, ddI, and ribavirin. Of these agents, suramin has been shown to be highly toxic and appears to have no benefit to individuals with HIV disease. The rest of the reverse transcriptase inhibitors are either in Phase 1 or Phase 2 trials, with the exception of ribavirin, which is in Phase 3 testing.

Of the aforementioned medications, one has stirred considerable recent excitement. In July 1989, the results of a Phase 1 study involving the drug ddI were announced.[11] The drug was shown to be effective in a small group of patients without producing the bone marrow toxicity that has been observed with AZT. On the basis of these early trials, ddI will be further advanced into larger studies. The new ddI information, along with the additional AZT data, have resulted in a new optimism about treating AIDS that was notably absent just four or five years ago. At that time researchers were considerably skeptical that there would ever be any drugs available for combating the infection.

Another step in the HIV replicative cycle at which antiviral drugs are being developed is the initial stage, in which the virus attaches to the T-helper cell. Drugs in this regard are Peptide-T and soluble rCD4, both of which are in Phase 1 or Phase 2 trials. The most promising of these therapies is soluble rCD4, which is a synthetic replica of the binding site of the T-helper cell to which HIV attaches. Soluble rCD4 "fools" the virus by binding to it, thereby preventing attachment and infection of the cell.

The final steps in the HIV replicative cycle include the point at which new viruses are assembled within the T-helper cell and then released to infect other cells. Compounds that interfere with HIV at this point are known as interferons, which are naturally occurring proteins actually made in the body itself and which act against a variety of different DNA and RNA viruses.

Interferon alpha (Roferon-A) has recently been approved for the treatment of Kaposi's sarcoma.

The other two categories of anti-HIV therapy—the immune modulators and cytokines—have numerous representatives in all phases of testing. It is beyond the scope of this book to cover these medicines, and the reader is directed to several references in this regard.[12] (See also note #2.) It should be noted that incredible advances have been made in AIDS research to screen candidate drugs in the fight against HIV. Recently a simple test has been developed for high-volume screening of different agents for activity against HIV. This was announced in April 1989 and will allow more than 40,000 agents to be screened yearly by 1990. Since the National Cancer Institute began its large-scale screening program, approximately 7,000 synthetic agents and about 8,000 natural-product extracts have been screened. As noted, about 350 new agents are now being tested weekly, and this number is expected to rise to nearly 1,000 per week.[13]

Vaccine Development

Since the discovery of HIV as the causative agent of AIDS, a great deal of effort has been aimed at the development of an effective and safe vaccine. A broad variety of strategies for vaccine development is being pursued. The research to find a vaccine has been filled with a number of considerable challenges related to the virus itself.

The development of a vaccine is based on the traditional premise that pre-existing immunity to HIV that is induced by vaccination would protect against actual HIV infection. In this regard, it is not clear that any vaccine will be protective, since the body's natural production of antibodies against HIV following infection does not appear to prevent disease progression. This is probably because most of the virus lives inside of cells (i.e., T-helper cells and macrophages, etc.), and therefore cannot be reached and eliminated by antibody production. Other problems in this regard include the fact that infected HIV cells can remain dormant and therefore escape immune recognition. Also, since HIV infection involves the integration of the virus into the genetic machinery of the infected cell, only the killing of the infected cell will actually eliminate the virus.

Another major challenge in vaccine development has to do with the marked genetic variability of HIV, with a 40 percent-to-50 percent variation between different viral isolates. This genetic variability was recently emphasized at the Fifth International Conference on AIDS in Montreal, Canada. At that meeting, investigators reported isolating as many as a hundred variants of HIV-1 from a single individual over time. Presumably, variability contributes to the virulence of HIV; therefore, holding HIV in check may depend on controlling it very early on after initial infection (i.e., before it has the chance to change its genetic composition).

Much of the genetic differences between HIV isolates lie in the envelope region, or outer covering of the virus. This fact has caused considerable concern, since presumably this area of the virus will be the most effective inducer of protective antibody response by the immune system. Despite the extreme variability of the HIV envelope, there are regions in the envelope that do not change between different HIV isolates. Therefore, targeting this part of the virus for vaccine development still appears to be most promising.

A third area of concern in vaccine development surrounds the fact that vaccination may actually induce antibodies that enhance HIV infection rather than prevent HIV infection of cells. This fact was pointed out at the Fourth International Conference on AIDS held in Paris, France (June 1988), where the theoretical possibility was raised that some vaccines could produce exactly the opposite effect of what they are designed to produce (i.e., instead of protecting against HIV, they actually enhance HIV).[14] In a related area, it has also been found that portions of HIV resemble the body's own normal cellular constituents; therefore, immunization could lead to the development of antibodies that act against normal body cells (i.e., autoimmune antibodies).

A fourth issue in vaccine development surrounds the lack of an adequate animal model to test viable vaccine candidates. Since HIV is uniquely pathogenic for humans, the value of animal models will be limited. One of the few animals actually known to be susceptible to HIV is the chimpanzee, but because of the rarity of this animal, other models are needed. Two possibilities are a mouse and rabbit model.

A fifth issue in vaccine development surrounds the ethical and liability dilemmas that will attend HIV-vaccine trials. One ethical dilemma is the balance that must be reached between the obligation to counsel research subjects about avoiding high-risk behavior for HIV infection and the ability to obtain vaccine efficacy data. Therefore, successful education of vaccine trial volunteers so as to bring about a decrease in high-risk behavior could theoretically diminish the possibility of obtaining adequate vaccine information. Closely related to ethicality are the liability issues, with the number of vaccine manufacturers declining over the last twenty years because of concerns over vaccine-related injuries, liability, and expense, for example.

A number of possible candidate HIV vaccines have been proposed: (1) vaccines that contain live virus; (2) vaccines that contain live but incapacitated virus; (3) vaccines that contain killed whole virus; (4) vaccines that contain portions of the virus (subunit vaccines); and (5) vaccines that protect the target cell of HIV (T-helper cell). Of all these mentioned, it seems unlikely that a live viral vaccine would ever be utilized, so most of the research has surrounded the other possible candidates.

As of September 1989, there were seven vaccines in human development trials within the United States. The race to develop a vaccine is moving at breakneck speed and has included a number of familiar names, such as Dr. Jonas Salk, who announced at the Montreal AIDS Meeting his experience using a killed whole-virus vaccine. In one series of experiments, Dr. Salk's group showed that previously HIV-infected chimpanzees could rid themselves of their original infection after being vaccinated with the killed-virus vaccine. Early studies in human beings using this vaccine have shown it be safe in regard to serious side effects, although the numbers were too small to draw any conclusions regarding its effectiveness in preventing AIDS.[15] Further optimism was generated using a killed vaccine in rhesus monkeys as reported in December 1989.[16] In this report a similar virus to HIV called simian immunodeficiency virus (SIV) was studied in an inactivated form in nine of these animals. The vaccine was found to be highly effective, protecting eight out of nine monkeys from becoming infected.

It is unclear how long it will be for an AIDS vaccine to be ready for widespread human use. Because of the very long incubation period of AIDS, a vaccine will need to be evaluated over a minimum of five or even ten years. In the development of the effective hepatitis B vaccine, it has been pointed out that it took ten years just to identify the part of the hepatitis B virus that was eventually used within the vaccine to stimulate a protective immune response. This is the stage of AIDS vaccine development at present.[17,18] (See also note # 2.)

There do appear to be many overwhelming obstacles, yet research to find an AIDS vaccine will continue to progress at an unprecedented rate. Great success in the development of vaccines against other viruses, such as polio, smallpox and hepatitis B, provides the background for legitimate hope that a similarly effective vaccine against HIV will eventually be developed.

Since the phrase "an ounce of prevention is worth a pound of cure" could not be more true than with HIV infection and AIDS, it is to prevention strategies that we next turn.

6

The Prevention and Control of AIDS

In spite of the incredible explosion of knowledge regarding AIDS and its causative agent, HIV, the epidemic continues to grow at an alarming rate. There have been few instances in medical history where so much was known about a disease without a definitive cure being offered. Until a cure is found or until an effective preventative vaccine is developed, the prevention and control of AIDS will largely arise out of massive educational endeavors, combined with applying methods to test and screen individuals for the presence of the virus.

The encouragement for persons in high-risk groups to seek testing for HIV has been increasingly promoted. Several years ago a sort of pessimism reigned over the issue of testing because it was viewed as a relatively useless endeavor because no therapies were available. This has considerably changed with the development and use of the drug AZT, which has now been shown to delay the progression of HIV-related disease, with subsequent prolonged life expectancies. Persons who view themselves in high-risk categories should therefore promptly seek testing, since an effective therapy does exist, albeit not a cure.

The application of screening techniques to detect the presence of HIV has been in place since early 1985, when blood banks across the country made it standard policy to screen all blood donors. Certain other groups of people are tested on a mandatory basis, including military personnel, prison inmates, and immigrants coming into the United States.

Educational efforts regarding AIDS prevention in the United States have been quite prolific, using every form of media possible. The first major push from the federal government came in the Surgeon General's report on AIDS, published by the U. S. Department of Health and Human Services in October 1986. Another major effort occurred in June 1988 with the publishing and release of *Understanding AIDS,* a document that was distributed to every household in the United States.

To further understand the various aspects of HIV prevention and control, this chapter will be divided into several sections dealing with prevention of AIDS (1) as a sexually transmitted disease; (2) in the I.V. drug user population; (3) in the blood-banking system; and (4) in low-risk populations. Sections will also be devoted to additional public-health concerns, AIDS in the school, and prevention of HIV infection in the health-care context. We will also briefly touch on the prevention of AIDS in Third World countries.

Prevention and Control of AIDS as a Sexually Transmitted Disease

AIDS continues to be predominantly a sexually transmitted disease within both the homosexual and heterosexual community. Although male homosexuals were identified early on as the predominant group at risk in the U.S.,[1] it has become increasingly clear that HIV is also transmitted heterosexually. The African AIDS epidemic conclusively demonstrates the heterosexual transmission risk of HIV.[2,3,4] Therefore, preventative measures must be directed toward all people who engage in high-risk sexual practices.

Education and counseling have been shown to be effective in changing sexual behavior, but these efforts will be greatly influenced by the prevailing sexual practices. It is evident from a multitude of studies on sexual behavior in the United States that people have become more "experimental and non-traditional" in their sexual activity.

The Risk Factors

Studies going back all the way to the 1940s, such as the Kinsey report, showed that activities such as oral sex were occurring in about 50 percent of the population.[5,6] Since that time, the reported prevalence of oral sex has increased to nearly 70 percent of subjects questioned.[7] The incidence of anal intercourse has also increased from 8 percent in the Kinsey data to current estimates of 25 percent in heterosexuals between the ages of twenty-five and thirty-four years of age, as well as 50 percent in homosexual males. Clearly, an increasing number of individuals are engaging in high-risk sexual practices and are therefore more vulnerable to HIV transmission. When discussing prevention of HIV transmission, it is important to remember that not all sexual practices are equivalent in terms of risk. It is useful to re-emphasize those highest risk factors as well as those that may represent lesser risks.

Receptive/passive anal intercourse between males has been proposed to be the major sexual risk factor for HIV transmission in the United States.[8,9] The mechanism of viral transmission is likely related to the significant trauma that results from anal sexual practices. The lining of the rectum, unlike that of the vagina, is quite thin and therefore does not confer the same type of protection against injury or invasion from microorganisms such as HIV, which may enter the body as semen and blood are mixed. Insertive anal intercourse would appear to carry a risk of its own, but studies suggest that it represents a less efficient mode of viral transmission than receptive anal intercourse. Although little data exist regarding heterosexual anal intercourse, it would logically follow that women who engage in receptive anal intercourse would be at increased risk. Other anal sexual practices may be associated with a lesser risk of HIV transmission.

The transmission of HIV between male and female may involve a number of different sexual activities, including penile vaginal intercourse, oral genital contact, anal sexual practices, and kissing. Information from Africa as well as increasing amounts of data from the United States show that the efficiency of HIV transmission is probably equal between the sexes. (See notes #3 and 4). The number of sexual contacts certainly affects risk, as does contact with partners who would be at a greater risk of having HIV (e.g., prostitutes). A major risk between heterosexuals is penile-vaginal intercourse, whereas such other activity as oral genital sex (fellatio and cunnilingus) is less well documented as to the degree of risk.

Additional sexual activities that appear to present a much less risk in terms of transmission would include "deep kissing," mutual masturbation, and contact with urine. The risk of transmission of HIV by saliva via kissing is extremely low, but it theoretically could occur on occasion.

On the prevention side, the person who practices sexual abstinence and does not have any other independent risk factors for acquiring HIV is in a "no risk" category for acquiring AIDS. Additionally, it is also apparent that couples who do not have other risk factors for HIV infection and who are mutually monogamous are not at risk for infection, unless one or both partners have had a previous history of high-risk sexual activity. In this case, HIV testing would be suggested. The risk for HIV infection within the sexually active population is clearly lowered by limiting the number of sexual partners as well as selecting partners who are not from high-risk groups. Even though "limitation" and "selection" do have an impact on transmission risk, the overall increasing prevalence of the virus in the population, especially in certain geographic areas, makes the chance of acquiring HIV through a single sexual encounter much greater. ("Premarital testing" is discussed below in the section on prevention and control of AIDS in low-risk populations.)

"Safe Sex"

The term *safe sex* has been grossly misunderstood and is in fact a misnomer. The better term is "safer sexual practice," which has come to mean both the practice of those sexual activities with a low potential for transmission and the use of barrier contraceptives and spermicides.

Barrier contraceptives and, in particular, condoms have been shown to decrease transmission of a variety of sexually transmitted diseases including herpes, Chlamydia, gonorrhea, syphilis, and now also HIV.[10,11,12] The type of condom determines the effectiveness of prevention, with latex condoms being found more impermeable to HIV in the laboratory as opposed to the so-called natural-membrane condoms.

The actual effectiveness of condom use in the prevention of HIV transmission has been difficult to assess. Certainly in other sexually transmitted diseases (e.g., gonorrhea), a lower frequency of transmission is seen in persons who use condoms.[13] One study, which evaluated the heterosexual spouses of patients with AIDS, showed that consistent condom use was associated with lack of HIV transmission.[14] Another study showed a protective association between condom use and HIV transmission among a group of prostitutes in Zaire.[15]

The success of condom use in HIV prevention is related to two factors: (1) the actual frequency of condom use; and (2) the failure rate of the condom itself. Recent data suggests that condom use in general is increasing but is still infrequent. Trends in this regard are changing, especially in the homosexual population, where condom use was seen in only 1 percent prior to the AIDS epidemic as compared to present figures of 80 percent in those reporting anal intercourse activity.[16,17] Similar trends among the heterosexual population are less well known, although a study of female prostitutes in the United States in 1986–87 showed only 4 percent reporting condom use with each sexual encounter.[18] To be effective, condoms must be used routinely and correctly, and guidelines have been developed for their use in decreasing HIV transmission.[19,20]

The failure of the condom itself is related to quality-control issues. There is indication that the average leakage rate of domestically produced condoms is approximately 1 percent, whereas foreign-manufactured condoms have a much higher failure rate, in the 20 percent range. The Food and Drug Administration has set strict government standards that state that a batch of condoms may be discarded if as many as four out of a thousand condoms leak water. (See note #20.)

The use of spermicides such as nonoxynol-9 suggests a possible increased effectiveness in preventing HIV transmission when used along with condoms. Nonoxynol-9 inhibits HIV replication in the laboratory as well as kills the lymphocytes that carry the virus.[21] Whether or not these laboratory findings will be borne out in the real world remains to be established. The use of condoms has been encouraged by the Surgeon General, the Public Health Service, and the Centers for

Disease Control for those who do not abstain from sexual activity and who engage in high-risk sexual practice. It should be pointed out that condoms will not eliminate the risk of HIV infection, just as they do not eliminate the risk of pregnancy, which is in the 10 percent-to-20 percent range per condom-using couple over a year's time. Therefore, condom use is a part of *safer* sexual practice but does not provide a total "safe" haven.

The Prevention of AIDS Among I.V. Drug Users

I.V. drug users are the second largest group in the United States to have developed AIDS, and intravenous drug use is a risk factor in 28 percent of adult cases. Among these, 21 percent had I.V. drug use as their only or predominant risk behavior and another 7 percent were both homosexual and used drugs intravenously. Besides being an important means for transmitting HIV, this population serves as possibly the largest reservoir for the transmission of HIV into the heterosexual community. In New York City, for example, almost 90 percent of heterosexually acquired cases are contracted from I.V. drug users.[22] Additionally, the predominant risk factor in women giving birth to children with AIDS is I.V. drug use.

The control of HIV transmission within this high-risk group probably presents one of the greatest challenges in AIDS prevention, since historically the rehabilitation rate of I.V. drug users has been very discouraging. This is dramatized by the fact that only 10 to 15 percent of such drug users are in drug treatment programs at any one time.

An additional issue seems to be the lack of an educational impact on stemming the rate of HIV acquisition among I.V. drug users. Of particular concern in this regard is the overrepresentation of I.V. drug users within inner-city minority communities, such as blacks and Hispanics who are not being adequately reached by current educational efforts.[23,24] This is evidenced by rising rates of sexually transmitted disease (STD), particularly syphilis, in these groups. At the same time, declines in STD's are being seen in other groups, such as homosexual and bisexual white males. Both improved education and expansion of drug-abuse treatment policies must be developed if controlling HIV within I.V. drug users is to become a reality. Specifically on the drug treatment side, increased funding will be necessary, since many who desire treatment are placed on waiting lists because of the lack of available immediate resources.

In addition to improved education and expansion of drug treatment programs, others have promoted strategies that utilize risk-reduction counseling to those who are not in treatment. This approach may include specific instruction on sterilizing drug paraphernalia, using substances such as bleach, which inactivates HIV. Programs in San Francisco involve outreach workers who work with I.V. drug users and provide small bottles of bleach for the use of needle and syringe sterilization. The San Francisco bleach-distribution project showed great increases in the numbers of I.V. drug users using bleach—from less than 5 percent prior to evaluation and distribution to over 60 percent thereafter.[25] The actual impact on HIV transmission through the use of sterilization techniques has not been extensively studied and therefore represents only a theoretical "help" to those who persistently use intravenous drugs.

Another initiative has been the establishment of public programs for the exchange of sterile needles and syringes for used contaminated I.V. equipment. Several other countries, including the Netherlands, the United Kingdom, Australia, and Switzerland, have begun government-supported needle-exchange programs that are free to those participating.[26] There has been some evidence presented by the World Health Organization that high-risk needle sharing actually declines among those who exchange for sterile needles. In the United States, needle-exchange programs have been started, beginning in New York City in October 1988.[27]

Opposition to these practices has been based on the belief that nothing should be done that could be seen as encouraging I.V. drug use. However, in the face of an alarming increase of HIV infection within these users, there has been an increasing openness to the possibility of needle exchange. It is too early to know for certain that needle-exchange programs actually reduce the rate of infection transmission.

Legitimate ethical and moral concerns surround many of these risk-reduction initiatives, especially as they apply to high-risk populations for HIV and AIDS. Much of the argument surrounds whether or not it is morally acceptable to provide information and implement programs that will allow people to realize a less-than-full consequence from their behaviors.

Two ethical schools of thought have been applied. The more "idealist" ethic states that certain risk-reducing initiatives—such as needle sterilization, exchange programs for I.V. drug users, and/or the promotion of condom use within the sexually promiscuous community—are ethically unacceptable. This way of thinking advocates that the only risk-reducing activity that should be taught is avoidance of the activity. This position articulates a "way things should be" approach.

The second school of thought suggests a "way things are" approach. This "realist" ethic states that persons in high-risk groups for AIDS will to a great extent not avoid the activities that threaten them with HIV contact. Therefore, AIDS-prevention endeavors must promote risk-reducing behavior in the context of these high-risk activities.

This book endorses a combination of both ethics. This "interventional" approach holds up the standard of the ideal but recognizes that we live in a less-than-ideal world and are still responsible to help those who cannot at any one time live up to the ideal. Therefore, while calling for the ideal, it is important that we pursue those programs that legitimately and objectively reduce HIV transmission, particularly among high-risk populations.

Prevention and Control of AIDS in the Blood Supply

Highly specific and sensitive screening techniques for the presence of HIV were made available in early 1985.[28] By the middle of that year, virtually all blood banks within the United States were screening every donated blood unit for the presence of HIV antibodies.

In addition to the screening of the donated blood itself, educational approaches are being employed by blood-collection agencies to identify and screen out those persons who are at high risk for AIDS. The aim of specific questions asked each donor is to eliminate from the donor pool the following individuals:

1. Those having homosexual or bisexual contact since 1977
2. Users of intravenous drugs, past or present
3. Those who have had sexual contact with intravenous drug users
4. Hemophiliacs and their sexual partners
5. Residents of Haiti and central African nations such as Zaire and Rwanda who have entered the United States since 1977, as well as their sexual contacts
6. Persons who have had sexual contact with an individual with AIDS or ARC or who have been identified as being HIV positive
7. Persons who have engaged in the practice of prostitution since 1977 or who have had sex with a prostitute since then
8. Persons who have had sexual contact with individuals who themselves have had sexual contact with a homosexual or bisexual, I.V. drug user, prostitute, or hemophiliac[29]

The combination of question-oriented donor screening and testing of all donated blood for the presence of HIV has essentially reduced the risk of transfusion-associated HIV infection to nil. Therefore, transfusion-associated AIDS, at least within the United States, is predominantly a disease of the past.

The very rare case of transfusion-associated AIDS may continue to occur because all HIV-positive individuals may not have antibody present at the time of their blood donation. Therefore, a unit of blood could possibly slip through the current screening procedures. Most individuals who have been infected with HIV will develop antibody by three months, with an outer limit of six months (i.e., 95 percent).[30,31] A very few persons who are HIV infected have gone for several years without having detectable HIV by current antibody-detecting methods.

Several studies have been performed to look at the risk of acquiring HIV from an antibody-negative donor unit. As noted previously, this is extremely rare and probably occurs on the order of 1 in 150,000 to 1 in 250,000.[32] It should be emphasized that the blood supply has never been completely "safe," as there are a number of other blood-mediated organisms that can be transmitted from one person to another. The AIDS epidemic has only heightened this reality.

Although transfusion-associated AIDS has occurred predominantly via whole blood, blood components and plasma derivatives also have the potential to transmit virus to transfusion recipients. Each unit of whole blood may be broken up into different components, including packed red blood cells, platelets, fresh frozen plasma, cryoprecipitate, and leukocytes (white blood cells). In addition, the plasma portion of blood may be broken down into different protein components, such as albumin, Factor VIII and IX, as well as different antibody (immunoglobulin) preparations. These various blood and plasma components are derived by different physical and chemical means.

In the case of some of the plasma-derived components, such as Factor VIII and IX, many different whole blood units are used to make up one unit of plasma-derived clotting factor. As mentioned in a previous chapter, hemophiliacs lack Factor VIII and IX, and exposure to one unit of Factor VIII concentrate could expose the individual to multiple donors. Prior to screening procedures, up to 90 percent of hemophiliac patients in some studies who required frequent infusion of Factor VIII concentrate became infected with HIV.[33,34]

Precautions for the hemophiliac population have been instituted in addition to donor-unit screening, and these involve a process of heat-treating the coagulation factor products.[35] This has essentially eliminated any risk for HIV transmission to hemophiliacs. Other plasma derivatives, such as various protein substances like albumin and immune globulin preparations, undergo specific treatment methods of their own, which removes the risk of HIV transmission.

An understandable concern involves those individuals who received blood transfusions between 1978 and the late spring of 1985. The Centers for Disease Control has estimated that during this period of time as many as 12,000 people living in the United States may have acquired HIV infection by transfusion.[36] This risk would have been increased in those people who received multiple transfusions and those who were transfused closer to the time when screening procedures were initiated (i.e., later in the epidemic). No clear-cut recommendations exist regarding whether or not all individuals who have been transfused between 1978 and 1985 should be tested for HIV. Clearly, anyone who desires to be tested for HIV should be offered the test. Individuals who are sexually active may also want to consider having themselves tested for HIV so as to protect their sexual partners as well as to benefit from therapies such as AZT. Any person in this category who develops signs or symptoms suggestive of HIV infection should certainly be tested and properly evaluated by his or her physician.

Although the risk of developing HIV infection from transfusion of either whole blood or its components is extremely small, there is a fair amount of anxiety among many people who require these therapies. Such is the case with those who anticipate surgery or who will require transfusion for other reasons. Medical technology has progressed so that now there are alternatives to traditional transfusion therapy.

The most popular of these is autologous transfusion, whereby the patient actually receives his or her own blood. Unlike homologous transfusion (blood from another person), there is no risk of transmitting any infectious agent when the patient and donor are the same.

Autologous transfusion is managed in two different ways. The first involves the individual's donating blood prior to anticipated need. This is especially seen in those who are contemplating elective surgery and who are healthy enough to serve as their own donors. The limitations on this form of blood donation are few and can easily be investigated through the patient's personal physician. It should be noted that blood can be stored in a frozen state up to approximately three years.

The second way in which the person's own blood may be utilized is through intraoperative autotransfusion, which involves a process of collecting blood from a wound or body cavity at the time of operation. This blood is processed and then reinfused into the patient. Intraoperative autotransfusion is offered in a number of settings, including trauma situations as well as for those persons undergoing cardiovascular surgery or hip replacement, for example.

Another way in which patients can respond to the need for transfusion is to choose their own blood donors. The motivation for using these "directed donations" arises from the presumption that a particular friend or relative might be a "safe" donor. Several problems exist in this area. The directed donor may not be entirely truthful about possible past high-risk exposures for fear of arousing distrust. An additional problem involves genetically related blood units (i.e., from relatives). Such blood units might have the potential to alter certain immune responses within the recipient so that these donors might be eliminated as a blood source for this person in the future. An example is patients who have malignancies and, because of chemotherapy, develop deficiencies in their platelet counts. In this situation they may require a so-called "matched" platelet donor such as a relative.

The development of a safe blood-banking system has been one of the highest priorities in AIDS prevention. Although the system is not perfect, the risk of transfusion-associated AIDS is at a negligible level, and efforts to further improve testing for HIV are now being implemented with already-available technologies that detect the virus directly rather than the antibody to it.

Prevention and Control of AIDS in Low-Risk Populations

Much has been said about the predominant need to test high-risk groups for HIV, but it is also necessary to address the issue of prevention within the larger population context. There has been considerable pressure to expand HIV testing to groups that are at low risk for HIV. In the United States, mandatory HIV testing already applies to several groups, including blood donors and organ donors, military personnel, prison inmates, and incoming immigrants. (As mentioned above, the rationale for the mandatory screening of blood donors is obvious.)

Screening Within Specified Groups

In the military, reasoning for mandatory screening has been based on concern that, during a time of war, the military becomes its own blood-banking system and requires the same sort of safety profiles as in the civilian population. It has also been recognized that HIV-infected personnel who might become ill could be deployed to areas of the world where only suboptimal medical care is available. Additionally, military recruits receive several other live-virus vaccines, which could pose a threat to the person if significant HIV-related immunosuppression had already occurred. The military maintains that its testing policies are not truly mandatory, since those joining the service do so on a voluntary basis and therefore are submitting by choice to policies in place.

Justification for testing prison inmates is based on the high incidence of previous intravenous drug use in that population, as well as ongoing sexual activity and drug use after incarceration. Statistics vary as to the prevalence of HIV within the inmate population, but it may range up to 17 percent in some institutions. Concerns regarding HIV testing within prison facilities include how the results are managed. These concerns center on the confidentiality of positive HIV results, the civil rights of the individual tested, and whether or not too much weight is placed on screening rather than emphasizing proper education regarding HIV transmission.

The basis for testing of immigrants is consistent with past health-screening programs for people entering the United States. In general, the nation has maintained the right to bar entrance of people with potentially communicable diseases.

Drawbacks to Mandatory Screening

Except for the above-mentioned groups, the application of mandatory testing is unlikely to decrease the spread of HIV. A number of segments of the general population have been advocated for screening, such as all those seeking marriage licenses or all individuals admitted to hospitals. Several reasons for *not* using mandatory testing as a preventative measure within low-risk populations deserve comment.

In the first place, mandatory screening more likely drives people away from the health-care system. There is considerable validity to this concern, in view of the rather unique character of the AIDS illness. There is no question that AIDS clearly stigmatizes an individual, not only physically but also in many other ways. If potentially HIV-infected persons feel that they have no control over their being tested, one might expect avoidance as the initial reaction in a significant number of cases.

Second, the cost of testing large numbers of low-risk individuals would be monumental. In view of the limited funds available, such a proposal would be grossly cost-ineffective and would divert funding away from education and counseling, which prompt real behavioral changes that result in decreased HIV transmission. Finally, if HIV testing were applied broadly to low-risk populations, the problem of false positive testing comes into play. False positivity simply means that a person might test positive by the current HIV screening method (ELISA test) but actually be negative for HIV when further tested by confirmatory methods (Western Blot test). Any test, no matter how accurate, will have problems with false positives when applied to populations who have a low prevalence of the factor being tested for (e.g., HIV). This phenomenon is described by the concept of "predictive value."

The predictive value of a test measures how well the test performs in a given population and often changes dramatically, changes depending on the population being tested. When applied to populations with low prevalence for HIV, the false-positive rate of the ELISA screening test becomes unacceptably high, and therefore the predictive value of a positive test is low. Conversely, the predictive value of a positive test rises with corresponding increases in the prevalence of HIV infection within the population being tested (e.g., the homosexual community). The costs and possible confusion regarding the false-positive phenomenon are potentially great.

Premarital Testing

The above concerns regarding mandatory testing for HIV in low-risk populations have led such agencies as the Public Health Service and the Centers for Disease Control to advocate a predominantly voluntary testing program, coupled with pre- and post-test counseling. This policy has not evolved without objection, especially in the area of premarital screening, which has had considerable political and popular appeal.

Historically, couples have been screened for sexually transmitted diseases prior to obtaining marriage licenses (e.g., syphilis). However, in the last decade many states have discarded their premarital blood-test requirements, leaving less than half of the states currently testing for syphilis. Much of this has to do with the cost and inefficiency of detection in this relatively low-risk population.

Another reason to question the rationale for premarital screening has been emphasized by the former Surgeon General, C. Everett Koop, who rightly maintained that marriage is no longer the precursor to either sexual contact or childbearing. Indeed, the estimated percentage of those having sexual intercourse by age nineteen is very high for both men (75 percent) and women (60 percent). Therefore, mere *premarital* screening for AIDS does not serve the function of protecting sexual partners nor the future children born into a union.

Despite these limitations, several states have passed premarital screening proposals, including Louisiana, Illinois, and Texas. In 1986, seventeen states considered legislation that would require premarital HIV screening. In 1987, Louisiana and Illinois enacted such legislation, while Texas took the approach of requiring screening only if the prevalence of HIV reached 0.83 percent. By the middle of 1988, Louisiana had repealed its law six months after enactment, leaving Illinois as the only state currently legislating mandated premarital screening. The Illinois experience has been recently reviewed, and some very interesting results have surfaced. During the first six months of mandated testing, 8 out of 70,846 applicants for marriage licenses were found to be positive for HIV. This yielded a prevalence of 0.011 percent (approximately 1 in 10,000). The cost of this testing program for six months was estimated at 2.5 million dollars, which translated into $312,000 per positive individual identified. Also, during this same six-month period, the number of marriage licenses issued in Illinois went down by 22.5 percent. This was contrasted to the significant *increase* in the number of licenses issued to Illinois residents in surrounding states during that time period. The conclusion of the Illinois experience was that mandatory premarital testing was certainly not a cost-effective method to control HIV infection.[37]

It should be noted that attitudes concerning mandatory screening of the larger population base may change as the prevalence of HIV rises, and there may certainly come a point where the benefits of testing large numbers of people outweigh the possible detractions.

Additional Public Health Concerns

Several other issues that may affect the general public have included the areas of contact notification and warning potential third-party individuals who might be at risk. Additionally, there are controversies surrounding whether or not physicians should be required to report HIV-positive cases. Finally, concerns have surrounded what measures should be taken against those HIV-positive persons who knowingly transmit HIV to unaware partners.

Concerning contact notification, physicians are encouraged to motivate their HIV-positive patients to notify any sexual or needle-sharing partners. In addition to relying on the doctor/patient relationship, contact notification may also occur through each state's public health office, and several states currently give public-health officials the authority to investigate sexual partners of HIV-infected persons. Although concerns about breach of confidentiality have been expressed in this area, the track records of both the medical community and the public-health sector have been excellent, holding to the highest of professional confidentiality standards.

The rationale for requiring physicians to report HIV-positive cases has considerable merit. Besides broadening the information base about the prevalence rate of HIV in the state, the reporting of HIV-positive individuals enhances contact-notification potential and is consistent with the view that HIV is a communicable disease.

Although there have been some well-publicized cases of irresponsible HIV-positive persons who knowingly transmit HIV to unaware partners, this appears to be rare. Despite this, increasing attention has been given to establishing laws that provide for the quarantining and/or the "punishing" of these types of individuals. The restriction of personal liberty in these cases should remain an option that has only had to be exercised occasionally up until the present.

Prevention of AIDS Within the School Context

It has been emphasized throughout this book that HIV is not transmitted through casual contact. Therefore, there is little rationale for prohibiting HIV-infected persons from participating in community, business, or school activities. Of all of these situations, the most controversial, and indeed the most heated, has been within the school setting.

The famous case of Ryan White, a hemophiliac youngster from Indiana, focuses this point. Ryan had contracted AIDS through blood transfusions and was prohibited from attending school for over a year until the court mandated his return. Unfortunately, Ryan and his family had to move to another town, where (thankfully) he was greeted with open arms. Clearly, the measure of how a community will respond to AIDS will be to a great extent measured by its response to the child with AIDS in the classroom. False assumptions must be dispelled in regards to how HIV is transmitted if the community is to become appropriate in its response to these unfortunate children.

There are only two possible situations where a child who is HIV infected might be restricted in attending school. The first would be that child who has open draining sores or is unable to control certain bodily functions, such as bladder and bowel excretion. The other restriction would apply to those children who exhibit aggressive behavior (such as biting), a scenario that would be quite rare.

Specific guidelines for AIDS education within the school have been published in the *MMWR,* and many (if not most) school boards have an AIDS-education policy in place.[38] For educational programs to be successful, they must involve parents, students, and school officials. Most experts agree that education about AIDS should begin in the early elementary years, with appropriate information being tailored to the understanding and needs of each particular age group. Although only 1 percent of all persons in the United States with AIDS have been diagnosed under age twenty, this remains an important target population for education, in view of prevailing sexual practices and the rising problem of drug abuse within the youth population of America. Additionally, it should be pointed out that 20 percent of AIDS patients are in the age bracket of twenty to twenty-nine years, demonstrating that many of these were likely infected while still teenagers, given the relatively long incubation period of HIV (mean incubation approximately ten years).

Prevention of HIV in the Health-Care Context

The risk of HIV transmission to the health-care worker has been commented on in a previous chapter. As noted before, fortunately the risk is quite low, with most studies estimating a less than 1 percent risk of acquiring HIV from such contacts as needle stick injuries and so on. Clearly, not all health-care workers are in the same category as to risk. This is influenced not only by where the worker serves in the health-care delivery system, but also by the area of the country in which he or she resides. This has been pointed out in a recent study evaluating the risk to health-care workers at the Johns Hopkins Hospital Emergency Department in Baltimore, Maryland. This study found that 152 of 2,544 consecutive patients coming to that emergency room were HIV positive. This represented a figure of 6 percent, which had considerably increased from the previous year. In addition to this high prevalence rate, the study found that precautions were in general poorly followed by health-care providers (e.g., physicians, nurses, ancillary staff). The study concluded that HIV infection will "directly and significantly impact on the demand for Emergency Services in the foreseeable future, particularly as patients with unrecognized infection increasingly become symptomatic from HIV." This study also called for strategies to use emergency resources appropriately and also to maximize health-care provider protection.[39]

In general, health-care workers can minimize the risk by following specific infection control guidelines, which stress that all patients should be assumed to be infectious for HIV and other blood-borne infections.[40]

Prevention and Control of AIDS in Third World Countries

Preventing AIDS in less well-developed countries, such as those in central Africa, presents unique problems. Much of what has already been stated regarding prevention could be applied here, although there are obvious cultural differences that would play an important role as to how specific measures are brought into practice. Differences in the ability to educate and to deal with different cultural norms will present unique challenges to those promoting AIDS-prevention efforts worldwide. The reader is referred to several good reviews that evaluate the specific problems existing in those countries where Pattern 2 HIV transmission is seen.[41,42,43]

The Question of Quarantine

Although it may seem unnecessary to even mention the idea of quarantining patients with AIDS, this concept as a preventative measure in the spread of HIV seems to linger. On the surface this measure seems noble, but experts realize that quarantining will not work.

First, HIV is not a casually contracted infection but rather requires certain high-risk exposure situations. Therefore, HIV is totally unlike the four internationally recognized quarantinable infections—plague, cholera, yellow fever, and smallpox—which can be spread by nonsexual modes (fleas and airborne spread in plague, food and water contamination in cholera, mosquitoes in yellow fever, and close personal contact, inanimate objects, and airborne spread in smallpox). None of these modes has been shown to spread HIV.

Second, HIV is so ingrained into our society and world that even if there was some rationale for separating the infected from the uninfected, it would be an almost impossible task with incalculable logistical problems. As accurate as HIV testing is, there would always remain groups of people carrying HIV but testing negative. Quarantining, therefore, has no place in the control and prevention of AIDS except possibly in that extreme and rare case of an HIV positive person who tries to spread HIV with premeditated and malicious intent.

Part Two

Theological Perspectives and Context

7

Overcoming Barriers

The Background for an AIDS Ministry

The perception of many Christians that AIDS is a "sinners' disease," is linked to human sexuality, and is terminal and contagious often gives rise to what may appear to be insurmountable barriers to ministry in the midst of this crisis. Considerations of the risks involved in contact with AIDS patients and ingrained human fears of the disease are genuine and must not be simply dismissed. At the same time, the AIDS epidemic presents a ministerial challenge to the people of God. The church is called to overcome the barriers for the sake of ministry in this crisis. The first step toward developing such a ministry can be taken as we come to view the disease in its medical context. Accordingly, the purpose of Part One was to provide sound medical perspectives and advice concerning AIDS.

To this first major step must be added a second. We must also view the epidemic in a theological context.

That is, we must come to see it in terms of certain spiritual realities. To this end, this chapter offers a theological understanding of the causes of sickness in general (and thus of AIDS), which is then employed in an attempt to view this epidemic as a mouthpiece for the voice of God, who is seeking to speak through the AIDS crisis.

Sickness and Sin

Important for ministry in the midst of the AIDS epidemic is a theological understanding of the causes of sickness in general. This is the case because one significant question with which the church struggles concerns the relationship between sickness and sin. Is sickness the mark of God's displeasure with sin? Is it a product of sin? Is sickness an occasion for Christian ministry? Quite obviously the answers we give to questions such as these have a profound effect on our response to the AIDS crisis.

The sickness-and-sin issue constituted an important question in the biblical era. Perhaps nowhere in the Old Testament is it more vividly presented than in the Book of Job. Although Job's friends came to console him in his misfortunes, they resolutely maintained that Job's calamities were due to his own sinfulness or to that of his family. This opinion was articulated by Bildad the Shuhite, for example, who declared to Job, "Does God pervert justice? Does the Almighty pervert what is right? When your children sinned against him, he gave them over to the penalty of their sin" (Job 8:3–4). As an outworking of this outlook, Bildad's advice was simple: "But if you will look to God and plead with the Almighty, if you are pure and upright, even now he will rouse himself on your behalf and restore you to your rightful place" (vv. 5–6).

The understanding concerning the relationship between sickness, calamity, and sin that was reflected by Job's friends forms the background to the perplexing question that Jesus' disciples raised when faced with a situation that did not fit with their preconceived understandings: "Rabbi, who sinned, this man or his parents, that he was born blind?" (John 9:2). The disciples' question, arising as it did from the viewpoint prevalent among the Jews of that day, may also be voiced today in the midst of the AIDS epidemic: "Who sinned, that these people have AIDS?" This question is but a reformulation of another: "What is the relationship between the disease and sin?" The answer to this question may break through the preconceived understanding of many Christians, just as Jesus' response to his disciples broke through theirs.

The Causes of Sickness

The search for an answer to the question about AIDS and sin begins with several general considerations. The Bible indicates that the ultimate cause of *all* sickness is indeed sin, in that sickness is an evil effect, resulting from the fall of humanity. Because of the fall we are living in an imperfect world, one characterized by the presence of many evils, including the various sicknesses that plague humans.

Beyond pinpointing this general cause, however, we can be somewhat more specific concerning the causes of the diseases that beset us. In fact, most illnesses can be seen as the product of one or more among three basic causes.

First, sickness is the result of contact with a fallen environment. Paul points in this direction when he declares, "For the creation was subjected to frustration, not by its own choice, but by the will of the one who subjected it, in hope that the creation itself will be liberated from its bondage to decay and brought into the glorious freedom of the children of God" (Rom. 8:20–21). According to Paul, creation is not yet the perfect order that God intends it to be. Rather, our world lies in bondage, and this bondage includes the imperfections of the present. Even nature awaits the full liberation that will come only in the future. This means that living in the presently imperfect environment brings illness and eventually death. We are susceptible to sickness by virtue of our existence in a not-yet-perfect universe.

A second cause of sickness is more closely related to sin, specifically to the sins of society. We are prone to certain sicknesses because of our membership in a people group or nation. Such illnesses may be related to the lifestyle characteristic of a specific social order or to the structures inherent in it. Thus, we who reside in this land are susceptible to certain sicknesses that arise out of the general way of living connected with Western society, including the hectic pace so much a part of life in our culture. Among such illnesses one could list high blood pressure, heart diseases of various types, and certain varieties of cancer. Other diseases are a result of societal dietary customs or the way foods are grown, processed, and prepared. Even the prevailing approach to health care present in a given society may foster a susceptibility to certain illnesses.

A third cause of sicknesses lies with personal sins. Some illnesses are in part connected to harmful personal lifestyles and therefore quite readily arise among persons who practice certain activities. For example, smoking may dispose an individual to lung cancer, alcoholism can lead to liver problems, and obesity may contribute to a host of conditions related to the heart and the circulatory system. A few diseases can even be contracted through one isolated, specific act a person chooses. For example, one act of sexual infidelity can be the channel for being infected with a venereal disease. Illnesses such as these are in part the outworking of the harm that people do to their own bodies.

In the Bible, specific sicknesses were sometimes allowed by God as an indication of God's displeasure concerning sin present in a person's life and as a warning that repentance is needed. A vivid example of this is found in a situation faced by the church in Corinth. Some within the fellowship were guilty of dishonoring the Lord's Supper. As a result, sickness—even death—came on them (1 Cor. 11:29–30). This divine response was both an act of judgment on the perpetrators and a call to repentance directed toward the community as a whole.

AIDS and Personal Sin

The above considerations relate to the AIDS epidemic, in that they raise the important question concerning the relationship between sin and AIDS. This relationship may appear on the surface to be quite uncomplicated. In actuality, however, it must be viewed under two dimensions if its full significance is to surface. The relationship between AIDS and sin has both personal and social aspects.

Often those who suggest any direct relationship between personal sin and the disease are roundly criticized. Such criticisms are sometimes just, for these pronouncements can easily be merely condemnatory, rather than offered in a spirit of reconciliation and healing. Nevertheless, the honest inquirer cannot avoid the conclusion that certain actions and lifestyles increase the risk of contracting the AIDS virus. Homosexual activities, heterosexual promiscuity, and I.V. drug abuse do place an individual into a high-risk category, as medical research has demonstrated. In cases in which persons living these lifestyles have become infected, Christians must forthrightly declare that a relationship may indeed exist between this disease and the chosen activities of the sufferer.

These comments may at first appear somewhat brash. Yet, it is instructive to note that our society is now willing to draw similar connections between other illnesses and lifestyle choices. For example, in contrast to the widely held viewpoint of past decades, a link between smoking and lung cancer is now acknowledged by nearly everyone. In fact, our government has gone so far as to demand that explicit warnings be placed on cigarette packages. There seems to be only one reason for this drastic change in attitude. Smoking, it appears, has fallen into sufficient societal disfavor to allow the connection between this harmful lifestyle and the specific disease it causes to be readily admitted.

One wonders, however, why people are often reluctant to draw similar connections between AIDS and the lifestyles that propagate the disease. Why are some persons reticent to issue similar warnings against these harmful lifestyles? The histories of the public response to other social ills, such as smoking, suggest that lifestyles that increase the risk of AIDS must first become the objects of widespread societal disfavor if public pressure is to be mounted and the spread of this deadly epidemic arrested.

However, while admitting an unavoidable link between certain lifestyles and susceptibility to AIDS, Christians must avoid generalizing. It is obvious that not all who follow such lifestyles contract the disease. Why AIDS strikes some members of so-called high-risk groups and not others remains a mystery. This aspect of the epidemic and related facts, such as the presence of the disease among homosexual men but its relative absence among lesbian women, provide a needed caution against a simple equating of the contracting of AIDS and personal sin. Nor dare we declare that all incidents of the AIDS disease are the result of unholy living. This generalization is disproven by the undeniable reality of the innocent victims of AIDS.

Therefore, while Christians ought to declare that both promiscuity of all types and drug abuse bear a large responsibility for the spread of the disease, we must avoid being judgmental, refusing to utter pronouncements of sin and doom as we seek to minister to individuals affected by this dreaded epidemic. Further, it must be kept in mind that AIDS is not *caused* by promiscuity and drug abuse. Rather, such practices increase the risk of contagion and are vehicles of the transmission of a virus that does not discriminate on the basis of the morality of its potential host.

AIDS and Social Sin

Equally significant is the question of a possible relationship between social sin and AIDS. This link is forged in several ways. First, it arises from certain basic orientations of contemporary American society. For example, it is undeniable that ours is a sex-crazed culture. Sexuality is glorified in the United States. Each day we are bombarded with a seductive lie concerning human sexuality. "All you need is love," we are continually told. But this "love" is understood mainly in sexual terms and often is nothing other than pure lust. Such a message is one contributing factor to the rise of promiscuity and to the dishonoring of the Christian perspective concerning the boundaries of sexual expression given by God.

The emphasis on sex is coupled with an equally strong and devastating emphasis on "experience." We are continually bombarded with tantalizing claims concerning the experiences one ought to enjoy if life is to be full and carry meaning. The result is a glorification of self-gratification, leading to a never-ending search for new thrills as a way of satisfying the insatiable human appetite for pleasure. Among other outlets, this orientation encourages the use of drugs to experience ever greater "highs."

Given these twin emphases—the glorification of sexual pleasure and the quest for greater thrills in general—it is not surprising that AIDS would quickly reach epidemic proportions in America. As a society, we are now reaping the consequences of the attitudes we have developed over the last several decades. There *is* an undeniable connection between societal sin and the spread of AIDS.

A second side to the relationship between AIDS and societal sin begs to be mentioned, however. This aspect focuses more specifically on the victims of the disease. The AIDS epidemic forces us to ask hard questions concerning its victims in our society. These questions center on two different groups of persons with AIDS: those who have contracted the disease through a harmful personal lifestyle and those who have been infected apart from their own actions.

On the one hand, we must consider to what extent AIDS "sinners" are at the same time the "sinned against." To date, the largest group of persons contracting AIDS in the United States has been individuals with a homosexual orientation. While most Christians find homosexual practices sinful, we must nevertheless consider the extent that current attitudes toward homosexuality in society and in the church actually serve to compound the problem and thereby contribute to the spread of the AIDS epidemic. To what degree are homosexually oriented persons driven to the gay community, even to impersonal sex practices and promiscuity, because they are unable to find community within the wider society and more specifically within our churches? To what extent have we as Christians been guilty of sinning against persons with a homosexual orientation because of our failure to show love and to offer them the true fellowship they are seeking?

The church is called to be a community in which fallen creatures can find fellowship and reconciliation with God and with one another. Our calling is denied, however, when we exclude from our ranks, whether willfully or merely through oversight, persons who are unlike ourselves or who are caught in deviant lifestyles.[1] If the door to the church and the fellowship offered there are closed to such people, where can they go to find the experience of community that all persons so desperately need?

We must raise a similar question with respect to drug

abusers. The church must condemn such practices, of course, because of the destructive effect they have on the individuals involved and their relations with others, including their families and society as a whole. Yet, at the same time, we must raise difficult questions concerning the causes of drug abuse. The ranks of drug abusers are filled with people from the lower classes of American society, persons experiencing the ill effects of poverty and ghetto living. Their numbers are swelled by persons of all socio-economic levels who find no purpose in life and therefore are suffering from a sense of sheer boredom. How are we providing alternatives and answers for these situations? And do we care about those caught in this evil web?

The spread of AIDS among homosexually oriented persons and drug abusers raises difficult questions. To what extent are these sinners likewise the sinned-against, the product of a society gone awry and of a church whose doors appear at times to be only partially opened to them? Although raising such questions does not excuse the choices that persons make, it nevertheless serves to indicate that more than personal choice is involved when an individual follows a sinful lifestyle.

For most Christians, a more obvious category of the sinned-against are the innocent victims of the AIDS epidemic, persons who have contracted the disease apart from any involvement in questionable lifestyles. The AIDS epidemic forces Christians to ask hard questions concerning these people as well. Why has this disease spread to spouses of unfaithful partners, persons who have contracted AIDS through normal marital relations? What about the babies who have been born with this dreaded disease? What about hemophiliacs who have been infected with AIDS through blood-product transfusion? Consideration of these victims moves us beyond any simple or one-sided understanding of the relationship between sickness and sin, whether personal or societal in nature.

There is no answer to the problem of the innocent victims of this epidemic. In our fallen world, the innocent do indeed suffer with the guilty. And the sinful actions of some affect others. For the Christian, this means that AIDS cannot be viewed merely as a moral problem, merely as a situation reflecting the morality of the infected. In the final analysis, AIDS itself is not a moral issue. It is a disease, an enemy of humanity, and therefore is to be fought like all other enemies. Nor (as we have seen) can we view AIDS as solely a "gay problem." Rather, it is *our* problem. If this understanding is correct, we must join together in a concerted effort to attack and overcome the epidemic. A victory over AIDS is not only a victory for some; it is also a victory for all of us.

This takes us back to the incident involving a man born blind, recorded in John 9. There is, of course, a major difference between this story and the current AIDS epidemic. The man's blindness appears to have been the result of a birth defect and therefore apparently unconnected with any personal, parental, or societal sin. The contracting of AIDS, in contrast, is not always so "innocent." Past acts of patient, parent, or spouse can provide the entry point for the virus. Nevertheless, there are the cases of innocent people becoming infected—and in all cases there are the additional factors discussed above.

For this reason, the response of Jesus to the disciples— ". . . this happened so that the work of God might be displayed in his life" (John 9:3)—is not without application to the AIDS epidemic. Similar to the situation lying behind the incident in John's Gospel, the current crisis offers an opportunity for the work of God to be displayed. But, for this to occur, the church must rise to the challenge of seeing the AIDS epidemic through the eyes of Christ. The church must truly be his body, responding to the crisis in a way that is in keeping with his attitude and with the church's role as the instrument for carrying on his ministry. (The theological basis for this is developed further in subsequent chapters.)

God's Voice

A step may likewise be taken toward overcoming the barriers to ministry in the midst of the AIDS epidemic as Christians come to see AIDS as a vehicle for God's speaking to us and to our world. We must listen for God's voice. What is God trying to say to us? What is the tone of the divine utterance? It seems that God's voice may be speaking at least three words to our society and to the Christian community in particular.

Judgment

To understand fully the significance of the current crisis, we must realize that God's voice is speaking a word of judgment through the AIDS epidemic. This theme, AIDS as the judgment of God on human sin, has been repeatedly sounded by various Christians. Others vehemently object to and categorically reject this suggestion, declaring that viewing AIDS as "judgment" reflects an undue fear of homosexuality and is counterproductive. In spite of arguments to the contrary, however, the conclusion that AIDS constitutes a divine word of judgment is unavoidable. This declaration arises in several ways.

First, AIDS is a vivid reminder of the relationship between acts and consequences. The principle that actions bring consequences is not popular in contemporary society. On the contrary, people today often maintain that they can live as they please without suffering any adverse effects themselves or negatively affecting others. The AIDS epidemic constitutes a conclusive counter-example to such thinking. It is a reminder that personal actions do have their implications and carry consequences. In this sense, AIDS is the voice of judgment on irresponsible living. It is a bold declaration that the age of such naive innocence is over.

Second, AIDS is the voice of judgment on the privatization of morality. Our age popularizes the idea that what is done between consenting adults behind closed doors is solely a private matter. The age of naive innocence presupposed by this outlook, however, is likewise over. The AIDS epidemic declares that a relationship does exist between "private" acts and the public good and between a society's mores and its health. No people can allow God's norms to be ignored or eroded and expect to suffer no ill consequences. Rather, a relationship exists between the guidelines for personal living found in the Bible and a healthy society. Because these guidelines have been given for human benefit, they are ignored only to the peril of individuals and also of society as a whole. Cardinal George Basil Hume, the Archbishop of Westminster, articulates this point well: "The spread of AIDS and the peril it represents for our society illustrate dramatically what has happened to the attitudes and values of society and what price it now has to pay for its previous disregard of moral standards."[2]

Third, the AIDS epidemic should be seen as the voice of judgment on the callousness of God's people. If, in some sense, the victims of the disease are also the sinned-against, AIDS speaks a word of condemnation on our complicity in this sin. To the extent that our unwillingness to become "community" to persons whose lifestyles we see as abhorrent has contributed to their fleeing to unwholesome communities for fellowship, we have contributed to the spread of the epidemic. AIDS calls us to account for whatever prejudice, apathy, and inaction may have characterized the church in the past.

Hearing God's voice of judgment through the AIDS epidemic demands that the call to repentance accompanying it be heard as well. This call comes, of course, to individuals who are practicing sinful and harmful lifestyles. To such persons God declares, "Repent! Turn from your sinful ways, for the wages of sin is death." But the call to repentance is not limited to persons engaged in sinful lifestyles. It moves beyond them to society as a whole and to the trend setters and influential persons in our world. God's challenge to our nation is to turn from those harmful attitudes and actions that have opened the door to this epidemic and facilitated its spread, whether they be the use of sex in marketing, the promotion of self-gratification, or the erosion of morality in general. To the church God also issues a call to repent. We are challenged to forsake our complicity with the spirit of the age, our complacency with our comfortable clique, and our hesitancy to fulfill our mission to reach out in the name of Jesus to persons who do not meet our standards of righteousness.

The Unity of Life

To understand the AIDS epidemic, we must likewise listen for God's voice as it offers a needed reminder of the unity of life. For a time, many people viewed AIDS as a "gay disease" from which they could remain unaffected, but we are now beginning to see that this is a fallacious and dangerous attitude. The spread of the AIDS plague has offered a profound declaration concerning the nature of society. No longer are groups allowed the privilege of thinking they can shield themselves from society as a whole or from any subgroup in society. No one can withdraw from the world into some safe enclave. Rather, society is an organic whole, and we are an integral part of that whole. What Paul stated concerning the church is true of any society or people group—when one part suffers, eventually all parts suffer as well (1 Cor. 12:26).

This reality is borne out by the distressing fact that the AIDS epidemic has quickly jumped the boundaries of the homosexual community in which it first multiplied and now carries the potential to infect all population groups of American society. This should not surprise us, given the biblical understanding of the unity of humanity. Solidarity, however, is not limited to the human family at any given moment. Rather, it also transcends any one generation. Right now, even future generations are at stake in the AIDS controversy. This grim reality is evidenced in that the disease has already moved to the next generation, from parents to children. Our decisions and our response to the current crisis will affect not only ourselves, but also our children and our children's children.

For this reason, those who would hear God's voice speaking through the AIDS epidemic must listen for God's call to responsibility. We are indeed "our brother's keeper." We must shoulder the responsibility that comes to us as members of society and as part of the ongoing link from the past to the future generations.

The Way of the Cross

Finally, to understand the AIDS crisis we must hear in it God's voice speaking a word of admonition. The AIDS crisis reminds us that the way of the Christian is the way of the cross. God demands that the church of Jesus Christ follow the example of the Lord by being willing to take risks for the sake of others. Repeatedly in his ministry, Jesus spoke of the cost of discipleship. He clearly stated that being his follower entailed risk, sacrifice, and the willingness to pay a price, that is, the willingness to lose one's life for the sake of the gospel. God's voice issues a call to suffer with the afflicted, just as Christ suffered and died for us. For this reason, even if AIDS presented a serious medical risk, would not the gospel of Christ ask and even demand that we risk our lives and well-being in order to minister to these needy persons?

As we have seen, the AIDS epidemic can easily give

rise to certain barriers that hinder ministry in the midst of this crisis. Yet, these barriers can be overcome for the sake of the kingdom of God and for the ministry of Christ in the world. The foundation for overcoming the various barriers is laid as we come to a theological understanding of the causes of sickness in general and of AIDS in particular, and as we are open to hear the voice of God speaking to us and to our world through this awful disease. These considerations offer a means to deal with the barriers. If ministry is to occur, we must not only eliminate the barriers that hinder our task. We must also cross over and touch the needy persons plagued by the AIDS disease. For this to happen, we must sense a compelling urge to minister in the midst of the AIDS epidemic. The development of a theological basis that compels such a ministry is the subject to which we now turn.

8

Crossing the Barriers Through Compassion

We have noted that three major barriers hinder ministry in the midst of the AIDS epidemic: its perception as a "sinner's disease," its link to human sexuality, and its terminal nature. As Christians, however, we are called to overcome these barriers. The previous chapter laid a foundation for this by developing a theological understanding of the causes of sickness and by attempting to describe what the voice of God may be saying through the AIDS crisis.

If ministry in the midst of the AIDS epidemic is to be successful, the barriers must not only ultimately be overcome, they must first be crossed. Since this action requires a compelling motivation, we now turn our attention to the development of a theological basis for such a ministry. The goal of this discussion is to encourage the people of God to cross the barriers for the sake of persons in need.

Christians *can* minister in the midst of the AIDS epidemic. For this to happen, however, we must sense a strong central motivation for such a ministry. At this important juncture the Bible speaks clearly and thereby provides such a motivation, one that is actually many-sided. This chapter focuses on one compelling motivation for action in the midst of the AIDS crisis: compassion. Our ministerial response to this epidemic arises in part as we are gripped by godly compassion for persons in need.

Compassion is crucial for genuine ministry, although this emotion is not readily present nor easily developed in contemporary society. In fact, total compassion is beyond the ability of humans to produce. True compassion is a divine trait and is present in the world only as the fruit of the Holy Spirit in the lives of believers. If compassion is to be present, we must open ourselves to the working of the Spirit. A first step toward the fulfillment of this challenge is taken when we come to understand more fully the divine compassion we are called to emulate.

The obvious beginning place lies in the meaning of the concept itself. Compassion means literally "to suffer with." This forms the background to a standard dictionary definition: "a sympathetic emotion created by the misfortunes of another, accompanied by a desire to help."[1]

Compassion for others in the face of their misfortunes does not arise in a vacuum, however. Its source lies in a more foundational emotion—love—that is, *agape,* whereby persons give of themselves unconditionally for the sake of others. Such love is seldom experienced in our world. On the contrary, a perfect example of this emotion can be found only in the compassionate love shown to us by God. It is for this reason that Christians look to divine revelation, especially the revelation of God in Jesus Christ. There they discover the loving nature of God. As we come to view the perfect love of God, the Holy Spirit is able to create in us the kind of compassionate love needed for ministry in the midst of crises such as the AIDS epidemic. The biblical revelation of the divine heart, its incarnation in Jesus, and our response to it will occupy our attention in the following pages.

The Compassionate God

A persistent theme in the Bible is the presentation of God as the Compassionate One. This theme is developed in several related ways.

1. *God's compassionate response to creation is an outworking of the divine love.* The Bible indicates that God's compassion, just like human compassion, is a secondary attribute, dependent on this more fundamental divine characteristic. This viewpoint requires further elaboration.

According to Christian theology, love is the foundational moral attribute of God. Love is visible in a primary way within the Godhead, for God is the Triune One, the community of Father, Son, and Spirit. These three trinitarian persons constitute one God, in that they are bound together by the cord of divine love. John, the apostle of love, characterizes God in this way. In his first epistle, John makes a simple, yet profound declaration: "God is love . . ." (1 John 4:16). This seemingly obvious statement is filled with meaning. It offers the bold declaration that the eternal God is characterized by love.

Throughout all eternity, the triune God is characterized by love, in that the Father, Son, and Spirit constitute one God, a community of love. For this reason, it is not surprising that the fundamental character of God—love—shines toward creation as well. Love, which describes God's own essence, also characterizes God's relationship to creation. Because God *is* love, God loves the world. Again John describes this love for us: "For God so loved the world that he gave his one and only

Son . . ." (John 3:16). God relates to the world out of the abundance of his own character, which is love.

This theme is not unique to the New Testament understanding of God. In the Old Testament, the people of God already expressed the foundational relationship of God to the world in terms of God's compassion, a compassion related to the divine love. In fact, God as the Compassionate One is a foundational theological theme of the Old Testament. This is reflected in a theological formulation that stood at the center of the faith of the Hebrew community. The Book of Exodus even describes this assertion as having its source in a divine self-affirmation. In the account of God's appearance to Moses on Mount Sinai, after revealing the divine name, Yahweh declares "the compassionate and gracious God, slow to anger, abounding in love and faithfulness" (Exod. 34:6).

This formulation—God as abounding in love and filled with compassion—is found repeatedly throughout the Old Testament, forming as it were a central faith affirmation concerning the divine nature (e.g., Neh. 9:17; Ps. 86:15; 103:8; 111:4; 116:5; 145:8; Isa. 54:10; Joel 2:13; Jon. 4:2). Writing in the *International Standard Bible Encyclopedia,* Williston Walker reaches a conclusion related to this observation: "Nothing therefore is more prominent in the Old Testament than the ascription of compassion, pity, mercy, etc., to God. The people may be said to have gloried in it."[2]

2. *Because of the divine love, the plight of God's creatures evokes compassion from God.* Not only does the Old Testament declare God to be the Compassionate One, it also links this compassion to the human predicament. This understanding is bound up with the Hebrew word employed to speak of compassion: *racham.* Robert Girdlestone declares that this term "expresses a deep and tender feeling of compassion such as is aroused by the sight of weakness or suffering in those that are dear to us or need our help."[3] *Racham,* or

"compassion," aptly portrays the response that arises when the divine love views the struggles of God's people.

3. *God's covenant people are the special object of this compassion.* In keeping with the above understanding, the Old Testament asserts that God longs to have compassion on his people (Isa. 30:18). Jeremiah, for example, describes God as desiring to have compassion on Ephraim, "my dear son" (Jer. 31:20). In this way, God's covenant love for his people and God's fidelity to that covenant form a crucial foundation for the divine compassion.

This observation leads Elizabeth Achtemeier, writing in the *Interpreter's Dictionary of the Bible,* to define God's mercy (which in the Old Testament is synonymous with compassion) as "a loving act of Yahweh by which he faithfully maintains his covenant relationship with his chosen people."[4] In Achtemeier's opinion, the covenant relationship is foundational to God's compassion. It even overshadows the meaning that arises from the original derivation of the Hebrew term *racham:* the idea of family relationships. The stem from which the Hebrew term is derived means "womb," she notes. Following this development, compassion would be seen as referring to "the feeling of those born from the same womb" or "the love of a mother for her child." Achtemeier, however, finds this etymological meaning supplanted by an understanding of compassion as God's covenant faithfulness.

4. *God's concern moves beyond Israel to encompass all creatures.* Although in the Old Testament God's compassion is especially directed toward the covenant people, the Bible clearly indicates a wider outreach. The Psalmist, for example, declares, "The Lord is good to all; he has compassion on all he has made" (Ps. 145:9). This theme is reiterated in the New Testament. It is found in Jesus' teaching, especially in the Sermon on the Mount. And Paul employs the same theme in speak-

ing of God's intent to save all sinful humanity (Rom. 11:32).[5]

5. *Divine compassion is evoked especially in the face of the distress and suffering of God's people.* Isaiah articulates this well: "Shout for joy, O heavens; rejoice, O earth; burst into song, O mountains! For the LORD comforts his people and will have compassion on his afflicted ones" (Isa. 49:13). Elsewhere Isaiah reflects on Israel's history and declares, "In all their distress he too was distressed, and the angel of his presence saved them. In his love and mercy he redeemed them; he lifted them up and carried them all the days of old" (Isa. 63:9). Similar considerations cause Hosea to conclude concerning God, ". . . In you the fatherless find compassion" (Hos. 14:3). The foundational moral attribute of God, love, evokes the emotion of compassion in the face of the plight of God's creatures.

6. *This divine compassion or mercy arises from God's grace, not from human merit.* The Scriptures firmly declare that God's compassion is the product of his sovereign mercy (Exod. 33:19; Rom. 9:15–16, 18). For this reason, the divine grace toward humans can be present in spite of human rebellion. Daniel, for example, boldly declares this truth: "The Lord our God is merciful and forgiving, even though we have rebelled against him" (Dan. 9:9).

Perhaps the most moving illustration of God's love for humans, despite their rebellion, is found in the parable of the prodigal son. While the son "was still a long way off," the father saw him "and was filled with compassion for him" (Luke 15:20). Here Jesus gives us a picture of God's compassion toward wayward creatures, even when they have been in rebellion against their Creator and Father.

This sovereign, gracious compassion of God forms the basis for Daniel's bold assertion that God answers the request of God's people not because of their righteousness, but because of God's great mercy (Dan. 9:18). The same understanding lies behind the repeated plea in the Book of Psalms for God to remember the covenant and to act compassionately toward his people in the midst of their trials (Ps. 25:6; 40:11; 51:1; 69:16; 77:9ff.; 79:8; 119:77).

The belief in a gracious, compassionate God likewise forms the foundation for the repeated hope expressed by the prophets, that at some future day God would again be compassionate on the people of Israel (e.g., Isa. 14:1; 54:7; Jer. 12:15; 30:18; 33:26; 42:12; Ezek. 39:25; Hos. 1:7; 2:23; Joel 2:18; Mic. 7:19; Zech. 1:16; Mal. 3:17). Isaiah stands as an example of the prophetic movement as a whole in anticipating a day when God's compassion would be experienced as an expression of his everlasting kindness: "'In a surge of anger I hid my face from you for a moment, but with everlasting kindness I will have compassion on you,' says the LORD your Redeemer" (Isa. 54:8).

7. *Although divine compassion is the result of God's grace and not human merit, the Bible declares that the reception of this compassion is connected to a proper human response to God.* Holy living, for example, evokes the compassion of God (Deut. 13:17). God's compassion comes likewise as the response to human repentance and the forsaking of evil ways (Deut. 30:16–18; Prov. 28:13; Isa. 55:7). The fear of God also brings divine compassion (Ps. 103:13; Luke 1:50 [Mary's Song]). On the other hand, continued involvement in disobedience and sin hinders the reception of God's compassion. Ezekiel declares that God responds not in compassion but in judgment in such situations (Ezek. 5:11; 7:4, 9; 8:18).

8. *Divine compassion leads to divine action.* The Old Testament repeatedly appeals to the history of Israel as an illustration of this principle. Isaiah, for example, desires to proclaim the deeds that the compassionate God has done (Isa. 63:7). Reflecting on Israel's experiences in the exodus and in the wilderness wandering,

the psalmist asserts that out of compassion God atoned for the iniquities of the people and did not destroy them (Ps. 78:38).

In the post-exilic era, reflection on Israel's history became especially important. On the basis of this history as a whole, the Book of Nehemiah declares that God did not abandon his people (Neh. 9:7–31). And the author of 2 Chronicles summarizes Israel's story as the repeated reception of divine compassion: "The LORD, the God of their fathers sent word to them through his messengers again and again, because he had pity on his people and on his dwelling place" (2 Chron. 36:15).

For Israel the foundational divine action on their behalf stood at the beginning of their history in the Exodus. Williston Walker describes the relationship between divine compassion and this event. Compassion, he writes, "lay at the foundation of Israel's faith in Jehovah, for it was out of his compassion that he by a marvelous act of power delivered them from Egyptian bondage and called them to be his own people."[6]

God's activity in the history of Israel was not merely viewed as belonging to a dead past, however. Rather, it remained as a living presence and held out the promise of a future renewal. This anticipation forms the context for the understanding reflected in the New Testament. As the New Testament era began, God's past expression of compassion called forth a heightened anticipation of renewed divine action arising out of the divine compassion. This is evident in Zechariah's hymn at the birth of John. For Zechariah, John's arrival entailed an act of God, who in this event demonstrated "mercy to our fathers" and was now remembering the covenant with Israel (Luke 1:72).

According to the New Testament, however, the supreme action that arose out of the divine compassion is the salvation available in Jesus Christ. That this event is the expression of God's mercy is reiterated throughout its pages. A specially beautiful declaration of this truth is found in the Book of Ephesians: "But because of his great love for us, God, who is rich in mercy, made us alive with Christ even when we were dead in transgressions—it is by grace you have been saved" (Eph. 2:4–5). The same theme is reiterated in Titus: God "saved us, not because of righteous things we had done, but because of his mercy . . ." (Titus 3:5a). In a similar way, Peter declares that "in his great mercy" God has given Christians "new birth into a living hope . . ." (1 Peter 1:3).

9. *The goal of God's compassion is that God be praised.* A far-reaching awareness of this idea is important for the biblical understanding of the compassion of God. This theme is summarized by Paul, who—in writing to a church consisting of both Jews and Gentiles—declares:

> For I tell you that Christ has become a servant of the Jews on behalf of God's truth, to confirm the promises made to the patriarchs so that the Gentiles may glorify God for his mercy, as it is written: "Therefore I will praise you among the Gentiles; I will sing hymns to your name." Again it says, "Rejoice, O Gentiles, with his people" (Rom. 15:8–10).

The goal of God's loving compassion, which leads to divine action on behalf of God's creatures in the midst of their plight, is that all the peoples of the world may together offer praise to the glory of the God who has saved them.

Jesus—the Compassionate One

The compassion of God is a theme of the Bible as a whole, but the New Testament takes this point a step further. It declares that God's loving compassion finds concrete manifestation in Jesus of Nazareth. For Christians, following the New Testament, Jesus stands as the grand example of godly living, in that our allegiance is to him, and we are his disciples, his followers. This means that Jesus is also our model of compassion. Because of Jesus' status as the incarnation of divine love and the example to the believing community, the compassion necessary for crossing the barriers and ministering in the midst of the AIDS epidemic can be learned only at the feet of Jesus. At least six themes concerning Jesus' compassion are found in the New Testament.

1. *Expressing compassionate love lay at the heart of Jesus' understanding of his mission.* The Lord's outlook is revealed, for example, in his response to the request of James and John for the positions of honor in the coming kingdom. This incident indicates the fundamental misunderstanding concerning the nature of prominence in the minds of the disciples. Jesus, linking himself to the eschatological figure of the Son of Man, declares in response: "[For even] the Son of Man did not come to be served, but to serve, and to give his life as a ransom for many" (Matt. 20:28; cf. Mark 10:45). His mission was one of compassionate service to others, arising from a self-giving attitude, that is: love.

John's Gospel explains Jesus' mission not in terms of judgment and condemnation, but in terms of salvation: "For God did not send his Son into the world to condemn the world, but to save the world through him" (John 3:17). Using the imagery of "the good shepherd," the Johannine Christ reiterates the point made in the Synoptics, declaring that he came to give life in its fullness, even to the point of sacrificing his own life for the sake of others (John 10:10–11).

In the synagogue in Nazareth, Jesus appealed to Isaiah to explain to his audience the nature of his mission. His purpose included the practical goals of bringing freedom, healing, and release to people in distress (Luke 4:18–19). In short, Jesus understood and defined his own mission in terms of expressing the compassionate love of God.

2. *Jesus sensed compassion in the face of ignorance,*

hunger, sickness, and death. The Gospels report that on at least two occasions the compassion of Jesus was evoked by the sorrow others were experiencing at the loss of loved ones. When he saw a woman weeping over the death of her son, Jesus' "heart went out to her," and he comforted her (Luke 7:13). At the tomb of Jesus' friend Lazarus, John reports, the master "wept" (John 11:35). Those observing the Lord could not help but exclaim, "See how he loved him!" (v. 36).

Jesus was gripped by compassion when he saw the aimlessness of the common people as "sheep without a shepherd" (Matt. 9:36; Mark 6:34). The heart of the Master was also moved when he saw the sick among the multitudes (Matt. 14:14). This compassion was kindled by the plight of specific individuals, such as the two blind men whom Jesus confronted outside the city of Jericho (Matt. 20:34). A similar response was evoked by the crowds who grew hungry as they intently listened to his teaching (Matt. 15:32; Mark 8:2).

3. *Jesus' compassion expressed itself in ministry.* As he saw the needs of people around him, needs that sparked his emotion, Jesus did not stand aside. On the contrary, he engaged in action to alleviate the misery of the people and minister to their needs. To those who had lost loved ones, Jesus responded by raising the dead (John 11:1–44; Luke 7:1–15). To people lacking guidance, Jesus offered instruction and teaching (Mark 6:34). And in response to the sick, Jesus healed their diseases (Matt. 4:23; 9:35; 14:14; 19:2).

4. *In his ministry, Jesus was not afraid to make physical contact with those in need.* The Gospels abound in examples of Jesus' touching of people. He often took the hand of sick persons to help them stand as he healed them. Jesus laid hold of the hand of Peter's mother-in-law, for example, to help her up as he cured her fever (Mark 1:31). On another occasion he took the hand of a girl presumed to be dead and raised her to life (Matt. 9:25). Jesus was even willing to take the hand of a boy

possessed by a demon and liberate him from his tormentor (Mark 9:27).

Not only did Jesus take the hand of others, he also was willing to put his hands on those in need of his ministering touch. A crippled woman was one recipient of this healing action (Luke 13:13). Likewise, the fingers of Jesus often reached out to those to whom he ministered—touching blind eyes to make them see (Matt. 9:29; 20:34; John 9:6), deaf ears to bring about hearing (Luke 22:51), silent tongues to give the gift of speech (Mark 7:33).

Most significantly, however, Jesus was not afraid to touch the outcasts of his day, those suffering from the dreaded and contagious disease of leprosy (Matt. 8:3; Mark 1:41; Luke 5:13). This debilitating illness exacted an impenetrable wall between the afflicted and the society of the healthy. Laws against any kind of contact with lepers were strictly enforced, and the victims of this disease were treated as the living dead. One man, however, was willing to cross the barriers and touch these outcasts—Jesus.

The willingness of the Master to touch those to whom he ministered becomes more significant when it is remembered that actual physical contact was not necessary for Jesus to heal. He appears to have had the power to cure the sick without the least amount of physical contact or even physical presence (e.g., Luke 7:1–10). Nevertheless, he freely chose to touch the untouchables. These acts demonstrate Jesus' great compassion.

The Book of Acts indicates that Jesus' example of fearlessly making physical contact with those in need was followed by the early church. Peter and John extended their hands to the crippled beggar outside the temple gate to heal him (Acts 3:7). And, reminiscent of Jesus' own practice, Peter took the hand of a dead woman, Dorcas, as he raised her to life (Acts 9:41).

5. *Jesus' compassion was all-encompassing.* It

extended beyond the circle of his friends to include the multitudes. It included his enemies and those who rejected him. Even when his arrest and death were imminent, Jesus' heart still went out to others. Anticipating the final rejection he would experience by the nation he loved, Jesus wept over the city of Jerusalem (Matt. 23:37). Then, during his arrest, Jesus offered his healing touch to the soldier whose ear had been injured in the scuffle (Luke 22:51). In his hour of death, his thoughts were directed toward the needs of those who rejected him. Jesus prayed that the forgiving mercy of his Father be extended even to the soldiers who were crucifying him: "Father, forgive them, for they do not know what they are doing" (Luke 23:34).

Jesus' actions stand as apt illustrations of his teaching. He declared that compassion is to be given to all without exception, even to enemies. In the Sermon on the Mount, for example, he appeals to the universal merciful goodness of God as a basis for enjoining a similar compassion in the lives of his disciples:

> "You have heard that it was said, 'Love your neighbor and hate your enemy.' But I tell you: Love your enemies and pray for those who persecute you, that you may be sons of your Father in heaven. He causes his sun to rise on the evil and the good, and sends rain on the righteous and the unrighteous" (Matt. 5:43–45; cf. the parable of the good Samaritan, Luke 10:30–37).

Jesus' life comprises a vivid illustration of this principle.

6. *The loving compassion of Christ is not merely that of an exemplary man; it reveals the heart of God.* Foundational to the understanding of Jesus' person that developed in the early church is the acceptance of Jesus' life as the revelation of God. The New Testament clearly presents Jesus as God incarnate in human form. At the heart of this understanding of the incarnation is

Jesus' life as the Compassionate One. Paul, for example, summarizes the incarnation in terms of Jesus' self-sacrifice on behalf of miserable human beings: "For you know the grace of our Lord Jesus Christ, that though he was rich, yet for your sakes he became poor, so that you through his poverty might become rich" (2 Cor. 8:9).

Reflecting on the earthly life of Jesus, who is now the exalted Lord at the right hand of God the Father, the author of Hebrews offers a practical Christological implication of that exemplary life: "For we do not have a high priest who is unable to sympathize with our weaknesses, but we have one who has been tempted in every way, just as we are—yet was without sin" (Heb. 4:15). Even now in his exalted state, our Lord remains the Compassionate One who sympathizes with us in our trials.

According to the New Testament, then, Jesus stands as a vivid example of the meaning of compassion. He is the revelation of the compassionate, loving heart of God. In him we find the God who responds with loving compassion to the plight of God's creatures.

Compassion and the People of God

According to the Bible, the compassionate nature of God is revealed in God's actions in history, climaxing in the coming of Jesus Christ. This central attribute of the divine nature places a great responsibility on Christ's church. As God's people we are to be emulators of the compassionate Lord. His example calls us to be the compassionate ones and thereby to reflect the divine character.

This understanding is so well ingrained throughout the Bible that compassion is without question a central aspect of biblical piety. Job's rhetorical question, "Have I not wept for those in trouble? Has not my soul grieved for the poor?" (Job 30:25), indicates that this kind of compassion was simply assumed to be characteristic of every member of the Old Testament covenant community. The New Testament reaffirms the same outlook. For example, James declares, "Religion that God our Father accepts as pure and faultless is this: to look after orphans and widows in their distress, and to keep oneself from being polluted by the world" (James 1:27). Not only personal holiness, i.e., freedom from sin, but being compassionate toward others both in attitude and in action lies at the center of what is assumed to be normal religion.

In keeping with this, the New Testament Epistles repeatedly admonish the Christian community to be compassionate. Colossians, for example, declares, ". . . clothe yourselves with compassion . . ." (Col. 3:12). Likewise, Peter commands his readers to be compassionate and sympathetic (1 Peter 3:8). Paul forges the link between compassion and the example of Christ. To the Galatians he writes, "Carry each other's burdens, and in this way you will fulfill the law of Christ" (Gal. 6:2). Burden lifting and sharing the load of others are important aspects by which believers follow the example of the Lord. And Hebrews offers some specific ways in which the Christian community can live out the compassion that is to characterize it: "Remember those in prison as if you were their fellow prisoners, and those who are mistreated as if you yourselves were suffering" (Heb. 13:3). Christians are to be characterized by compassion—they are to display true sympathy for those in distress, even to the point of sharing in that distress.

Perhaps the grandest illustration and admonition to the disciples of the Lord to be a compassionate people, however, is found in Jesus' parable of the good Samaritan. In narrating the story, Jesus clearly sought to emphasize that it was this outcast individual, not those who stood in traditional positions of leadership within the Jewish community, who was compassionate to the man in need. The Samaritan saw the battered man lying along the road and "took pity on him," Jesus declares. It is interesting to note that the same verb the Gospel writers employed to speak of Jesus' outlook toward the needy is utilized here to describe the Samaritan. The emotion of compassion, so characteristic of the Master, was translated into action by this man as he bandaged his wounds, took the injured person to an inn, and offered to pay the innkeeper to look after the needs of the battered traveler.

After delivering the parable, Jesus then asked the crucial question of the expert in the law to whom he was speaking: "Which of these three do you think was a neighbor to the man [in need]?" (Luke 10:36). The response of his listener was significant: "The one who had mercy on him," and it evoked Jesus' command: "Go and do likewise" (v. 37). By means of this vivid parable, Jesus' followers are commanded by the Lord to have compassion for, and show mercy to, those who are suffering or are in distress.

The compassion of God revealed throughout the Bible and incarnate in Christ leads to the obvious conclusion: As Christians, we are called to be a compassionate people. As imitators of God, we are to respond to persons in distress with actions motivated by compassion. As disciples of the Lord, we are to follow his example by reaching out to the untouchables of our society. Among the ranks of modern-day "lepers" we must place persons with AIDS. Like their first-century counterparts, they, too, are often placed on the fringes of society and shunned as "unclean"—as contagious, unloved, and unwanted. The compassionate God, however, challenges us to action. Just as the divine heart longs to act on behalf of all sufferers, God is moved by AIDS patients. We, therefore, ought also to be moved by their plight. The Lord, who offered his healing touch to so many, challenges us to be his fingers and hands in reaching out in compassionate touch to those around us who are suffering, including persons struggling with AIDS.

Yet, godly compassion goes beyond what is humanly

possible. As has been noted previously, this kind of compassion can be present only as it arises from love. But love in its full biblical sense must be created in us by the Holy Spirit. As Paul declares, love belongs to the fruit of the Spirit (Gal. 5:22). Our task must therefore begin with a prayerful and conscious attempt to be sensitive to the presence, working, and filling of the Spirit in our lives and in our churches.

As Christians, we are compelled by the divine compassion to minister to those in need, including persons struggling with AIDS. Such ministry, however, is possible only as we are filled with the Holy Spirit and thereby are flooded with the divine love, the love that responds to the needs of all suffering persons with compassionate action.

Godly compassion is central to ministry. It provides the impetus to reach out to others. It gives tenacity when the life of ministry is difficult. Without compassion, ministry is reduced to a heartless veneer, often of greater comfort to the one who ministers than to the sufferers in need of care.

9

Other Motivations for an AIDS Ministry

Although the people of God can cross the barriers and minister in the midst of the AIDS epidemic, ministry requires a biblical motivation. As already noted, the primary source of the compelling motivation needed for action in response to this crisis lies in the compassion that arises from the love produced by the Holy Spirit in the hearts of believers. There are, however, other aspects of the biblical message that also contribute to a strong motivation for ministry in this arena. Two of these will be explored in this chapter.

God and Evil

One motivation for ministry in the midst of the AIDS epidemic arises from an understanding of God's relationship to evil. Scripture offers two fundamental insights concerning this relationship.

God's Struggle Against Evil

First, the Bible declares that God is engaged in a struggle against evil. In this struggle, God is battling against everything that seeks to thwart the divine plan for creation: God's intent to bring creation into fullness of life. These enemies of God attempt to undermine the divine purposes by destroying the very life God creates. Evil, regardless of the form it takes, is ultimately life destroying and death producing. Insofar as they produce these effects, all diseases, including AIDS, must be seen as evil, as opposing God's purposes.

Jesus repeatedly alluded to the reality of a cosmic struggle in his ministry. In the context of describing himself as "the good shepherd," for example, he draws a contrast between his mission and that of the opposing forces: "The thief comes only to steal and kill and destroy; I have come that they might have life, and have it to the full" (John 10:10).

In keeping with the outlook of the Master, the Book of Ephesians offers an important insight concerning the identity of these forces: "For our struggle is not against flesh and blood, but against the rulers, against the authorities, against the powers of this dark world and against the spiritual forces of evil in the heavenly realms" (Eph. 6:12). The enemies of God and of human life, therefore, are not human beings; God has reconciled humanity to Christ (2 Cor. 5:19). Rather, behind the evil in the world lie spiritual forces of evil—authorities and powers in the cosmic realm. Because these are God's enemies, they are our enemies as well. Within the ranks of these enemies of humanity, we must place sickness, including AIDS and the diseases related to it.

Although acknowledging the presence of a divine struggle against the powers of evil, the Bible leaves no doubt as to the final outcome of this battle. Evil may appear to be on the offensive. Sometimes it may even seem to be carrying the day. However, the end result of this struggle is already decided. The good news of the Bible is that the decisive victory in the battle against evil has been won by Christ himself. On the cross and through his resurrection, he has dealt a decisive blow to the forces of evil.

Nevertheless, the final victory in this cosmic battle lies still in the future. According to the Bible, it comes only at the end of the age, at the eschaton, when Satan is forever banished from God's kingdom. At that point all evil will be eliminated from the human realm, and the new creation in its full perfection will be brought into existence. In speaking of that day, John declares that God "will wipe every tear from their eyes. There will be no more death or mourning or crying or pain, for the old order of things has passed away" (Rev. 21:4). In one sense, then, the Bible views history as a drama, a stage, the field in which God's struggle against evil is played out. This battle will be completed at the return of Jesus, when Satan and all of God's enemies are ultimately defeated.

According to the Bible, the divine struggle against evil has an important implication for Christians. In the midst of the battle, God issues a call to us, one that moves in two directions. First, we are enjoined to become God's agents who participate in the cosmic struggle against evil. Of course, the victory over evil comes only by God's action and is the product of God's grace. Therefore, we must continually caution ourselves against thinking that victory will be won by our actions. At the same time, however, although God's grace gives the victory, the triumph over evil is to come through our activity and with our cooperation. We are to engage as agents of God in the fight against evil on all fronts.

This principle applies to the struggle against all our enemies, including the AIDS disease. Victory over this evil, too, belongs to God. But we are to join the struggle, to enlist as God's partners and agents and do battle with AIDS.

Peter's second epistle gives evidence of this principle. He suggests that Christians are to hasten the day of the Lord's return. After describing the coming day of the Lord, he asks, "Since everything will be destroyed in this way, what kind of people ought you to be?" (2 Peter 3:11a). Peter then offers an answer to his query: "You ought to live holy and godly lives as you look forward to the day of God and speed its coming" (vv. 11b–12). The apostle indicates that Christians can speed the coming of the eschaton through appropriate living, which, as God's agents, includes concerted action against the evils we face. Among these evils is the disease called AIDS, which we are to confront as an enemy on many levels.

In addition to calling us to participate as God's agents against evil, God issues a second call to us. In the midst of this struggle, we are to keep before our eyes the vision of God's ultimate victory. Even in situations where it appears that evil is gaining the victory, we can look to the biblical promise of the eschatological triumph of God. One day God's kingdom will be present in its fullness. Then all evil, including all sicknesses, will be banished from God's realm. Death will be eradicated and epidemics such as AIDS will no longer threaten humanity. If we would maintain fervency in battle, we must maintain this vision as we struggle against this epidemic.

The eschatological hope of God's final victory serves as an inspiration to Christians in our struggles against evil in this age. It provides inspiration toward steadfastness and courageous involvement. Paul employs the Christian hope of victory over death through the resurrection to this purpose. After his lengthy discussion of various aspects of, and problems associated with, this doctrine, he admonishes his readers: "Therefore, my dear brothers, stand firm. Let nothing move you. Always give yourselves fully to the work of the Lord, because you know that your labor in the Lord is not in vain" (1 Cor. 15:58). The knowledge that our efforts are "not in vain," but carry eternal implications, should serve to encourage Christians today in the battle against AIDS.

This eschatological hope likewise serves as a source of consolation in the face of death and in the struggle against death-producing diseases. Once again Paul stands as a vivid example. After asserting the marvelous declaration of the return of the Lord and his glorious meeting of the saints in the air, the apostle adds, "Therefore encourage each other with these words" (1 Thess. 4:18). We, too, can console those who are touched by the crushing blow of death, even death at the hand of the AIDS epidemic. This defeat will one day be changed to victory, when God's reign comes in its fullness, marking the end to the struggle against evil.

Overcoming Evil in the Present

God engages in an ongoing struggle against evil, a struggle that will climax in the eschatological victory. But the Scriptures assert yet a second truth concerning God's relationship to evil. Evil's defeat is not merely an eschatological reality, for even now God is bringing good out of evil. Paul was aware of this great truth. Therefore, he offered an important certainty to the Roman believers: "And we know that in all things God works for the good of those who love him . . ." (Rom. 8:28). God's victory over evil need not be relegated solely to the realm of eschatological hope. In the current evil situations of life, including the AIDS crisis, God is present and working in all things for our good.

The divine activity in bringing good out of evil arises from a fundamental aspect of God's character. Our Lord is the Omnipotent or All-powerful One. This means that evil is no match for the Ruler of the Universe. Primarily, omnipotence is directed to the entire flow of history. It indicates that God's goal for creation will be attained. The attainment of the divine purpose will occur specifically at the eschaton, when evil is banished from God's kingdom.

Yet, omnipotence refers not only to the future. God's power is a present reality as well. Although God's sovereign omnipotence over evil will indeed be demonstrated in the future, even now the Lord of the Universe, who is stronger than the forces of evil, is at work overruling evil for the sake of the divine purposes. God is so mighty and so good that even those situations that are intended by the enemy to thwart the divine plan can be transformed by God's power so as to become instruments of God.

For the Christian, this has several important implications. In the context of present sufferings, it means that the evils of life can be used by God's Spirit as aids to growth in faith. James articulates this truth: "Consider it pure joy, my brothers, whenever you face trials of many kinds, because you know that the testing of your faith develops perseverance" (James 1:2–3). The same theme is echoed by Peter, who writes concerning the inheritance in heaven awaiting the believer:

> In this [i.e., in the inheritance] you greatly rejoice, though now for a little while you may have had to suffer grief in all kinds of trials. These have come so that your faith—of greater worth than gold, which perishes even though refined by fire—may be proved genuine and may result in praise, glory and honor when Jesus Christ is revealed (1 Peter 1:6–7).

The evils of life, such as AIDS, can therefore be a means to strengthen the faith of God's children.

Evil may also become the agent of God's purposes as it serves as a means to encourage repentance. James says this about the Christian's response to sickness:

> Is any one of you sick? He should call the elders of the church to pray over him and anoint him with oil in the name of the Lord. And the prayer offered in faith will

make the sick person well; the Lord will raise him up. If he has sinned, he will be forgiven (James 5:14–15).

This advice appears to be primarily intended for those situations in which sickness has been allowed by God as a warning concerning some personal sin. Such sickness serves its intended purpose as it draws the sick person's attention to the spiritual condition in need of repentance. As this occurs, evil is turned into an agent for the purpose of disciplining God's child (Heb. 12:5–13).

God may also employ evil as a warning to others. This was the situation in the Corinthian church. Paul notes that sickness and even death came to some members of the congregation as a warning against desecrating the Lord's Supper (1 Cor. 10:29–30).

Because of God's action in the face of evil, Christians are encouraged to engage in ministry in the midst of the AIDS epidemic. God is struggling against the forces of evil, a struggle which God calls Christians to join as well. In the midst of the AIDS epidemic, the struggle entails fighting against this sickness and against the toll it extracts in terms of human misery. Christians serve with the calm assurance that one day God will banish from the eternal kingdom all evil and all sickness, including AIDS. The prayers and actions of Christians are directed toward this goal, with the hope that the banishment of this disease will come even in history and will come quickly. At the same time, as Christians engage in such ministry, God is at work, seeking to bring good out of this evil even now.

The Mandate of the Church

We are likewise motivated to cross the barriers and minister in the midst of the AIDS epidemic as we are gripped by the mandate given to the church. When we see why the church exists and what our role as members of Christ's body entails, we can engage in the corporate task of ministering to those touched by this disease and of serving society, that this epidemic can be conquered.

According to the Bible, the fundamental purpose of the church, like the purpose of all creation, is to bring honor and glory to God. God is glorified through the church as the people of God fulfill their divinely given mandate, which is actually threefold. The people of God have been entrusted with a worship mandate, the joyous task of praising God and proclaiming the glory of the One who is worthy (John 4:23–24; Rev. 4 and 5). The church has also been given the mandate of edification, which consists of the members of the body in Christ ministering to one another, so that all might develop spiritually (Eph. 4:11–13). The third mandate is that of outreach, which takes the form of disciple making and ministry to the world (Matt. 28:19–20; cf. Luke 4:16–21). Taken in both its individual aspects and as a whole, this threefold mandate demands that the people of God engage in ministry in the midst of the AIDS epidemic.

Worship

The first aspect of our mandate, worship of God, carries several implications for ministry in the face of the AIDS crisis. One such implication lies in a central aspect of church worship relating to a unique characteristic of the people of God: that the church is a unity in diversity. We who are to praise the Lord as a diverse body are nevertheless one in Christ.

The New Testament envisions the church as a special type of unity, one that arises in the midst of diversity and encompasses that diversity. Within its walls, people from all branches of the human family and all walks of life praise God together as one united body. Although describing a heavenly vision, John's words are applicable to the church as the foregleam of the eschatological chorus of praise. He saw:

> . . . a great multitude that no one could count, from every nation, tribe, people and language, standing before the throne and in front of the Lamb. They were wearing white robes and were holding palm branches in their hands. And they cried out in a loud voice: "Salvation belongs to our God, who sits on the throne, and to the Lamb" (Rev. 7:9–10).

Jesus himself anticipated the nature of the church as a unity arising out of diversity when he said, "I say to you that many will come from the east and the west, and will take their places at the feast with Abraham, Isaac and Jacob in the kingdom of heaven" (Matt. 8:11). This statement actually forms the context for the giving of the Great Commission to the disciples: "Therefore go and make disciples of all nations . . ." (Matt. 28:19). The church, then, is to consist of a unified diversity, as people from all corners of the world and from all strata in society worship together as the one body of Christ.

The diversity of the church, however, is not only cultural and socio-economic, for the church is also a diversity of sinners. It is a fellowship of saints who are cleansed from the diverse sins in which they formerly lived. This point is emphasized by Paul. After listing a host of persons who would not inherit the kingdom of God—the sexually immoral, idolaters, adulterers, homosexual offenders, thieves, the greedy, drunkards, slanderers, swindlers—the apostle adds, "And that is what some of you were. But you were washed, you were sanctified, you were justified in the name of the Lord Jesus Christ by the Spirit of our God" (1 Cor. 6:11). For Paul, then, the church is a diverse body of persons saved from a multitude of sins. It is a community of cleansed sinners with all types of sordid backgrounds who, because they have been redeemed and sanctified through Christ, come together to praise the God of their salvation.

If the church consists of a worshiping body of people with diverse backgrounds, it is only natural that congregations can expect to find within their ranks persons who are suffering from AIDS. The church may indeed include within its fellowship those who have been forgiven through faith in Jesus Christ but whose former lifestyles made them vulnerable to this disease. Certain of these persons may have been touched by the regenerative power of the Holy Spirit only after contracting the disease itself. The church, which is to be "home" for repentant sinners of all stripes, would in this way become a community to those who have repented and been converted, but yet find themselves the victims of AIDS.

At the same time there may be present in the church the innocent victims of the disease, those who have contracted it through no immoral actions of their own. For example, the church fellowship may include faithful spouses of AIDS carriers. Or congregations may discover that they are called to minister to the families of AIDS-infected infants, whether these children be the adopted or natural offspring of church members.

In all these possible situations, the inclusion of persons touched by AIDS within the ranks of the church could have certain beneficial effects for the entire body. The most basic of those would be the vivid example that the presence of persons with AIDS would bring, as implicit in the statements of Paul and John (quoted above). What a grand and fitting praise can be offered to God by a congregation of believers who bear such a personal witness to God's ability to save from diverse backgrounds and thereby create for God's glory a redeemed people!

Further, the presence of AIDS victims can offer a new dimension to the actual worshiping life of the church. People with AIDS often have a profound sense of the importance of the present and a genuine zeal for making each day count. Richard L. Shaper notes the desire of persons with AIDS to think of themselves as living, not dying. "Confronted with a suddenly foreshortened future," he writes, they "frequently find an appetite for savoring and living fully the days of strength which remain to them."[1] Their involvement in the worshiping community can therefore offer a dimension of intensity. AIDS victims also are often characterized by a profound hope for life beyond death, a hope for the coming kingdom of God. The very presence of people with this fervent hope can spark a fuller understanding and awareness of the eschatological nature of worship for a Christian community.

The worship dimension can be enhanced as well through the personal testimonies of persons who are struggling with AIDS and drawn to God by this affliction. BettyClare Moffatt reports this aspect of her son's experience: "He talked often about the awakening that AIDS had brought into his life, the 180 degree turnaround that had led him to a deepening relationship with God."[2] As they bear testimony to God's goodness in the midst of suffering and of God's use of trial to awaken and strengthen faith, the involvement of persons who have been drawn to God through the fire of trial and pain can heighten the worship life of all God's people.

Persons struggling with AIDS can add a new richness to worship for the entire people of God as they join in Christian fellowship to express love for the One who has redeemed them from the sins of their past and from the fallenness of their present existence. For this reason, a ministry to persons with AIDS can be an important outgrowth of the worship mandate of the church.

Edification

The second aspect of the mandate of the church, edification, likewise has significance for ministry in the midst of the AIDS epidemic. The edification task means that the church is called to build up its members in the faith "until we all reach unity in the faith and in the knowledge of the Son of God and become mature, attaining to the whole measure of the fullness of Christ" (Eph. 4:13).

AIDS victims within the ranks of the church are to be a natural part of this edification mandate, and their relationship to the church's ministry moves in both directions. On the one hand, these individuals are to be edified by the church, by virtue of the very fact that they are part of the body of Christ.

The New Testament repeatedly emphasizes edification as including concern for the physical and material needs of others. John suggests that involvement in this ministry is a measure of the presence of God's love within the heart of a believer (1 John 3:17). The author of the Book of Hebrews ranks ministry to the physical needs of others as equal in importance with verbalizing praise to God (Heb. 13:15–16). Therefore, an important aspect of the edification life of the church is ministering to the physical needs of all persons within the body of Christ. For this reason, AIDS victims can expect their sisters and brothers in the Lord to exercise concern for them.

The edification mandate also includes concern for the psychological and spiritual needs of others. Christians are called to carry the burdens of sisters and brothers in the fellowship (Gal. 6:1–2). They are to pray for one another (James 5:16) and encourage each other (Heb. 10:24–25). This means that members of the body of Christ are called to ease the burdens of their sisters and brothers who are infected with the AIDS disease, just as they are to assist all others within the fellowship.

On the other hand, edification moves in the opposite direction as well. Not only are AIDS sufferers to be edified by the church, but *they* may be used by God's Spirit to help others. This ministry could have several dimensions. Most obvious may be the important ministry that persons with AIDS can offer to others in the congregation who are sick, especially those struggling with terminal illnesses, as they themselves are. Such persons can strengthen and encourage one another as they face the coming of death.

But AIDS victims can likewise minister to the healthy. They do so as they stand as a reminder of the need that all of us have for the grace of God to sustain us in life. And they minister as they transfer to the entire congregation their profound sense of the importance of living the present to the fullest possible and trusting God for the future, even one's future beyond death.

Further, AIDS victims can teach the body of Christ the significance and value of suffering. This role is aptly described by James Stulz:

> For many of us, admiration of the Greek notion of tragedy and assent to the Christian teaching of the redemptive value of suffering remain at a purely cerebral level. There is a truth here that we admit on faith, though reluctantly, but then put safely aside. A man with AIDS, however, can experience this truth in his very flesh even as Jesus did. Indeed, many AIDS victims report that their experience of the disease has somehow been positive. They report a new and intuitive grasp of the real necessity of suffering, the necessity of the cross—a truth they have experienced not only on the level of faith, but in their flesh.
>
> AIDS patients have also spoken of a heightened appreciation of God's gift of life itself. Some have searched for symbols to celebrate that gift or for ways to enrich whatever life they have here and now.[3]

In an age when suffering is a forgotten virtue, the church can be instructed by the presence in its midst of persons who are discovering through personal experience how to capitalize on suffering for the sake of personal spiritual growth.

Outreach

Finally, the third aspect of the mandate of the church, outreach, also has important implications for ministry in the midst of the AIDS epidemic. The outreach task includes evangelism. The church is called to preach the gospel to the lost, a challenge that knows no boundaries. The Great Commission given by Jesus to his disciples is not meant to exclude any group of people. Instead, we are to follow the example of the Lord, whose mission included preaching "good news" to the poor, proclaiming freedom for the prisoners, and releasing the oppressed (Luke 4:18). This commission offers the challenge to proclaim the good news, even in the midst of the AIDS epidemic. Persons with AIDS ought not to be shunned by the church. Rather, they are to become the recipients of the church's message of salvation and forgiveness in Christ.

Outreach includes service as well, for this mandate calls the church to serve the wider community in the name of the Lord. Jesus emphasizes the importance of service in the parable of the sheep and the goats (Matt. 25:31–46). The basis of the judgment of the nations at the end of the age, he declares, includes ministry to those in need—feeding the hungry, giving a drink to the thirsty, inviting the stranger in, clothing the naked, ministering to the sick, visiting those in prison. The service task of the church includes that of being salt and light in the world as well, that is, of seeking to be a preservative and enlightening force in society.

The challenge of Christian ministry does not stop where the AIDS disease begins. Rather, the church is called to serve everywhere in the world in the name of the Lord. In our context, this mandate to serve those who are suffering surely includes the call to minister to persons struggling with the AIDS epidemic.

Accepting the Challenge

The AIDS crisis quite naturally raises barriers to ministry, as we have noted. However, as Christians come to a theological understanding of the causes of sickness and listen to the voice of God speaking through this crisis, a step can be taken to cross these barriers. We are enabled to overcome these obstacles as we are challenged and moved by the Spirit to act compassionately in accordance with the nature of God and the example of Christ. We are called to engage in the struggle against evil and to fulfill the mandate Christ gave to the church. Discipleship and obedience to our Lord motivates—indeed, compels—ministry in the midst of the AIDS crisis.

As this occurs, the AIDS epidemic comes to be defined not in terms of the fear and death it represents, but in terms of what the church is: the ministering people of God. The reality that AIDS is a fearful enemy is not to be denied. But the church can, by the power of the Holy Spirit, assume a position of vulnerability and accept the risk of ministry. Through service in the name of Christ, it can indeed live out the divine principle of life, losing its life and thereby saving it. Our goal is to be God's instrument in the redemption and healing of the world. Practical ways as to how we, as the people of God, can so minister forms our next topic.

10

Caregiving to the AIDS Patient

"Do you believe in heaven and hell?" An AIDS patient in Boston directed this query not to a hospital chaplain but to his medical doctor—Wendell Hoffman. This incident is repeated daily in hospitals across the country. It indicates the great opportunity offered to sensitive, perceptive Christians by the current AIDS crisis.

In this book's introduction, we sought to identify the major barriers that hinder ministry in the midst of the AIDS epidemic. Part One then provided a medical perspective on the disease: its history, spread, clinical aspects, treatment, and prevention. Part Two deals with the theological context. Chapter 7 outlined a theological understanding of the crisis as a background for our attempts to cross and overcome the barriers. The previous two chapters have focused on the motivation for crossing the perceived roadblocks. Ministry in the midst of the AIDS crisis was seen as compelled by an understanding of compassion, of God's victory over evil, and of the church's mandate for worship, edification, and outreach.

With these materials in mind, we look now to the ministry itself. What can and ought the church as a whole, and individual caregivers as extensions of the body of Christ, do to minister in the midst of the AIDS epidemic? This chapter and the two that follow assert that the attempt to offer a full response to the current crisis requires that the ministry of the church move in several directions: to the sufferers themselves, to the family and friends of the sufferers, to the world on behalf of the victims, and finally to society in terms of prevention and containment of the AIDS disease. Our initial concern focuses on the first of these, namely, ministry to AIDS patients themselves.

If the church is to have an impact in the midst of the AIDS epidemic, it must develop a ministry aimed at persons with AIDS, those who are most directly struggling with this disease. Primarily, this ministry will be carried out by individual Christian caregivers, who are acting on behalf of all the people of God. Under their direction, however, or as a response to their recommendations, the congregation may enter into a more direct involvement in ministering to AIDS patients. Because the major task of this ministry will be fulfilled by individuals on behalf of the community—compassionate laypeople, chaplains, pastors, counselors—it is necessary to look more closely at the caregiver before discussing the type of care to be offered.

The Attitude of the Caregiver

Ministry to AIDS patients is made difficult by the very nature of AIDS: a deadly, contagious illness, linked largely with sexual promiscuity and drug abuse. For this reason, the attitude of the caregiver becomes especially important. The one who would seek to minister to

AIDS patients should prepare for this ministry by developing three characteristics: nonjudgmentalism, love that overcomes fear, and the attitude of a shepherd.

Nonjudgmental Compassion

First, it is crucial for the caregiver to separate one's caring response to the disease from the issue of morality, that is, from ecclesiastical and personal judgments concerning the ethics and lifestyles of most AIDS sufferers. It must be kept in mind that AIDS is a medical phenomenon. Of course, it also has moral overtones, for the AIDS virus is most readily spread by certain lifestyle choices and acts, and lifestyle is to some extent a moral issue. Obviously, then, there is an important relationship between the AIDS epidemic and morality. This connection is reflected in caregiving, insofar as ministry to the persons involved includes assisting them in taking ownership over past actions and in coming to repentance and faith in Christ. This aspect of ministry is discussed subsequently.

At the same time, however, apart from this aspect, the morality question is in a certain sense quite irrelevant for ministry to those who are now suffering from the disease. As far as caregiving is concerned, AIDS is a medical phenomenon, an illness that affects human beings. Persons with AIDS are to be viewed as humans who have contracted a disease caused by a deadly virus. These people are dying and are therefore in need of concerned, sympathetic care. They require support and caregiving that moves beyond assisting them in dealing with the past. How this virus was contracted is not to be the focus. More important is the recognition that theirs is a situation of human need. Christians are called to minister to persons in need, even if these persons are "publicans and sinners."

Willingness to separate one's response to the disease from the issue of morality, for the sake of ministering to the sick, is actually an outgrowth of the sensitivity that ought to characterize every caregiver in every situation of need. It is simply insensitive to make judgmental comments to terminally ill persons concerning the sources of the diseases from which they are suffering, when one's aim is to share their burdens. It is unhelpful, for example, to criticize an individual dying of lung cancer for being a chain smoker for several decades. Moralizing in the terminal ward is not only in bad taste, it is counterproductive. In the same way, moralizing concerning sexual conduct or other aspects of a person's lifestyle, when ministering to those dying of AIDS, may be irrelevant and uncaring. The response of the caregiver to the disease and its victims must be one of compassion, concern, and interest, regardless of the caregiver's views about such possible issues as sexual promiscuity and drug abuse.

This is not to say that issues of sinful lifestyle are not to be addressed. On the contrary, Christian care must include assisting persons in dealing with spiritual needs, including the need to experience forgiveness. Nevertheless, caregivers must keep in mind that their principal task is not to moralize concerning the sins in the patient's past. Nor ought their compassionate care be dependent on the patient's willingness to confess and reject what may have been a sinful lifestyle.

In offering compassionate care to all persons regardless of the relative "righteousness" of the sufferers, Christian caregivers are merely following the picture of God presented by Christ. Our Lord responded to persons in need without asking that they first join the ranks of the righteous. In fact, nonjudgmental compassion is one aspect of his ministry that the multitudes found so refreshing and his enemies found so disconcerting. Rather than moralizing concerning the sins of those who came to him for healing, he simply forgave their sins (e.g., Mark 2:1–12). This same Jesus taught that the heavenly Father "causes his sun to rise on the evil and the good, and sends rain on the righteous and the unrighteous" (Matt. 5:45). Of course, because God is holy, Christian caregivers cannot treat sin lightly. But the incarnate Jesus who reveals the Holy God offers to us all a model of a compassionate response to the lost. His was a loving concern that followed the pathway to the cross on their behalf.

Fear Overcome by Love

A second important characteristic of the caregiver's attitude relates to personal fears. To minister to persons suffering from AIDS, a caregiver must deal with his or her personal fears and anxieties. As noted earlier, fear is a formidable barrier to effective ministry to AIDS victims. Among the most commonly experienced fears are the uneasy recognition of our own mortality, anxiety concerning our personal weaknesses, and sometimes even insecurity concerning our sexuality.

But, in addition, there is the practical fear of contracting the disease. This fear has in part been perpetuated by false or faulty information concerning how the AIDS virus is carried from one person to another. Part One of this volume has provided medical information for the purpose of dispelling these fears. Yet, caregivers must continually deal with their fearful attitudes, which often persist despite an informed mind. Because our fears are often irrational, they are not simply eradicated once the facts are known.

To minister to the sick, then, caregivers must understand their own fears, seeking to know where they come from and how they arise, so that they can be dealt with. One helpful means of dealing with personal fear is to view sick persons simply as fellow human beings. Christians have the orientation to do so, since our theology gives us a basis for perceiving suffering individuals (such as AIDS patients) as—above all—*persons in need.* The Bible encourages us to view them as persons created to participate in the image of God, but in whose lives God's intention is being challenged by the forces of evil.

As we see the sick in this manner, the Spirit of God can create in us the divine love that translates into compassion in the face of need. This loving compassion then becomes the beginning point in the process of dealing with our fears.

John articulated this truth: "There is no fear in love. But perfect love drives out fear, because fear has to do with punishment. The one who fears is not made perfect in love" (1 John 4:18). In ministering to victims of the AIDS epidemic, genuine love, concern, and compassion for them in the midst of their need becomes a Spirit-utilized tool for eliminating the fears that lurk in the recesses of our hearts and short-circuit our desire to minister. This love forms the basis of a willingness to follow the all-encompassing principle taught and lived by the Master, namely, that the way to life comes through self-sacrifice, through giving oneself for the sake of others. On this basis, Christian caregivers can be willing to take risks in the face of the AIDS scare for the sake of ministry in Christ's name.

Shepherding

The caregiver must likewise be characterized by a shepherd's heart. In a sense, ministry to AIDS patients does not differ categorically from caregiving in any needy situation. Christian ministers and caregivers often act as shepherds toward others. In his article, "AIDS, the Pastor and the Patient Parishioner," J. Harold Ellens points out that a shepherd is one who engages in a ministry of healing, sustaining, guiding, and comforting. But the key to a shepherding ministry, Ellens declares, is compassion, understood in a special sense. Minister-shepherds are called "to sit where they sit," that is, to be among "the sheep," to use the imagery of the Book of Ezekiel.[1]

For this attitude the Christian has Jesus Christ's own example as a model to follow. As followers of Christ, believers are called to minister the good news of grace in the midst of the suffering that those in their care are facing. This attitude is particularly important for caregiving to AIDS sufferers. Persons with AIDS likewise need caregivers who are willing to "sit where they sit," that is, to seek to share the burden they carry.

Ellens correctly points out that the task of the caregiver includes as well the attempt to stand against the meaninglessness that AIDS sufferers are facing. He describes this as

> the task of preventing any experience from being meaningless, that means, standing against the trivialization of meaningfulness, that means, keeping alive the vision of the person with AIDS as a person made in God's image and cherished by God in his or her brokenness. It means keeping alive the inherent vocation of a person with AIDS as a person who is none the less called of God to be a kingdom builder, a compatriot of God and enhancement of his role of love and grace in human hearts and lives. It means guaranteeing to the person with AIDS the unconditional acceptance as a person which reflects the worth and esteem with which God views that person and all persons.[2]

Meaninglessness is a generalized and commonly felt threat in our Western society.[3] Yet, how much more dreadful is the specific hopelessness evoked by an incurable, deadly disease when it lays hold of persons in the prime of life. For some AIDS patients, a Christian caregiver may be the only person who can assist in standing against this feeling of meaninglessness. Only the Christian caregiver can speak about the eternal value that God places on each human life, no matter how short or shortened, and about the eternal significance that can belong to every individual.

In summary, caregivers who would be truly helpful must offer a compassionate response to AIDS patients, regardless of their personal stance on the morality issue.

Through love, they must deal with their own fears. And they must strive to be a shepherd to those in distress. Only the cultivation of this type of attitude can foster a truly meaningful ministry to AIDS patients.

The Specifics of Caregiving

When seeking to minister in the midst of the AIDS epidemic, the caregiver comes into a situation that is indeed difficult. Although no two AIDS cases are alike, and thus there is no "typical" AIDS patient, the caregiver may expect that many of the patients encountered will reveal a cluster of characteristics. Richard A. McCormick lists the following as typical:

> Young; alienated from family; frightened of isolation and abandonment, of pain and suffering, of dependency and loss of control; embarrassed and/or guilty; more or less alone; possibly angry; isolated further by societal attitudes, infection protection and backlash of anger at their consumption of beds and resources; without financial resources; incompetent, at least toward the end.[4]

In such a situation, the caregiver's ministry calls for a multifaceted program. Its goal is that of standing with the infected person from the early stages of the infection to the point of death.

Dealing with Guilt

The multifaceted ministry of the Christian caregiver includes assisting the person with AIDS in dealing with feelings of guilt. This is a delicate task, requiring keen sensitivity to the Holy Spirit's leading. Sensitivity is needed to combat the tendency prevalent in contemporary society to seek to eliminate guilt feelings too quickly, which often results in an attempt, even by well-meaning counselors, to assuage guilt prematurely. This tendency parallels, and is in part the result of, the loss of the concept of sin in our society.[5] With the elimination of "sin" from our vocabularies, guilt has come to be viewed as a negative and sometimes even a demonic emotion. When applied to AIDS, such a view gives rise to the tendency to dismiss any discussion of AIDS as God's judgment on homosexual behavior or drug abuse.

The Bible, however, indicates that a properly grounded sense of guilt can have a positive, healthy function. Guilt reflects a feeling of responsibility for personal actions that have come to be seen as morally wrong, that is, as having violated divine standards. Understood in this manner, a sense of guilt becomes a step in the process of conversion and sanctification. As a person is confronted with his or her involvement in sin, the need for a Savior is sensed, and the need for change is acknowledged. For this reason, the Christian caregiver ought not to seek to alleviate such guilt feelings *before* they have attained their intended purpose.

When faced with such situations, the caregiver must be sensitive to the possibility that God is seeking to speak to the person through the sense of guilt. In fact, the caregiver may be the instrument of God in assisting the patient in making peace with God. To facilitate this, the Christian may need boldly but gently to assist the person in probing the feelings of guilt: "Why do I feel guilty?" "Is the Holy Spirit seeking to speak to me?" The helpful caregiver seeks to bring the patient to understand which past actions are contrary to the divine standard, to agree with God concerning their sinful nature, and to recognize the personal need for reconciliation with God and others.

One caution is in order here, however. The Christian caregiver must avoid usurping the prerogative of the Holy Spirit, whose task it is to convince persons of God's judgment on their lives. Jesus anticipated this work of the Spirit in his declaration to the disciples:

> "When he comes, he will convict the world of guilt in regard to sin and righteousness and judgment: in regard

> to sin, because men do not believe in me; in regard to righteousness, because I am going to the Father, where you can see me no longer; and in regard to judgment, because the prince of this world now stands condemned" (John 16:8–11).

The convicting of the Holy Spirit is intended to bring an erring person to the point of repentance and faith in Jesus Christ. A true sense of guilt, therefore, must be produced by the Spirit's pressure, not that of another human being. Christians overstep their role, when they seek to manipulate others in an attempt to produce feelings of guilt in them.

While guilt may indeed be the result of the Spirit's ministry to an individual, there comes a point when guilt becomes negative and destructive. Such situations occur when sufferers engage in blaming themselves for the calamities that have come into their lives. These guilt feelings and self-blaming lead to a sense of alienation. In such cases, the task of the caregiver is to assist the sufferer in overcoming personal guilt. To do so, the caregiver may need first to assist the patient in repenting of any past destructive lifestyle and in making a commitment to Jesus Christ and to a life of discipleship.

Once repentance occurs, however, the thrust of the caregiver's ministry must be to emphasize the forgiveness available in Christ, who is willing and able to forgive, regardless of past sins. This forgiveness covers even an unwise and sinful lifestyle, which may have characterized a person's past. The good news the caregiver must bring to the sufferer includes the message that no sin puts us beyond God's compassion and love.

The task of the caregiver is not to be the agent of God's judgment nor that of attempting to develop a sense of guilt in a suffering person. Rather, the caregiver is to be God's messenger of reconciliation. Paul articulates the centrality of this role:

> All this is from God, who reconciled us to himself through Christ and gave us the ministry of reconciliation: that God was reconciling the world to himself in Christ, not counting their sins against them. And he has committed to us the message of reconciliation (2 Cor. 5:18–19).

Like Paul, Christian caregivers must sense their mission as being "Christ's ambassadors" (v. 20), imploring persons on Christ's behalf to be reconciled to God. This same message ought to be central in our ministry to AIDS patients.

Dealing with Fear

Second, the ministry of the caregiver to AIDS sufferers includes assisting them in dealing with their fears. The studies of Klaus Wendler indicate that several related fears are generally present in persons who have contracted the disease through homosexual practices.[6] These patients experience a sense of alienation as they come to feel rejected, overprotected, and misunderstood. This is due in part to the fatal nature of the AIDS disease. Persons with AIDS fear that family, friends, and caregivers may withdraw emotionally from them when these support people learn that the patient will soon die. A second fear that Wendler notes is that of disfigurement. This is a genuine fear, because disfigurement is often an outworking of the opportunistic diseases that persons with AIDS contract. The fear of disfigurement is especially crucial, given the fact that AIDS patients are usually persons in the prime of life. Individuals who have in the past prided themselves in their outward appearance and have led sexually active lifestyles face the loss of physical attractiveness with anxiety.

Another fear arises from the confrontation with one's own mortality. As a fatal disease, AIDS makes such a confrontation inevitable. Anxiety is produced not only by the thought of death, however. Often more devastating is the fear of the dying process itself.

The final fear that Wendler mentions is the anxiety connected with the sense of vulnerability and loss of control of one's own destiny that accompanies the AIDS disease. Especially as death approaches, the patient can be overwhelmed by the growing sense of dependency on others.

An important task of the caregiver is to assist the AIDS sufferer in dealing with fears such as Wendler outlines. Of all the fears, however, anxiety in the face of death is likely to be the most difficult and the most taxing on the resources of both patient and caregiver. Although this is the case in ministering to anyone with a terminal illness, the difficulties are most acute in AIDS cases, because they are usually persons in the prime of life. Helpful caregivers can assist the patient in maximizing the remaining time before death and then in coming to terms with death in a dignified manner. The caregiver seeks to work with patient, family, and hospital staff in seeking to provide as much as possible in terms of quality encounters between patient and the support community. AIDS victims ought to continue to be recipients of the dignity due everyone as a human being created by God. This means that support, concern, and love must not be withdrawn from the individual so long as that person continues to breathe.

When death is near, the caregiver becomes a strategist with hospital personnel and significant others to help the patient meet death most comfortably. This role is important, because death can be experienced in several ways, some of which are better, easier, or more beneficial than others. M. Pabst Battin offers an apt declaration of this:

> Certain conditions will produce a death that is more comfortable, more decent, more predictable and more permitting of conscious and peaceful experience than

> others. Some are better, if the patient has to die at all, and some are worse. Which mode of death claims the patient depends in part on circumstance and in part on the physician's response to conditions that occur.[7]

Although Battin's statement has in view caregiving to terminal patients in general, it is especially applicable to persons dying of AIDS. In such circumstances, the task of the caregiver is to assist the patient in meeting an unavoidable death on that person's own terms. To this end the caregiver may need to serve as an informed sounding board, assisting the patient in viewing and deciding among the various treatment options. In so doing, the caregiver can provide an immeasurable psychological comfort to the dying person.

Important in overcoming the fear of dying is an awareness of the stages through which a dying person moves. The studies of Elisabeth Kübler-Ross are especially helpful in bringing understanding to this process. She notes five major stages: denial and isolation, anger, bargaining, depression, and acceptance.[8] A helpful caregiver is not only aware of the presence of these stages in the patient's coping process, but is also cognizant of how best to minister in each stage.[9]

At the same time it must be remembered that Kübler-Ross's findings are descriptive, not prescriptive. These stages constitute a model derived from observation of the experiences of many cases. They do not comprise a rule concerning the cycle that a specific patient will follow. Therefore, a shepherding caregiver does not attempt to force the patient to move through these stages, but rather is conscious of their possible presence in the life of the person who has contracted a terminal disease.

As death approaches, the caregiver may need the sensitivity to facilitate the resolution of any remaining strained relationships or interpersonal problems involving the patient and family, friends, or others. Such reconciliation offers an important contribution and is a crucial factor in experiencing a more psychologically and spiritually comfortable death. This task becomes especially important when the patient has been hiding a homosexual orientation from parents or family.

Not to be overlooked are more practical matters as well. These include giving thought to a will and other social and legal aspects involved in preparing for death. Likewise, the patient's thoughts concerning the funeral should be aired. A Christian caregiver can be of invaluable assistance in helping the patient deal with these aspects of the dying process.

Above all, however, the process of meeting fears related to death requires that the patient make peace with God, although this may be a delicate task in the case of a homosexually oriented person. The sexual orientation itself often comprises a source of feelings of estrangement not only from the church but, more importantly, even from God. The helpful caregiver must therefore seek to be God's ambassador in the fullest sense, bringing to the AIDS sufferer the good news of reconciliation (2 Cor. 5:17ff.). Because no person lies beyond God's loving compassion, no person, regardless of sexual preference or past lifestyle, is beyond God's ability to work salvation in the lives of human beings. The Christian caregiver's greatest challenge may be assisting the AIDS patient to accept this biblical truth and, as a result, accept the salvation offered by the God of the Bible.

Providing Support Links

The caregiver also ministers to the person suffering with AIDS by providing links to other support bearers. One central hallmark of the church, and indeed a necessary aspect of full Christian living, is community. In fact, the church exists as a fellowshiping body, a community of people with various needs. Persons suffering with AIDS are often cut off from the experience of community. This is especially the case when patients become bedridden, for they are no longer in a position to take the initiative in participating in community life. Yet, such persons are in a situation that requires more fellowship and community support, not less.

Further, because of the fears existing in others, AIDS patients suffer a special depth of alienation. For this reason and because of the nature and effects of their disease, these individuals often have a special need for fellowship. A caregiver can provide an immeasurable ministry to persons suffering from AIDS by facilitating links of support between them and the Christian community. Here the role of the caregiver is to encourage contact between AIDS sufferers and the congregation. Such contact should include participation in regular church functions during the earlier stages of the disease or before the patient is bedridden. This ministry, however, may require educating the congregation concerning AIDS, including information about how the virus is and is not contracted and encouraging an openness on the part of church people to accept persons with AIDS in their midst.

In the case of bedridden patients, contact can obviously be initiated only from the side of the healthy. Here the caregiver can minister to an AIDS patient by encouraging the congregation to engage in the ministry of encouragement to AIDS sufferers. To facilitate this, the caregiver may need to foster a visitation program, in which people from the church come to the hospital to spend time with persons dying of AIDS.

Although such a program may seem initially threatening to many would-be callers, Christian compassion coupled with correct information about the disease can transform even the most fearful soul into a courageous minister to bedridden AIDS patients. Such potential caregivers may be assisted in overcoming their fears of infection by increased knowledge concerning how AIDS is transmitted. They may need to be assured that AIDS patients on their deathbeds are quite harmless, if for no other reason than because they are obviously no longer engaging in high-risk activities.[10]

Personal contact and fellowship can be developed in other ways as well. For example, the formation of support groups on various levels is often vital. The development of such support should include groups for persons with AIDS who are not yet bedridden. As long as they are physically able, these people should be encouraged to meet together to support one another as they face the physical deterioration that accompanies this disease. Care groups can be of immeasurable support as a source of fellowship for persons who are at the early stages of dealing with AIDS. This is an important ministry because the alienation that persons with AIDS experience often begins early in their battle. Persons who learn that they have contracted the AIDS virus may face problems immediately, including dismissal from their jobs and/or rejection by family and friends. They may discover that the social communities of which they once were a part have suddenly broken ties with them. In the face of this alienation, helpful caregivers seek to foster other links for the purpose of fellowship and community.

To facilitate this need, a congregation may be led to establish a Christian-oriented care fellowship solely for AIDS patients in the community. Or a care group focusing on patients struggling with other terminal illnesses may be expanded to include persons at various stages in the battle with AIDS. Local AIDS agencies may likewise serve as a resource for the development of care groups.

The support links provided by the church may at times even need to include aspects of the medical care of persons with AIDS. As hospital space becomes tight, or in the face of mounting hospital costs, care centers will become a growing need. Supporting or even initiating the founding of alternatives—AIDS hospices, halfway houses, and so on—is a challenge to which the people of God will need to respond if they would offer a multidimensional ministry in the midst of the AIDS crisis. In so doing, the church also serves as an advocate of the destitute and homeless, taking the lead in providing shelter for persons with AIDS who might otherwise be walking the streets.

Prayer

Finally, the ministry of the AIDS caregiver includes prayer. In prayer the heart of the believer is meshed with the heart of God. Through prayer the caregiver demonstrates the unconditional and universal nature of Christian ministry to others. As BettyClare Moffatt declares, "Prayer, like love, is unconditional."[11]

Prayer for AIDS patients ought to be a central aspect of the caregiver's personal ministry. It should be a natural part of visits, whether in the hospital ward, in the case of persons in the advanced stages of the disease, or in care groups, with persons in earlier stages. Also in need of intercession are medical personnel, family, and friends. Appropriate as well are prayers for researchers and petitions directed toward the finding of a cure for AIDS.

Prayer on behalf of AIDS patients ought to be a matter not only of the primary caregivers, but of the church as a whole. The Metropolitan Community Church of San Francisco, a congregation consisting mainly of individuals of a homosexual orientation, offers regular prayer and healing services for AIDS patients.[12] Although evangelicals generally question the validity of fellowships such as the MCC, their willingness to seek to meet the needs of persons with AIDS offers an unmistakable challenge. Can evangelical churches, which believe that Jesus Christ is the ultimate answer to all human needs, dare to do less?

Prayer for persons with AIDS ought to become a part of the intercessory ministry of every evangelical church. Such prayer would be offered on behalf of persons suffering with AIDS, with the goal being that the Spirit of God be present with them. Prayer could have as an additional result the mobilization of the congregation in the task of ministering to the spiritual, psychological, and physical needs of AIDS patients in their locale. This congregational prayer life would assume an even more personal and intense form if it were discovered that persons within the church community have been touched by the epidemic.

In all this, one crucial fact must be kept in mind: The intercessory life of the congregation on behalf of AIDS patients and the prayer ministry of caregivers form one united whole. Prayer is but a specific illustration of the fundamental principle of the interrelationship between the individual and the church community. In this activity, as in every activity, caregivers serve as an extension of the congregation.

The ministry of intercession, however, raises an important question concerning any prayer for the sick: the form such prayer ought to take. Some suggest that physical wholeness, which is indeed the ultimate will of God, is to be a present possession for Christians in the world. Building on such texts as "by his wounds we are healed" (see Isa. 53:4–5), such Christians conclude that prayer offered in genuine faith will always result in healing. But not only is this viewpoint contradicted by empirical evidence and biblical teaching, it can also be detrimental. It easily produces feelings of guilt in the lives of those who are *not* healed, for it implies that such persons lack sufficient faith.

While we cannot anticipate physical healing in every situation, Christian caregivers ought nevertheless to offer the request for healing to God, for indeed our desire would be that all persons suffering illnesses be restored to physical wholeness. This same principle is true in the case of a person suffering from AIDS.

Not to be overlooked, however, are prayers for the spiritual needs of the patient. In some situations, the need for salvation may be uppermost. Other times, additional aspects of spiritual healing may be the focus. In the case of Christian AIDS patients, certain petitions are always appropriate and needed. The Christian caregiver may ask that God grant wisdom in the midst of sickness, in accordance with the promise of James 1:5. Likewise, one ought to request that the infirmity be used by God to bring God's own spiritual purposes to fruition. This may focus on spiritual growth in the lives of the patient and those who observe the situation, or that God will bring some other positive result from this sickness.

Lying behind all such prayer is the assurance that God is able to bring good from every evil. On this basis, the Christian caregiver can beseech the heavenly Father to work, even in the midst of the AIDS disease, in order to bring good for the sake of God's kingdom. AIDS may lead to conversion, the strengthening of faith, or spiritual growth in the lives of the patient, loved ones, and onlookers.

Spiritual victory can indeed be attained through the struggle with AIDS. BettyClare Moffatt, for example, bears testimony to the spiritual awakening that contracting the disease eventually brought into the life of her son, Michael.[13] Similar stories have been compiled by researchers Earl Shelp and Ronald Sunderland. Among others, they chronicle the case of Jim, who "believed that he had always been searching for God, for a spiritual awakening, throughout his life. AIDS, in his mind, had enabled him to find God, to be awakened spiritually. The God in whom Jim believed was found in the midst of his experience with AIDS."[14] Such accounts ought to encourage Christian caregivers to be faithful in their ministry of intercession on behalf of other AIDS patients.

Finally, caregivers may intercede in order that spiritual illumination be brought by God's Spirit in the hearts of all persons concerned. Such illumination would enable them to see God's strengthening presence in the midst of the AIDS disease and thereby gain the resources to withstand the onslaught of Satan, who tempts persons in distress to discouragement and doubt. The prayer of Paul on behalf of the Ephesians is especially appropriate in the face of AIDS:

> I keep asking that the God of our Lord Jesus Christ, the glorious Father, may give you the Spirit of wisdom and revelation, so that you may know him better. I pray also that the eyes of your heart may be enlightened in order that you may know the hope to which he has called you, the riches of his glorious inheritance in the saints, and his incomparably great power for us who believe. That power is like the working of his mighty strength, which he exerted in Christ when he raised him from the dead and seated him at his right hand in the heavenly realms, far above all rule and authority, power and dominion, and every title that can be given, not only in the present age but also in the one to come. And God placed all things under his feet and appointed him to be head over everything for the church, which is his body, the fullness of him who fills everything in every way (Eph. 1:17–23).

The sufferers of AIDS are in dire need of the ministry of Christian caregivers. The goal of this care is to assist such patients not merely to cope with their situation but even to grow spiritually through it. The old adage, "As long as there is life, there is hope," is especially valid in the case of AIDS victims. They should be assisted in making the most of their remaining days to the glory of God. As death approaches, they should continue to be respected as persons and be assisted in coming to terms with death in a dignified manner. To this end, the resources of God's Holy Spirit and the church of Jesus Christ are crucial. The Christian caregiver is both a minister of these resources and a mobilizer of the people of God, who are called as a body to provide fellowship and support to all sufferers, including those suffering from the effects of the AIDS epidemic.

11

Ministering to Sideline Victims of the AIDS Crisis

The most obvious recipient of ministry in the midst of the AIDS epidemic—and often the person with whom such ministry begins—is, of course, the AIDS patient. Nevertheless, a truly helpful ministry must not be limited to the individual who is a direct victim of AIDS. There is often a host of other persons who are likewise touched by the disease, people engaged in a struggle against its effects, even though they have not contracted the AIDS virus themselves. This chapter will look at an appropriate ministry to several such "secondhand" participants: the AIDS patient's same-sex partner (in the case of patients with a homosexual orientation), the patient's family (and/or close friends), and the medical caregivers.

Ministry to a Same-Sex Partner

As in the case of ministry to the actual patient, giving care to his (or her) "significant other" will be especially difficult for the Christian caregiver when the AIDS victim has contracted the disease through homosexual activity. The homosexual orientation of an AIDS patient can introduce complicating factors into the caregiving situation. One such factor arises when the AIDS victim is intimately involved with one specific partner. In this case, the caregiver is generally called to minister to the dying patient's partner as well. Again, to be helpful, such ministry (with the exception of the aspect of dealing with guilt) must be carried out without regard to the caregiver's own judgments concerning the ethical legitimacy of homosexuality. Although caregivers may believe strongly that such relationships are sinful, as compassionate Christians they are called to extend the love of the Lord to such individuals as persons in need.

Dealing with Complicated Needs

Similar to providing support for a homosexual AIDS patient, attempts to minister to the needs of the partner are complicated by various factors. First, the partner in this situation, like the AIDS patient, may be unable to rely on the traditional support links that terminal patients and their loved ones otherwise have. It is possible that the partner, too, senses an alienation from church, family, and the wider society. At the same time, the support link to the gay community of which these persons may have been a part may now be jeopardized by the knowledge that one partner has contracted AIDS. The noninfected partner is also probably the victim of rejection and social stigma. In such a situation, the caregiver faces the difficult challenge of fostering links between the apparently healthy partner of the AIDS patient and various community groups.

Ultimately and most specifically, the caregiver will seek to build a bridge between the partner and the fellowship of the church. But other avenues of support may need to be explored as well. The wise caregiver keeps in mind that the friend likely has been providing care to the AIDS patient for some time and therefore has been shouldering a heavy burden. Outside support may be a necessary factor in maintaining his (or her) mental and physical well-being.

Second, ministry to the victim's partner may be complicated by that person's own fears,[1] the most immediate of which may be that of contracting the disease. Because of the long incubation period of the AIDS virus and the infectious nature of the disease prior to the physical signs of its presence, the partner may very well have already been infected through sexual contact with the patient. To this is added the possibility of contracting the disease by continued sexual relations with the AIDS victim (unless both have agreed to practice abstinence) or even through continued casual contact.

Here the caregiver functions as a means of emotional support to the partner, as well as a source of proper information. Obviously, the partners must be counseled to adopt abstinence immediately, if they have not already done so, both for medical and moral reasons. In addition, the caregiver should seek to encourage the partner to follow through with an AIDS testing program, offering assurance of continued support, even if such testing should determine the presence of the AIDS virus in the partner.

Third, ministry to homosexual partners of AIDS patients is complicated by the awkwardness of the situation. Although the gay community has sought to change cultural attitudes concerning sexual orientations, American society in general continues to look with disfavor on homosexual activity. Such disfavor may quickly surface when patient and partner move from what for them may be the relative security of the gay community to seek professional help in the wider society.

The problem may become most noticeable in the hospital context. This situation may be further exacerbated should the same-sex partner desire to continue to fulfill certain roles traditionally assigned to a spouse, including that of being involved in decisions concerning the patient's care. In fact, the very presence of a same-sex partner in the hospital ward may create an awkward situation for all persons involved, including the Christian caregiver. Conflicts may arise between the "spouse" and the patient's family, for example. The family may be intensely hostile toward the partner, perhaps blaming him for their loved one's sexual orientation or for his contracting the disease. Conflicts may focus on the care of the AIDS patient, for both partner and family may express strong but differing opinions as to how treatment and care in general should progress.

One's best interpersonal skills may be challenged as the caregiver attempts to act redemptively and compassionately in the midst of a group of people—patient, family, medical personnel—with conflicting attitudes about the existence of a gay couple. In these situations, the helpful caregiver seeks to facilitate as positive a relationship between the family and partner or friends of the patient as is possible in the circumstances.

One important practical question that may arise concerns the number of funeral services to be held after the death of the patient. The parents and family of the AIDS patient may be uncomfortable with the idea of their relative having a same-sex partner or being involved in the gay community. This discomfort may continue even after the patient's death. The patient's partner and friends from the gay community may not be welcomed by family members at the funeral service. If this is the case, the sensitive issue of a separate memorial service for the victim's homosexually oriented friends may need to be considered. This, in turn, raises additional, logistical questions, such as location of the second service and who will participate.

In such situations, the caregiver may be faced with both a personal and an ecclesiastical tension, desiring to minister to the friends of the AIDS patient while not appearing to condone a homosexual lifestyle. However, faithfulness to one's calling to emulate the compassion of Christ means that the will to foster a redemptive ministry to all persons involved must be the primary criterion for measuring every action. As disciples of Jesus, Christian caregivers may find themselves compelled to risk being misunderstood in their quest to meet the deep needs of hurting people.

Dealing with Emotional Needs

Certain aspects of the caregiver's ministry should attempt to focus directly on the partner's emotional needs. The partner may need a sympathetic ear to whom personal frustrations and anger can be vented. The caregiver must keep in mind that the partner may have moved with the patient through various stages of the disease and therefore has likewise suffered emotional turmoil and fractured nerves.

As death becomes imminent, this ministry shifts toward assisting the partner to envision life after the loss of the friend. Grief counseling becomes important as well.[2] Although this aspect of the ministry to the partner is similar to other situations of bereavement, the task is complicated by the alienation the partner may sense. At this point the resources of the Christian community may be especially welcome and helpful. This fits well with the ultimate goal of this ministry, namely, to assist the partner in experiencing the love and healing touch of God for the sake of personal reconciliation with God and others.

Ministry to Family Members

The case of a homosexually oriented AIDS patient also raises unique difficulties for a caregiver's ministry to parents and family. The task may be compounded by several related factors. Because many homosexually oriented persons tend to hide this aspect of their lives from parents and family, the news that their loved one has contracted this terminal disease may carry with it a double shock. The discovery that a son or sibling has contracted AIDS may be the first time that family members come to realize that their loved one is also homosexually oriented and homosexually active. It may even be more difficult for them to deal with the homosexual aspect than with the terminal nature of the disease.

A similar situation can arise within a husband-wife relationship. The disclosure that the husband has contracted AIDS, for example, could likewise be the first disclosure of his bisexual activity. Such a double disclosure could be devastating to the wife and other members of the family.

Another compounding factor is the shame and embarrassment that parents, spouses, and other relatives often experience after discovering that a loved one has contracted AIDS. An immediate problem becomes that of finding support links for family members. Who can they tell? To whom can they go to share their burden? Their sense of shame and embarrassment quite readily results in isolation, as they withdraw from their normal community groups emotionally and psychologically. In certain situations, families even change locations, leaving one city to take up residency in a place where they are totally unknown and can therefore remain anonymous.

Because of these compounding factors, in seeking to minister to parents and family of a homosexually oriented AIDS patient, the caregiver must deal with various aspects of family members' feelings. Most crucial are feelings of guilt and the fears that the family quite naturally faces.

Dealing with Guilt

First, Christian caregivers can minister to families of AIDS patients insofar as they assist them in coping with the feelings of guilt that often arise, whether expressed or unexpressed. Quite typically, the immediate response of family members is to raise the question of their possible failure to discharge personal responsibility. The theme is "What did we do wrong?" Parents may wonder, "How did we fail in raising our son?" A wife may ask, "What is wrong with me, which resulted in my husband engaging in bisexual activity?"

Helpful caregivers do not gloss over these feelings nor dismiss them prematurely. Rather, they look for ways to assist family members in taking constructive ownership of whatever responsibility they must legitimately accept for the present state of affairs, in the same way that AIDS patients are assisted in assuming responsibility for their actions. However, once the Holy Spirit has brought the divine intention to fruition—fostering repentance of whatever past sins have actually been contributing factors—the goal of ministry must be directed away from wallowing in guilt, regret, and remorse. Family members must be helped to accept Christ's forgiveness fully and also to overcome any unwarranted feelings of guilt. "If we confess our sins, he is faithful and just and will forgive us our sins and purify us from all unrighteousness" (1 John 1:9). This good news of forgiveness constitutes the central aspect of the caregiver's message to all concerned.

Coupled with the proclamation of divine forgiveness, the caregiver must assist family members in realizing that in the final analysis a person's choice of lifestyle is the responsibility of that individual, although family factors often play a significant role in the process. Nevertheless, loved ones need to come to realize that they may not be ultimately responsible for either the sexual orientation of the AIDS patient or, in most cases, for the fact that this person contracted the terrible disease. This is especially true in relatively stable family situations, in which parents (or the spouse) have honestly sought to discharge their duties to the best of their abilities. Even maintaining "a good home" is no guarantee that one's children will fulfill the parents' ideal. Nor does being a faithful and loving spouse always guarantee a happy marriage.

The situation is more complicated, of course, in cases of genuine failure on the part of parents or spouse. AIDS can be transmitted to children prenatally from an infected mother or by a sexually abusive infected father, and certain home factors may indeed contribute to a homosexual orientation. In all these situations, loved ones must assume a greater responsibility and may find themselves shouldering a heavier burden of guilt. Even for them, however, God's promise of forgiveness remains true. The helpful caregiver assists family members in moving from guilt to repentance and trusting acceptance of Christ's provision and forgiveness.

Regardless of who must share in the blame for the current situation, determination of responsibility is not the crucial task the family faces. Apart from bringing these persons to repentance and faith, the question "What did we do wrong?" is of only limited value. The helpful caregiver seeks to assist the family in moving beyond that concern to the more important question: "What can we do now to help our loved one in this person's hour of need?" Attention and energy must be channeled away from the past and its mistakes and directed to the present and the future. Regardless of the past, every family resource must be tapped for the challenge of acting redemptively in the situation confronting the entire family.

Dealing with Fears

The caregiver can also anticipate that family members are needing to deal with a variety of fears. They may be fearing for their loved one. How long will he (or she) live? What will happen to him? How much pain will be experienced? These and similar anxieties need to be expressed and faced openly, and the caregiver can play a vital role in this process.

One important service is that of being the interpreter

of medical information. The caregiver can assist the family in understanding what the medical personnel have determined concerning their loved one's prognosis and treatment. To serve in this way, however, the caregiver must be versed in the nature of the AIDS disease and current treatment programs. In addition to this, the Christian caregiver can provide a vital ministry to family members by assisting them to see the current crisis from an eternal perspective. Although the situation may appear bleak and therefore fearful, God is greater than AIDS. And God offers the hope of eternal life to all who rest in Christ as Lord and Savior. A helpful caregiver brings this spiritual perspective to each situation of human need.

Family members may likewise have personal fears. Especially acute may be the fear of contracting the virus through contact with the patient—casual contact with a son, daughter, or sibling; both casual and sexual contact in the case of a spouse. A helpful caregiver will help family members cope with these fears by offering current information concerning this aspect of the disease.

Finally, family members may find themselves confronted with fears relating to their own mortality. It is especially here that the spiritual resources of the caregiver and the entire Christian community are invaluable. Family members may need to hear the message of hope that only God's human messengers can articulate and embody. Only through faith in Christ can the fear of death give place to the hope of eternal life.

Anger and AIDS

An important aspect of ministry to persons struggling with AIDS—whether patient, friends, or family—is helping them deal with anger. The patient, for example, may sense anger at the prospect of having his or her life cut short by AIDS. Elisabeth Kübler-Ross maintains that such anger is an important step in coming to terms with personal death. Her studies offer insight for the caregiver in ministering to patients who are in this stage of the coping process.[3]

Not only patients, however, but also family members may struggle with bitterness and anger. This emotion may be most acute in cases involving "innocent" victims of the AIDS epidemic, especially persons who have contracted the disease through blood transfusions, but also infants born with AIDS. Family members often question why their loved one has been visited by such an apparent injustice.

In all situations relating to AIDS, the helpful caregiver seeks to direct each person involved beyond the present circumstances, so that each may find release in God. Through this process, all persons touched by the disease must be given permission to direct their anger even to God, if this is what they find themselves wanting to do. Expressing these feelings can become a catharsis, a cleansing experience. It can thereby be a step toward faith for patient, friends, and family, as they come to see that God alone holds the ultimate answer to the evil and injustice in the world (see chapter 7).

AIDS, like every evil, is unjust. Regardless of personal culpability, those who contract the disease are in some sense the victims of an injustice. We cannot know why God allows injustices to perpetuate themselves. But Christians discover that they have nowhere else to turn in the face of injustice but to God. When this occurs, they can find comfort by experiencing personal faith in the omnipotent God, the Holy One who is at work even now in bringing good out of evil, in overruling evil for good, and who one day will pronounce a final "no" to all evil and injustice.

The helpful caregiver proclaims this message. Yet, the proclaimer must be careful so that this message is not put forth as a simplistic, pious, quick response to what is a deep and complex problem. The Christian caregiver ought to sense genuine compassion for persons struggling in the depth of this situation. As a result of such compassion, the message of God's goodness and power, in the past, present, and future, can be articulated within the context of empathy. Needed is a true sense of struggling together with the sufferers and being at one with individuals who are victimized directly or vicariously by this awful disease. The caregiver must seek to assist family members in articulating their anger and their sense of loss. The goal is to help them come to rest in God and to find God's comfort and God's watchcare in the midst of their attempt to stand beside their loved one in the struggle with the AIDS disease.

Ministry to Medical Personnel

The major focus of caregiving in the midst of the AIDS epidemic, of course, will be those most personally affected by the disease—patients, as well as their families and friends. Not to be overlooked, however, is another group of people involved "on the front lines," the medical personnel providing care and treatment to hospitalized AIDS patients. They, too, need to be the recipients of the ministry of Christian caregivers.

The Multiple Medical Considerations

To minister effectively to medical personnel, a caregiver must come to understand the difficult and many-faceted nature of their task. Providing any medical care is taxing under the best of circumstances, but dealing with AIDS patients demands even greater personal resources. This is due to several factors specific to AIDS.

First, there are the physical complications. The hospitalized AIDS patient has generally contracted not just one disease, but several. As noted in Part One, various opportunistic illnesses may have infected the patient, due to his or her weakened immune system. This situation brings with it a more complicated treatment program and one generally involving more medical personnel than in other diseases. Additional physical considerations arise from the need on the part of medical personnel to take precautions against personal infection and the spread of the AIDS virus through the patient's blood products.

Second, there are the psychological complications found in AIDS cases. Because of the unique nature of their own fears, AIDS sufferers generally require more emotional support than other patients. Yet, as noted in chapter 10, they tend to have fewer support links outside the hospital. The stigma attached to the disease likewise adds to the difficulty of providing care. In cases of homosexual patients, medical personnel may be faced with the additional burden of dealing with and advising loved ones (family and same-sex partner) who may be hostile toward each other and have quite different expectations as to what their roles ought to be in managing the care of the patient.

Such psychological difficulties are further complicated by the terminal nature of the disease and by the relatively young age of the majority of patients. Members of the medical support team who find the task of facing these realities simply too difficult may attempt to shield themselves emotionally from AIDS patients by providing a minimum of hands-on medical care, performed in as detached a manner as possible. This tendency is particularly unfortunate for the patients who generally look to medical personnel for a sense of optimism and hope that they simply cannot offer.

These and other aspects of providing care for AIDS patients mean that medical caregivers may have special needs of their own. They may become exasperated as they discover that the number of persons with AIDS in their care steadily increases and when they realize that many will become chronic patients who require increasingly lengthier hospitalization. They may feel overworked and unappreciated when they discover that only a few of their colleagues are willing to care for persons with AIDS and as they are confronted with the low level of support for AIDS patients by family, friends, and other caregivers. Health-care workers may find themselves psychologically unable to provide the kind of emotional support demanded of them. And they may come to resent AIDS patients, not only because of the factors cited above, but because of their own negative feelings about "homosexuals and drug addicts" or because of such feelings among their colleagues and society in general.

The growing burden of caring for AIDS patients is placing increased pressure on medical caregivers. Some experts suggest that a crisis may even be in the making. An example of this is the current situation in San Francisco. In an article titled "AIDS: Seventh Rank Absolute," R. Fulton and G. Owen sketch the prognosis offered by Paul Volberding, director of the AIDS program at San Francisco Hospital:

> While the rest of the nation has come to look upon San Francisco as a model for coping with the AIDS crisis, Volberding is concerned that the burnout of health care workers, the ever-increasing number of AIDS cases, the competing needs of other patients, as well as the lack of coordinated long-range planning, may overwhelm San Francisco's health care system. Part of the problem is the sheer burden of caring for this group of patients given the increasing number of patients and limited resources, as well as the severe emotional stress upon caregivers of watching so many young persons die. While he notes that the most pressing current problem is one of chronic care, the situation will inevitably worsen, Volberding predicts, as the number of AIDS patients increases, making both the acute and the chronic care systems "hopelessly inadequate." In the face of these and other considerations, the moral and ethical cement that has traditionally bound caregivers to patients threatens to crumble.[4]

The Caregiver's Role

The difficulty of the task faced by medical personnel requires that sensitive ministering be directed toward them by Christian caregivers in the midst of the AIDS crisis. This ministry should have at least three aspects.

First, Christian caregivers can begin to minister to medical personnel through cooperation. When believers seek to provide support and care to AIDS patients and their families, they will inevitably find themselves involved with the medical support team as well. As this occurs, caregivers ought to place themselves in the position of being allies with medical personnel in their mutual goal of seeking the welfare of the patient. Their role is to do all they can to make the task of medical staff easier and to avoid complicating that task as far as possible.

One important way that Christian caregivers can cooperate in the overall task of providing care is by serving as a type of go-between. The caregiver should attempt to be a facilitator by assisting in the flow of information and understanding between medical personnel and the patient and family. This important responsibility works in two directions. On the one hand, it moves from medical staff to patient and family as the caregiver helps the patient and loved ones understand the information the medical team is providing. The goal of this assistance is to enable them to comprehend as best as possible the current status of the patient's illness and the prognosis for the future, including the various treatment options and their likely results. Thus informed, the patient and loved ones are better able to make responsible decisions.

On the other hand, this role moves information from patient and loved ones to medical staff. As one who is not as close to the situation emotionally, the caregiver may be in a position to articulate more cogently to the health-care team the feelings, fears, and thoughts of those touched by the disease. The caregiver is more able than the medical personnel to take the time necessary to help the patient and loved ones sort through their feelings and thereby uncover their deeper questions, which in turn can be relayed to the medical team.

Second, although nonmedical caregivers perform an important service, even when they seek merely to cooperate with health-care personnel, their ministry can move to a deeper level when they attempt to offer actual support to the medical team. Such support may take various forms, depending on the needs of the medical caregivers involved. It begins, however, with a sympathetic attitude and an openness to listen for and respond to their often only indirectly expressed cries for assistance. In every situation, support can be offered, if only in the form of genuine words of encouragement.

Christian caregivers also render an important ministry when they quietly and unashamedly seek to bring a broader, theological and eternal perspective to the medical caregiving situation. They can help medical personnel place the often-frustrating task of dealing with patients and their loved ones in the context of God's loving care for all his creatures. Thereby the mundane tasks of the daily routine can be lifted into the plane of the eternal value implicit in caring for the needy (Matt. 25:35–36).

The theological perspective is especially important in the face of the apparent futility of the medical war against AIDS. Personnel may be prone to discouragement as they realize that their medical successes will be meager. In such situations, they stand in need of a broader perspective, one that emphasizes the importance of their role as agents of divine care, if they are to withstand the temptation to discouragement that often confronts them. As patients in their care eventually die, medical personnel may need the ministry of Christian caregivers in assisting them to work through their own grief process.

Support Through Prayer

Not to be overlooked is the use of prayer in support of the medical team. Christian caregivers ought to be looking for opportunities to include medical personnel in their prayer ministry. Bedside intercession should be expanded beyond the patient and loved ones to encompass the medical caregivers. If health-care personnel are in the room when prayer is to be offered, they could even be invited to be a part of the circle. And such prayers should also include intercession for researchers, that they be given insight in their attempts to find a cure for AIDS.

The caregiver's prayer ministry may at times focus specifically on certain medical personnel who may be in special need or facing difficult struggles. As the Christian caregiver senses these needs and attempts to offer support to such a member of the health-care team, it may be appropriate to suggest that the two persons join together in a time of prayer.

Finally, the prayer support of medical personnel need not be confined to the hospital or hospice. Rather, concerned caregivers can intercede for their co-workers in the medical field during their own personal times of prayer. Likewise, the responsibility of supporting the medical team in prayer ought to be assumed by the entire church. Congregational and small-group prayer meetings as well as the prayers offered in formal worship services all provide opportunities to link church and medical personnel in their common task of ministering to persons in need.

Ministry to persons touched by the AIDS epidemic, then, is a challenging task. It extends not only to the patient, but also beyond, to encompass family, friends, and even medical caregivers. All persons affected by AIDS are at one time or another in need of the healing, encouraging touch of Christ, which comes as his disciples become servants in his name.

12

Broader Concerns of an AIDS Ministry

The primary focus of ministry in the midst of the AIDS epidemic will quite naturally be directed toward individuals touched personally by the disease—the patients, their friends and family, and their medical caregivers. Yet, other dimensions of this crisis must be addressed by the Christian community as well, if we would develop a full-orbed response to AIDS. This chapter introduces two of these dimensions: ministry in the wider society on behalf of persons touched by AIDS; and involvement in the efforts to contain and conquer the disease.

Ministry on Behalf of Persons Touched by AIDS

In addition to personal caregiving directed *toward* AIDS patients and their family, friends, and support personnel, an AIDS ministry should include action *on behalf of* persons touched by this epidemic. In the final analysis, all such action entails serving as advocates of the downtrodden and the outcasts in society, the powerless and the rejected. In assuming this role, the people of God are actually following the example of God as discovered in the pages of the Old Testament and as incarnated in the person of Christ.

The Biblical Basis of Advocacy

God's special care and concern for the victimized of society is a pervasive theme throughout the Bible. The Old Testament repeatedly announces God's concern. The psalmist declares, "The LORD works righteousness and justice for all the oppressed" (Ps. 103:6). Elsewhere the psalmist acts as God's mouthpiece: "'Because of the oppression of the weak and the groaning of the needy, I will now arise,' says the LORD. 'I will protect them from those who malign them'" (Ps. 12:5). God's concern for the oppressed forms a basis for human praise to God: "My whole being will exclaim," 'Who is like you, O LORD? You rescue the poor from those too strong for them, the poor and needy from those who rob them'" (Ps. 35:10).

The theme of acting as advocate on behalf of the oppressed forms a background for the ministry of the Messiah. The psalmist echoes Isaiah and anticipates Jesus' understanding of his own ministry when he writes, "The LORD sets prisoners free . . . gives sight to the blind . . . lifts up those who are bowed down, the LORD loves the righteous. The LORD watches over the alien and sustains the fatherless and the widow, but he frustrates the ways of the wicked" (Ps. 146:7b–9).

The immediate background for Jesus' understanding of his own ministry, however, lies in Isaiah 61:1, a verse that the Lord quoted as he began his work in Galilee. Luke describes that occasion:

> The scroll of the prophet Isaiah was handed to him. Unrolling it, he found the place where it is written: "The

> Spirit of the Lord is on me, because he has anointed me to preach good news to the poor. He has sent me to proclaim freedom for the prisoners and recovery of sight for the blind, to release the oppressed, to proclaim the year of the Lord's favor." Then he rolled up the scroll, gave it back to the attendant and sat down. The eyes of everyone in the synagogue was fastened on him, and he began by saying to them, "Today this scripture is fulfilled in your hearing" (Luke 4:17–21).

Followers of the Lord are called to imitate his example and serve as advocates of the downtrodden and the outcasts of society. In many respects, the description our Lord selected from Isaiah to indicate the special recipients of his ministry—poor, imprisoned, blind, and oppressed—metaphorically describes the person with AIDS. If the Lord were walking the earth today, he would indeed take their side and act as their advocate. This task, for now, has been mandated to his followers.

Education as Advocacy

Christian caregivers can act on behalf of those touched by the AIDS epidemic in several ways. One important way is by means of education, because information concerning the AIDS epidemic is needed both within the Christian community and in society as a whole. Because of our special concern for any persons who are the objects of unfounded prejudice, fear, or misinformation, we Christians ought to stand at the forefront of the dissemination of the facts about the AIDS epidemic. This task includes educating the congregation and the wider community concerning how the disease is spread and, most importantly, how the AIDS virus is *not* passed from one person to another.

As we serve as disseminators of factual information about AIDS, we engage in the important task of seeking to quiet the unreasonable fears widespread not only in society, but also sometimes present in the church. Further, by word and by example, we can encourage and admonish the Christian community and the world at large to continue to provide support links for those suffering from AIDS.

Advocacy in Rights Issues

We can also be advocates of the outcast as we speak out on the issues of the rights of AIDS patients. Societal viewpoints concerning the primary victims of AIDS—those with homosexual lifestyles or a history of intravenous drug use—plus the terminal nature of this awful disease and misinformation about how it is spread have combined to give human-rights aspects to the current AIDS crisis. These factors have already resulted in violations of the human rights of AIDS victims in recent years, including dismissal from employment and other forms of discrimination. Rather than diminishing, such violations will probably rise as the AIDS epidemic increases its impact. This situation raises many issues related to the human rights of AIDS patients in our society.

The people of God are called to be champions of the rights of the outcast and the powerless, and this calling is especially urgent in the midst of the AIDS crisis. We dare not allow our mandate to be set aside by our fear of involvement with persons with AIDS. On the contrary, we must be willing to follow the example of the Master who aligned himself with the downtrodden everywhere.

There is, of course, no simple solution to the crucial human-rights questions raised by the AIDS epidemic. Yet, one general principle has emerged that can serve to set the direction for Christians who would be advocates of the victimized. Glen T. Miller formulates this principle in an apt fashion when he suggests that Christians ask concerning any proposed legislation of public action, "Does the proposal contribute to the common good or does it only impose additional burdens on the sick?"[1] This principle forms a helpful context in which to ask hard questions concerning the various suggestions being put forth for dealing with the AIDS epidemic. It means that the human rights of AIDS patients can be set aside only in those situations in which the common good, that is, the public health of the nation, can truly be fostered and can be fostered in no other way. The church of Jesus Christ must take the lead in applying such a principle to current public policy proposals, thereby fulfilling the divinely given task of seeking to be advocates of the powerless in society.

The church's advocacy ministry, however, is not solely directed toward the wider society *on behalf of* persons with AIDS. Rather, its mandate demands that the people of God call all people to righteousness, a term that includes practicing responsible behavior. Therefore, the church must call HIV-infected persons and those in high-risk groups to forsake irresponsible practices and adopt responsible lifestyles. (This admonition, as will be noted in the following section, applies to the general population, too.)

This call should take the form of proclamation, disseminating sound medical information and solid theological understandings of what constitutes "responsible" living, while issuing a public challenge to follow proper guidelines. To be effective, our call must also take the form of providing assistance to persons who would heed the proclamation yet find themselves trapped in destructive habits and unhealthy situations. For them, the church must become a "halfway house" and a supporting fellowship, so that genuine change in lifestyle and attitudes can occur.

Ministry to Society as a Whole

Finally, Christian efforts in the midst of the AIDS epidemic must take the form of ministry to society as a whole. The major goal of this ministry is that of supporting steps to effect the prevention and containment of this awful disease. In this task, the church can provide an important service as it works in several directions.

Educational Efforts

The church can minister to society in a special way by offering a unique forum for education. The people of God have an important role in providing positive sex education for both church people and the wider society.

The last three decades have witnessed a widespread decline in appreciation for and adherence to the traditional Christian mores concerning human sexuality and its expression. During this time, the church has often been on the defensive, seeking to bolster a viewpoint that other segments of society have challenged as oppressive, narrow, and arbitrary. However, the AIDS crisis has triggered a reevaluation, at least by some, of the open stance toward sexual matters widely advocated and practiced in recent years. This changing situation offers us an opportune time to articulate in a positive way the sexual ethic of the Bible.

One intriguing result of the AIDS crisis has been a renewed interest in sexual fidelity. Several experts have concluded that despite the talk about "safer sex" there is ultimately no safe sex apart from practices that parallel the traditional Christian sexual ethic, which includes the fidelity of both partners within the context of a monogamous relationship and abstinence outside of marriage.

The AIDS epidemic has led several secular writers to advise abstinence in certain circumstances. For example, medical doctor Art Ulene declares, "If you can't be sure that you've got a safe partner, abstinence is the only sexual practice you can consider safe." He then boldly adds, "I believe that complete abstention from sexual activities with others is a choice that deserves serious consideration in the age of AIDS."[2]

Many persons have become aware of the importance of fidelity through tragic experiences. A letter printed in the widely read Ann Landers column bears witness to this. The author, after being reconciled to her adulterous husband, heard of his involvement in sexual orgies. She insisted that both of them be tested for AIDS and discovered thereby that he had infected her with the virus. Her advice to any woman in a similar situation is sobering: "Think about where and with whom [your] ex may have been, and if there is the slightest question, ask him to be checked out before you take him back." Ann Landers's comment is equally sobering: "AIDS has added a dimension to infidelity that no one dreamed of 10 years ago."[3]

Hancock and Carim cite several examples in the United States and elsewhere of persons who advocate monogamy:

> Because of these kinds of data, the warning notices are at last beginning to be posted for heterosexuals all over the world. Neal Blewett MP, Australia's Federal Health Minister, observes that "Great media and public interest has been focused on the present high risk groups," but adds: "I cannot emphasize too strongly that the problem of infection by the virus extends beyond these groups and into the general community. *Both as individuals and as a community, AIDS poses a potential threat to us all.* . . . Monogamy is the best prophylactic." Striking a similar chord, George D. Lundberg, editor of the *Journal of the American Medical Association*, advises: "People who do not wish to get AIDS must adjust their lifestyles so as to practise living defensively. . . . This is a great time to practise sexual monogamy."[4]

Even the Surgeon General, America's chief medical official, has noted the importance of this traditional stance. In his report on AIDS, he declares, "Couples who maintain mutually faithful monogamous relationships (only one continuing sexual partner) are protected from AIDS through sexual transmission."[5] Statements such as these suggest that the traditional position of the church may be able to gain a new hearing in the current situation generated by the AIDS epidemic.

The church's contribution to the discussion of human sexuality is crucial. Focusing on the negative aspects of certain lifestyles, secularists can propose abstinence outside of marriage and fidelity within a monogamous relationship as the way to protect oneself against contracting AIDS. But only the church can provide the positive theological rationale for the biblical outlook toward human sexuality. Only the church places the call for abstinence outside of marriage and fidelity within marriage in the context of God's design for humans and their society, as found in the Scriptures.

To have a lasting influence, however, we must go beyond advocating abstinence and fidelity just because they constitute safeguards against diseases such as AIDS. For, should the crisis pass, adherence to the Christian ethic would quickly wane, and the apologetic for this position would evaporate. Instead, we must indicate the positive relationship between this sexual ethic and human well-being as a whole.

Further, in the face of the risks that AIDS poses to the heterosexually active segments in our society, such as the high school and college-aged population,[6] we must hasten to direct other biblical teaching endeavors to the youth of America, in an effort to instill in them the importance of abstinence prior to marriage and fidelity within the marital bond. If this is to come about, however, the people of God must move beyond the apparently natural human embarrassment concerning the topic of human sexuality and the silence that this discomfort often produces.

One of the most troubling aspects of AIDS for society in general is that this disease links sexuality and death, two of the deepest dimensions of human experience. AIDS raises the specter that, when misused, the most intimate human expression of self-giving can actually result in a senseless and meaningless forfeiture of personal life. For this reason, the AIDS crisis provides a timely opportunity for us to present a Christian view on these realities, and this within the context of understanding the mystery of evil's destructive influence on human life.

The forum for education provided by the church ought to include education concerning homosexuality as well. We must rise to the challenge put forth by the gay community that homosexuality is to be accepted as "an alternative lifestyle" on equal footing with heterosexuality. To formulate a response, Christians need to come to grips with the actual factors that result in the homosexual orientation and place these within the context of a total understanding of human sexuality.

The development of such a response must, of course, look closely at the relevant biblical texts on the subject. But it must also address other difficult questions, to which no specific biblical passages may actually refer. For example, what is the genesis of the homosexual orientation in an individual? That is, what is the relative importance of genetic inheritance, environment, and behavioral response? Is homosexuality a sin of parents that is "visited on" their children, whether genetically or in the process of childrearing? Or is it a chosen lifestyle? Another important issue concerns the validity of a differentiation between disposition and action. Is the possession of a homosexual orientation itself sinful? Or is the orientation "neutral" until it is given expression through thoughts and overt acts? The issue of disposition versus action carries far-reaching practical implications.

Further, we should seek to become fully conversant in the psychology of lifestyle changes. In so doing, through the educational forum of the church the people of God are enabled to disseminate correct information concerning the possibility of homosexually oriented persons going through a change of lifestyle. For some this change will entail only a move to abstinence.[7] For others an additional and more radical move may be envisioned: an actual change in sexual orientation, perhaps to the point of maintaining heterosexual fidelity within a marriage bond. Both of these behavioral shifts form a stark contrast to the superficial "change" proposed by the gay community in the face of the AIDS crisis, a change characterized only by a reduction in its members' level of promiscuity. In fact, the gay community seeks chiefly to assist AIDS patients to continue to "accept" themselves for who they are, avoiding thereby any suggestion that their lifestyle or sexual orientation is somehow "bad" or abnormal.

As its educational forum develops, the church must not fail to remind its own members of the importance of welcoming a person of homosexual orientation within their midst. This includes standing beside such people as they seek to move away from promiscuity in every form and toward the wholesome options that God enjoins—abstinence within the single life or fidelity within a heterosexual marriage.

Encouraging Research

The church's ministry to society in the midst of the AIDS epidemic must include the encouragement of research aimed at finding a cure for the disease. It is unfortunate that certain segments of the body of Christ have come to be perceived as opponents of governmental funding of AIDS research. The church's concern and compassion for the sick and the victimized is incomplete without a strong stance in support of efforts to eradicate this evil from God's created world. If God does indeed fight against the evils that overtake humanity, linking ourselves to the divine cause includes seeing God's hand at work in the struggle to discover the cause and the cure for all sicknesses, including AIDS.

Moral Revival

Finally, a ministry whose goal includes prevention and containment of the AIDS epidemic can ultimately occur only as the people of God spark a moral revival in our nation. This is the only real solution to the AIDS crisis. The spread of AIDS is enhanced by lifestyles that are contrary to God's design for human life. Such lifestyles are expressions of human alienation from God, the Creator and Savior. To turn the tide, a moral revival is necessary, a turning of men and women to God and to committing themselves to follow God's design for life. In other words, a change of heart—a conversion—is the only lasting means whereby the widespread acceptance and presence of harmful lifestyles in American society can be altered.

The voice of God is speaking through the AIDS epidemic. In part the word spoken is a declaration of judgment, for our society is reaping what it has sown over recent years. The solution to the problem, then, is ultimately spiritual in its orientation. The world is being called to repent and to embrace the God who alone is the Author of Salvation. As God's people, we must sound this message clearly and plainly.

A moral revival in our land, however, requires more than merely preaching about sin and salvation. Any such reawakening of biblical values must begin within the church itself. God's people must repent of their own sins. We must admit to God that we, too, have become participants in the irresponsible spirit of the age. And we must also confess whatever lack of compassion toward the needy has characterized our past attitudes and actions.

Tolerant complicity with the ways of the modern world and the absence of compassion go hand in hand. People today often appear increasingly callous to persons in need. Even Christians do not always act as mercy givers to others within the church fellowship, much less to those whom they disdain and dismiss as unworthy sinners. This callousness has arisen in an age of materialism and self-gratification. Unfortunately, Christians are not immune to this modern-day infection. In fact, even entire congregations can be affected, as the quest to grow larger and richer becomes the central motivation in church life and activity. This connection between the spirit of the age and disinterest in the needy is understandable in human terms, because those who focus on themselves and their own "prosperity" have little interest in, or surplus resources for, the needs of others.

To the extent that the people of God are guilty, the church stands in need of genuine repentance. And just as true repentance always entails change, so also repentance of whatever failure may have characterized our response to the AIDS epidemic in the past must result in an openness to a redirection by the Holy Spirit. Such redirection begins with rediscovery of the ways of Christ in the world. The people of God can spark a moral revival in the land only as we are characterized by the servant motif so central in the life of the Master. With him we must take up the towel and the basin of water and wash the feet of the outcasts of society, ministering to needy people around us. When this occurs, Jesus' promise will be fulfilled—others will see our good works and glorify our Father who is in heaven (Matt. 5:16).

The AIDS epidemic offers to us a unique occasion to begin anew to live as servants. It offers us an opportunity to respond with compassion to the needs of all unfortunate persons in our world. The AIDS crisis gives us a context in which we can emulate God's love, the divine attribute that is the very nature of the Triune One whom we worship. This is indeed our calling as the people of God, to reflect in our lives the image of the eternal God. Given the crucial and timely significance of the AIDS crisis, we must rise to the challenge and be who we are called to be: the loving, compassionate people of God who serve others to the glory of God and for the sake of suffering people.

Epilogue

Toward an Interventionalist Ethic

The world is witnessing the spread of an epidemic that could threaten the future of all humanity. Because of its magnitude and the dire threat it presents, the AIDS epidemic poses both a great challenge and a crucial opportunity to the church. The thesis of this book is that all Christians are called by our Lord to seize this opportunity and respond to this challenge by taking action to combat the AIDS crisis. We—the people of God—are called to engage in a multifaceted ministry, which is directed both to persons—those touched by the disease and those battling on the front lines—and to society as a whole. We believe that this call to involvement, this "interventionalist ethic" to which God calls the church, is built on a foundation that is both theologically sound and consistent with the great tradition of the medical profession.

On the one hand, an interventional ministry in the midst of the AIDS epidemic arises from the medical perspective. The obligation to treat and care for persons infected by HIV is rooted in medical tradition and motivated by the ethical commitment lying at the basis of the practice of medicine.[1] The medical profession and physicians in particular have always been admired for their willingness to respond with expertise and compassion to critical situations, even when intervention posed risks to the health-care professionals themselves.[2] Organizations including the American College of Physicians and the Infectious Diseases Society of America have been willing to apply this traditional understanding to the current AIDS epidemic: ". . . physicians, other health care professionals and hospitals are obligated to provide competent and humane care to all patients, including patients with AIDS and AIDS-related conditions, as well as HIV-infected patients with unrelated medical problems."[3]

The preceding chapters issue a call to this type of ethic, based on virtues that reflect the essence of the medical profession as traditionally understood. These virtues include honesty, compassion, fidelity, and courage. Further, foundational to the health-care profession is the belief that all life is valuable. On the basis of considerations such as these, we conclude that the responsibility and willingness to intervene in the life of a needy patient despite possible personal risk—even when that patient is infected with the AIDS virus—is inherent in what it means to be a physician.

An interventionalist ethic, however, indicates that the role of the medical profession includes not only the direct treatment of persons with AIDS and related disorders. It also encompasses the task of supporting measures designed to help the uninfected avoid contracting the virus. In keeping with this role, many physicians and other health-care personnel and officials stand behind efforts to encourage the use of condoms by sexually active persons in high-risk categories and needle sterilization and distribution programs among chronic I.V. drug users.

However, all such measures are ultimately insufficient in the face of the spreading AIDS epidemic. The medical establishment must also become more vocal in calling society to a higher moral ideal. This social ethic would include sexual abstinence as a legitimate form of preventing the transmission of the virus. It would also refuse to assume that I.V. drug abusers are hopelessly beyond rehabilitation. In other words, when viewed from the medical perspective, the current AIDS crisis indicates the importance of the Christian perspective on ministry to the needy and emphasis on the ethics of prevention.

The call for an interventionalist ethic emerges from theological considerations as well, for the responsibility to intervene in the lives of needy persons is rooted in the ethics of the Bible. The foundation for this ethic is derived from God, who—acting from divine love, mercy, and grace—continually intervenes to bring healing to hurting people. Israel and the church bear testimony to the activity of God in human history, through which God has revealed to humanity his divine nature. The biblical ethic is rooted likewise in the concept of the value of human life. According to the Scriptures, this value is derived from God's concern for all the children of Adam.

Jesus of Nazareth stands as the greatest illustration of God's intervention on behalf of needy humanity. Jesus' earthly sojourn is filled with examples of intervention in situations of need. The lifestyles of many who received the Master's touch certainly failed to meet the standards of morality we would want people to follow. Nevertheless, Jesus' heart went out to them. The love, grace, and mercy of the Savior translated into involvement as he ministered to their needs. His example forms a great contrast to the "morally upright" of his day, who merely condemned their sins and avoided such "publicans and sinners." Although Jesus called all people to God's ideal of righteousness, his call was accompanied by his own willingness to engage in the risky business of ministering to people despite their less-than-ideal state of existence.

The theology of grace characteristic of the apostle Paul's preaching provides further confirmation of the interventional ministry derived from the actions of God in history and from the example of Jesus. Paul repeatedly speaks of himself as saved by the grace of God. His life would have continued along the path of disaster, he declares, had the Living Christ not intervened to rescue him from bondage.

Theological and medical considerations, then, converge. Both point to the same conclusion. Intervention is needed in order to deal with the AIDS epidemic.

AIDS poses a grave medical crisis unparalleled in history. Medical findings suggest that humanity is standing on the brink of a worldwide catastrophe. For the people of God, however, the AIDS epidemic offers a responsibility and a challenge. The church is called to demonstrate the compassionate love of God through concrete action in the name of the risen Lord Jesus, by the power of the Holy Spirit. For this reason, AIDS poses a crisis not only for the world as a whole but also for Christians, although the crisis we face as Christians is of a different sort. For most of us, AIDS is primarily an ethical challenge, a crisis of obedience. Through the AIDS epidemic, our Lord is offering us an opportunity to intervene in the lives of needy people, many of whom are searching for God. We are being given an occasion to minister to the physical and spiritual needs of our neighbors and thereby to follow the example of Christ, who willingly touched the leper and washed the dirty feet of his sinful disciples.

Appendix A

Figure 1

Structure of HIV

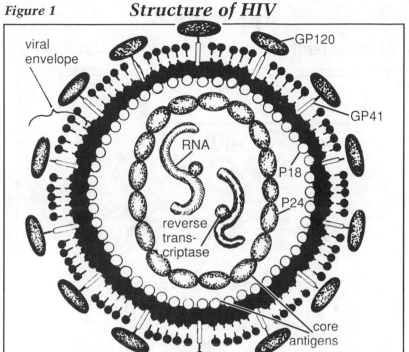

Infection of T-Helper Lymphocyte
The Life Cycle of HIV: RNA to DNA to RNA

Figure 2

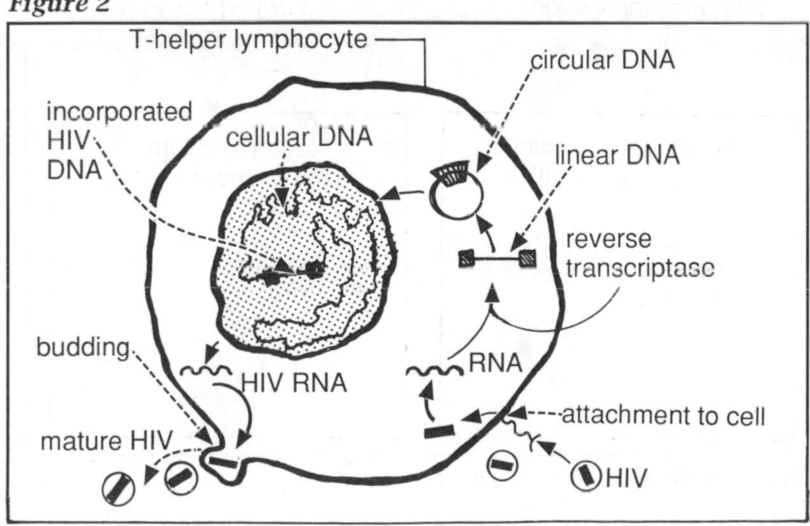

Adapted from *Science*, Vol. 239, page 619.

Appendix B

Mechanisms of How HIV Affects the Body

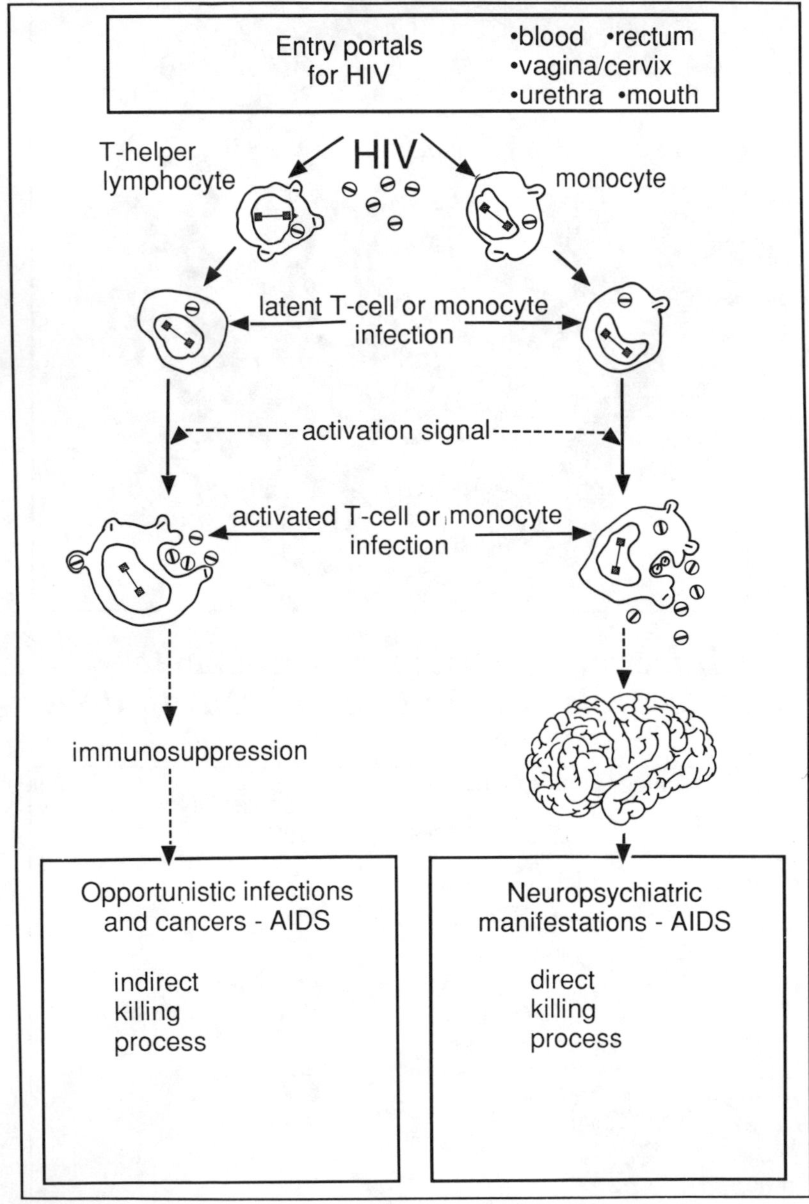

Adapted from *Science*, vol. 239, page 620.

Appendix C

How HIV Is Transmitted

Intercourse anal/vaginal between infected partners	**Maternally** • transmitted during pregnancy or time of delivery • transmitted by breast feeding
Sharing Contaminated Needles in I.V. Drug Use	**Receiving Contaminated Blood Products During a Transfusion**
Contact with Oral Secretions • oral sex* • biting* *rare case reports	**Receiving Donated Contaminated Body Parts and Tissues Such As Used in Organ Transplants**

Appendix D

How HIV Is Not Transmitted

Personal Contact with HIV Infected Person	**Services Given by HIV Infected Person**
• coughing • sneezing • talking • handshake • hug	• handling food/drink • serving food/drink • handling eating utensils • handling paper products
Touching Inanimate Objects Used by HIV Infected Person • table • doorknob • toilet seat	**Casual Contact with HIV Infected Person** • home • church • household • community
Insect Bites	**Donating Blood**

Appendix E

Patterns of HIV

Figure 1

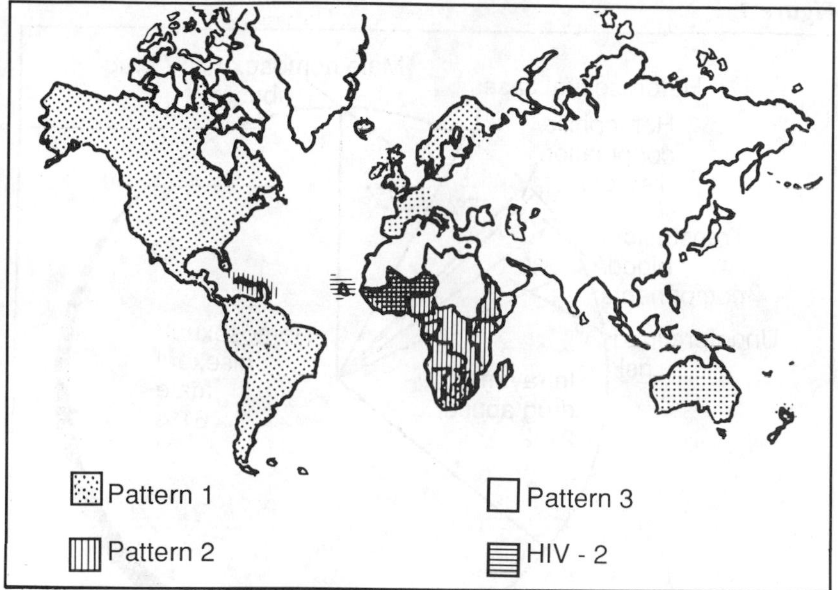

Adapted from *Science*, Vol. 239, page 577.

Figure 2

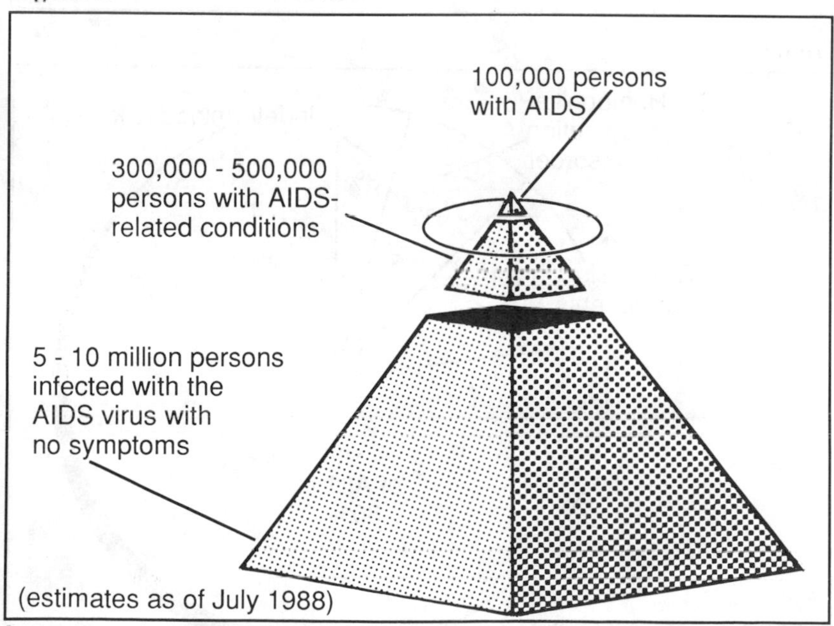

Adapted from the World Health Organization.

Appendix F

Risk Factors for AIDS in the United States

Figure 1

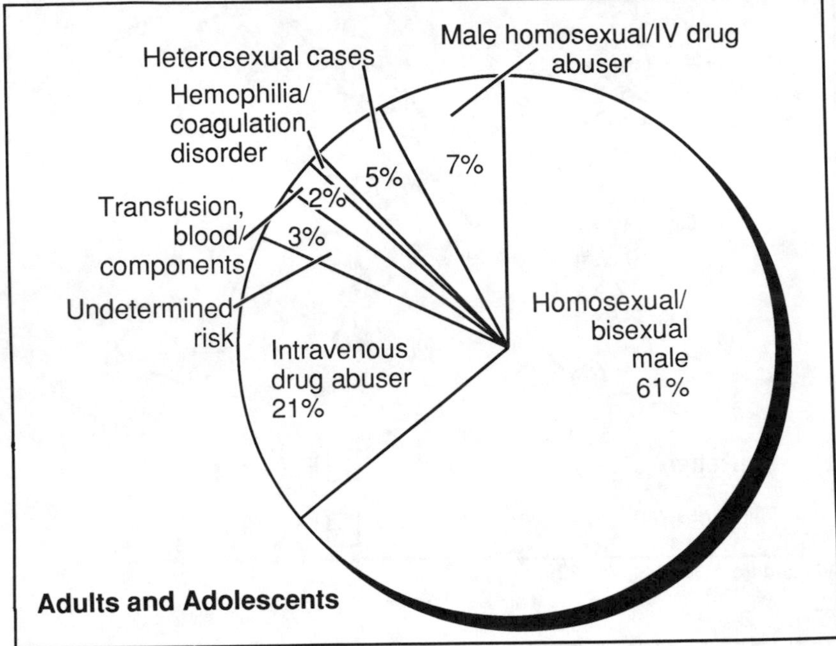

Figure 2

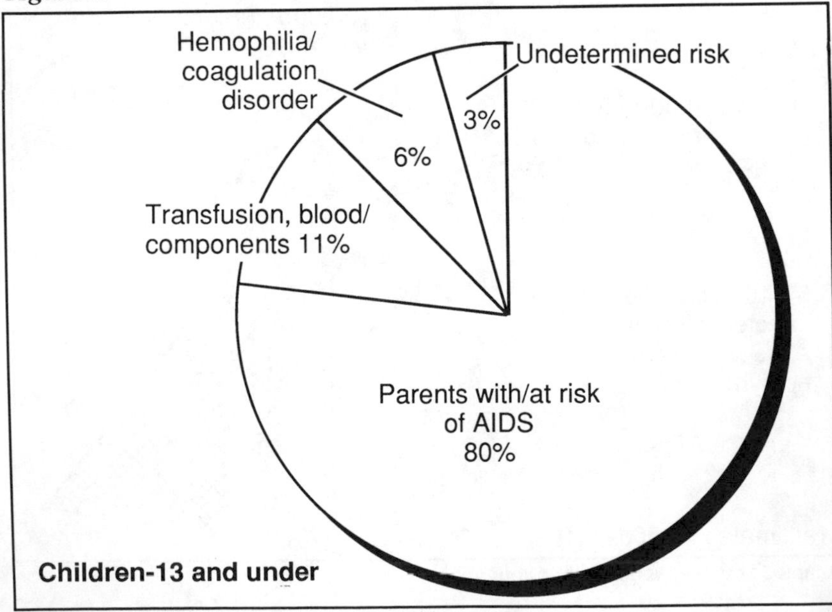

Adapted from Centers for Disease Control, Atlanta, Georgia

Appendix G
Current CDC Case Definition for AIDS

Introduction

The following case definition for the acquired immunodeficiency syndrome (AIDS) was developed by the Center for Disease Control in collaboration with public health and clinical specialists. It represents a revision of the prior definitions of AIDS and reflects increased knowledge about the disease. The objectives of the revision are (a) to track more effectively the severe and disabling manifestations associated with HIV infection (including HIV-1 and HIV-2); (b) to simplify the reporting of AIDS cases; (c) to increase the accuracy of the definition through the application of improved diagnostic laboratory techniques; and (d) to be consistent with diagnostic practice, which in some cases includes the diagnosis of AIDS presumptively without definite laboratory evidence of HIV.

The definition of AIDS is organized into three sections that depend on the status of the laboratory evidence of HIV infection (HIV antibody). The major proposed changes in this current definition apply to patients who have laboratory evidence for HIV infection and include those who have involvement of the brain by HIV (encephalopathy), the HIV wasting syndrome, and a broader range of specific diseases that indicate the patient has entered the AIDS phase of his or her illness (see below, Section II, A). The definition also includes patients with AIDS who have indicator diseases, which are diagnosed on the basis of clinical presentation of the disease and not on laboratory techniques (Section II, B). Finally, the revised definition eliminates those exclusions due to other causes of immune deficiency when the patient has evidence for HIV infection (Section I, A).

Application of the definition for AIDS in children differs from

Adapted from "Morbidity and Mortality Weekly Report Supplement," 36, #1S (August 14, 1987): 3S-6S.

that for adults in two ways. First, multiple or recurrent serious bacterial infections and lymphoid interstitial pneumonia are accepted as indicative of AIDS among children but not among adults. Second, for children less than fifteen months of age whose mothers are thought to have had HIV infection during pregnancy, the laboratory criteria for HIV infection are more stringent. In this situation the presence of HIV antibody in the child is, by itself, insufficient evidence for HIV infection because of the persistence of HIV antibody acquired from the mother up to fifteen months after birth.

1987 Revision of Case Definition for AIDS for Surveillance Purposes

For national reporting, a case of AIDS is defined as an illness characterized by one or more of the following "indicator" diseases, depending on the status of laboratory evidence of HIV infection, as follows.

I. Without Laboratory Evidence for HIV Infection

If laboratory tests for HIV were not performed or give inconclusive results and the patient has no other cause of immunodeficiency listed in Section I, A below, then any disease listed in Section I, B indicates AIDS, if it was diagnosed by a reliable diagnostic method.

A. *Causes of immunodeficiency that disqualify diseases as indicators of AIDS in the absence of laboratory evidence for HIV infection*

1. High-dose or long-term steroid therapy or other medications that could suppress the immune system about three months before the onset of the indicator disease.
2. Any of the following diseases diagnosed about three months after diagnosis of the indicator disease: Hodgkin's disease, non-Hodgkin's lymphoma (other than primary brain lymphoma), lymphocytic leukemia, multiple myeloma, any other cancer of lymph or histiocytic tissue, or angioimmunoblastic lymphadenopathy.
3. A genetic (congenital) immunodeficiency syndrome or an acquired immunodeficiency syndrome not typical of HIV infection, such as one involving hypogammaglobulinemia (congenitally low antibody levels).

B. *Indicator diseases diagnosed by a reliable diagnostic method*

Note: A reliable diagnostic method is a method that can definitely pinpoint a particular indicator disease. Reliable diagnostic methods would include direct inspection of the organism or of body tissue under a microscope, as well as utilizing specific and special culture techniques for the isolation of a particular infectious agent.

1. Candida infection of the esophagus, trachea, bronchi, or lungs
2. Cryptococcal infection involving organ systems other than the lungs
3. Cryptosporidiosis with diarrhea persisting greater than one month
4. Cytomegalovirus disease of an organ other than liver, spleen, or lymph nodes in a patient greater than one month of age
5. Herpes simplex virus infection causing mouth or skin ulcers that persist longer than one month; or bronchitis, pneumonia, or inflammation of the esophagus caused by herpes simplex for any duration in a patient greater than one month of age
6. Kaposi's sarcoma affecting a patient less than sixty years of age
7. Lymphoma of the brain (arising initially in the brain) affecting a patient less than sixty years of age
8. Lymphoid interstitial pneumonia and/or pulmonary lymphoid hyperplasia (LIP/PLH complex) affecting a child less than thirteen years of age
9. Mycobacterium avium complex or mycobacterium kansasii disease that involves organ systems other than (or in addition to) lungs, skin, or lymph nodes in the neck or internal chest regions

II. With Laboratory Evidence for HIV Infection

Regardless of the presence of other causes of immunodeficiency (I, A), in the presence of laboratory evidence for HIV infection, any diseases listed above (I, B) or below (II, A or II, B) indicates a diagnosis of AIDS.

A. Indicator diseases diagnosed by a reliable diagnostic method

1. Bacterial infections, caused by Haemophilus, Streptococcus (including pneumococcus), or other bacteria, multiple or recurrent (any combination of at least two within a two-year period), of the following types affecting a child less than thirteen years of age: bloodstream infection, pneumonia, meningitis, bone/joint

infection, or an abscess in an internal organ or body cavity (excluding ear infections, mild skin abscesses, or abscesses of mucous membranes)

2. Coccidioiodomycosis involving organ systems other than (or in addition to) the lungs or lymph nodes in the neck or internal chest regions
3. HIV encephalopathy (also called "HIV dementia," "AIDS dementia complex," or "subacute encephalitis due to HIV"
4. Histoplasmosis involving organ systems other than (or in addition to) the lungs or lymph nodes in the neck or internal chest regions
5. Isosporiasis with diarrhea persisting greater than one month
6. Kaposi's sarcoma at any age
7. Lymphoma of the brain (primary) at any age
8. Other non-Hodgkin's lymphoma
9. Any mycobacterial disease, caused by mycobacteria other than mycobacteria tuberculosis, which involves organ systems other than (or in addition to) lungs, skin, or lymph nodes of the neck or internal chest regions
10. Tuberculosis involving organ systems outside the lungs
11. Salmonella (nontyphoid) bloodstream infections
12. HIV wasting syndrome ("slim disease")

B. *Indicator diseases diagnosed presumptively*

Note: Presumptive diagnosis occurs when the physician is able to determine which indicator disease is present based on symptoms that the patient has, physical signs on examination, or characteristic appearance on x-ray study.

1. Candida infection of the esophagus
2. Cytomegalovirus infection of the retina with loss of vision
3. Kaposi's sarcoma
4. Lymphoid interstitial pneumonia and/or pulmonary lymphoid hyperplasia (LIP/PLH complex) affecting a child less than thirteen years of age
5. Tuberculosis or tuberculosis-related infection that involves organ systems other than (or in addition to) lungs, skin, or the lymph nodes of the neck or internal chest regions (specific type of tuberculous organism not identified by culture)

6. Pneumocystis carinii pneumonia
7. Toxoplasmosis of the brain affecting a patient greater than one month of age

III. With Laboratory Evidence Against HIV Infection

When laboratory test results are negative for HIV infection, a diagnosis of AIDS is ruled out unless:

A. *All the other causes of immunodeficiency listed above in Section I, A are excluded;* and

B. *The patient has had either*

1. Pneumocystis carinii pneumonia diagnosed by a definitive method; *or*
2. a. Any of the other diseases indicative of AIDS listed above in Section I, B diagnosed by a definitive method; *and*

   b. A T-helper lymphocyte count less than $400/mm^3$

Appendix H
CDC Classification System for HIV Infections

Introduction

This classification system organizes the manifestations of HIV infection into four mutually exclusive groups designated by I–IV (Table 1). The classification system applies only to patients diagnosed as having HIV infection. This classification system does not utilize the traditional terms AIDS and ARC.

Table 1
Summary of Classification System for a Human Immunodeficiency Virus (HIV)

Group I	Acute infection		
Group II	Asymptomatic infection*		
Group III	Persistent generalized lymphadenopathy		
Group IV	Other disease		
	Subgroup A	Constitutional disease	
	Subgroup B	Neurologic disease	
	Subgroup C	Secondary infectious diseases	
		Category C-1	Specified secondary infectious diseases listed in the CDC surveillance definition for AIDS+
		Category C-2	Other specified secondary infectious diseases
	Subgroup D	Secondary cancers+	
	Subgroup E	Other conditions	

*Patients in Groups II and III may be subclassified on the basis of a laboratory evaluation.

+Includes those patients whose clinical symptoms fulfill the definition of AIDS used by CDC for national reporting.

Adapted from "Morbidity and Mortality Weekly Report," 35 (May 23, 1986): 334-39.

Definitions of the groups and subgroups are as follows:

Group I. *Acute HIV infection.* A mononucleous-like syndrome, with or without meningitis, associated with the subsequent appearance of the antibody to HIV.

Group II. *Asymptomatic HIV infection.* HIV positive test results but no physical signs or symptoms of HIV infection. To be classified in Group II, patients must have had no previous signs or symptoms that would have led to classification in Groups III or IV. Patients whose clinical findings cause them to be classified in Groups III or IV should not be reclassified in Group II if those clinical findings resolve.

Patients in this group may be subclassified on the basis of a laboratory evaluation. Those patients with normal test results should be differentiated from patients whose laboratory test results show HIV-related abnormalities (lower numbers of T-helper lymphocytes, thrombocytopenia, etc.).

Group III. *Persistent generalized lymphadenopathy.* HIV positive test results with palpable lymph node enlargement (of at least 1 cm) located in at least two or more sites other than the groin area. These findings must be present for at least three months in the absence of another cause to explain the lymph node enlargement.

Group IV. *Other HIV disease.* Clinical manifestations of patients designated by assignment to one or more subgroups (A–E) listed below. Each subgroup may include patients who are minimally symptomatic, as well as patients who are severely ill. Each of these subgroups may be characterized (but not necessarily so) by the presence of lymphadenopathy.

Subgroup A. *Constitutional disease.* One or more of the following: fever persisting more than one month, involuntary weight loss of greater than 10 percent of baseline, or diarrhea persisting more than one month. There should not be a concurrent illness or condition other than HIV infection to explain these findings.

Subgroup B. *Neurologic disease.* One or more of the following: dementia, myelopathy, or peripheral neuropathy. There should not be a concurrent illness or condition other than HIV infection to explain these findings.

Subgroup C. *Secondary infectious diseases.* Infectious diseases associated with HIV infection or at least moderately indicative of a defect in cell-mediated immunity. Patients in this subgroup are divided further into two categories:

Category C-1. Patients with symptomatic or invasive disease due to one of the specified secondary infectious diseases listed in the surveillance definition of AIDS. Pneumocystis carinii pneumonia, chronic cryptosporidiosis, toxoplasmosis, extra-intestinal strongyloidiasis, isosporiasis, candidiasis (esophageal, bronchial, or pulmonary), cryptococcosis, histoplasmosis, mycobacterial infection with mycobacterium avium complex or mycobacterium kansasii, cytomegalovirus infection, chronic mucocutaneous or generalized herpes simplex virus infection, and progressive multifocal leukoencephalopathy.

Category C-2. Patients with symptoms due to one of six other specified secondary infectious diseases: oral hairy leukoplakia, generalized herpes zoster (shingles), recurrent Salmonella bacteremia (bloodstream infection), nocardia infection, tuberculosis, or Candida infection of the mouth (thrush).

Subgroup D. *Secondary cancers.* One or more kinds of cancer noted to be associated with HIV infection as listed in the surveillance definition of AIDS and at least moderately indicative of a defect in cell-mediated immunity: Kaposi's sarcoma, non-Hodgkin's lymphoma, or primary lymphoma of the brain.

Subgroup E. *Other conditions in HIV infection.* The presence of other clinical findings or diseases not classifiable above, that may be attributed to HIV infection and/or may be indicative of a defect in cell-mediated immunity. Included here are patients with chronic lymphoid interstitial pneumonitis. Also included are patients whose physical signs or symptoms cannot be attributed either to HIV infection or to another coexisting disease. Examples include: constitutional symptoms not meeting the criteria for Subgroup A; infectious diseases not listed in Subgroup C; and cancers not listed in Subgroup D.

Appendix I

Clinical Manifestations of HIV Infections

Opportunistic Infections

Parasites

Pneumocystis carinii
Toxoplasma gondii
Cryptosporidium
Isospora belli

Fungi

Candida species
Cryptococcus neoformans
Histoplasma capsulatum
Coccidioides immitis

Bacteria

Mycobacterium tuberculosis
Mycobacterium avium-intracellulare
Mycobacterium kansasii
Streptococcus pneumoniae (esp. pediatric)
Hemophilus influenza (esp. pediatric)
Salmonella species
Treponema pallidum (causative agent of syphilis)

Viruses

Cytomegalovirus
Herpes simplex
Herpes zoster
Epstein-Barr
JC virus

Neuropsychiatric Manifestations

AIDS dementia complex (chronic HIV-related encephalitis)
Acute HIV-related encephalitis
Meningitis (acute and chronic)
Peripheral neuropathy
Vacuolar myelopathy
Polymyositis and other disorders of muscle
Vascular disorders (strokes)
Progressive multifocal leukoencephalopathy (PML)

Aids Related Cancers

(1) Definite association with HIV
- Kaposi's sarcoma
- Malignant lymphoma (non-Hodgkin's type)
- Cancer of the anus (squamous cell cancer)

(2) Possible association with HIV
- Hodgkin's lymphoma

Appendix J

CDC Classification System for Human Immunodeficiency Virus (HIV) Infection in Children Under Thirteen Years of Age

Table 1
Summary of the Definition of HIV Infection in Children

Infants and children under fifteen months of age with perinatal infection

---

1. HIV cultured from blood or tissues

   or

2. HIV antibody

   and

   evidence of both cellular and humoral immune deficiency

   and

   one or more categories in Class P-2

   or

3. Symptoms meeting CDC case definition for AIDS

Older children with perinatal infection and children with HIV infection acquired through other modes of transmission

---

1. HIV cultured from blood or tissues

   or

2. HIV antibody

   or

3. Symptoms meeting CDC case definition for AIDS

Adapted from "Morbidity and Mortality Weekly Report," 36, #15 (April 24, 1987): 225-30.

Introduction to Classification System

Children having an HIV infection as illustrated above may be classified into one of two mutually exclusive classes based on the presence or absence of clinical signs and symptoms (see Table 2). Class Pediatric-1 (P-1) is further subcategorized on the basis of the presence or absence of immune abnormalities, whereas Class P-2 is subdivided by specific disease patterns. Once a child has physical signs and symptoms and is, therefore, classified in P-2, he or she should not be reassigned to class P-1 if signs and symptoms resolve.

Table 2
Summary of the Classification of HIV Infection in Children Under Thirteen Years of Age

- Class P-0 Indeterminant infection
- Class P-1 Asymptomatic infection
  - Subclass A Normal immune function
  - Subclass B Abnormal immune function
  - Subclass C Immune function not tested
- Class P-2 Symptomatic infection
  - Subclass A Nonspecific findings
  - Subclass B Progressive neurologic disease
  - Subclass C Lymphoid interstitial pneumonitis
  - Subclass D Secondary infectious diseases
    - Category D-1 Specified secondary infectious diseases listed in the CDC surveillance definition for AIDS
    - Category D-2 Recurrent serious bacterial infections
    - Category D-3 Other specified secondary infectious diseases
  - Subclass E Secondary cancers
    - Category E-1 Specified secondary cancers listed in the CDC surveillance definition for AIDS
    - Category E-2 Other cancers possibly secondary to HIV infection
  - Subclass F Other diseases possibly due to HIV infections

Explanation of Pediatric HIV Classes

Class P-0. *Indeterminate infection.* Includes infants and children exposed during pregnancy up to fifteen months of age who cannot be classified as definitely being infected but who have antibody to HIV, indicating exposure to a mother who has been infected.

Class P-1. *Asymptomatic infection.* Includes patients who meet one of the above definitions for HIV infection but who have had no previous physical signs or symptoms that would have led to classification in Class P-2.

These children may be subclassified on the basis of immune testing. This testing includes the measurement of the level of critical antibodies in the bloodstream (immuno globulins); measurement of the numbers of T-lymphocytes; and measurements of the white blood cell count, hemoglobin, and platelet count.

Subclass A. *Normal immune function.* Includes children with no immune abnormalities associated with HIV infection.

Subclass B. *Abnormal immune function.* Includes children with one or more of the commonly observed immune abnormalities associated with HIV infection, such as elevated antibody levels (hypergammaglobulinemia), low levels of T-helper lymphocytes, decreased T-helper/T-suppressor ratio, and low levels of lymphocytes in general. Other causes for these abnormalities should be excluded.

Subclass C. *Immune function not tested.* Includes children for whom no or incomplete immune testing has been done.

Class P-2. *Symptomatic infection.* Includes patients meeting the above definitions for HIV infection who have physical signs and symptoms of infection. Other causes of these physical signs and symptoms should be excluded. Subclasses are defined based on the type of signs and symptoms that are present. Patients may be classified in more than one subclass.

Subclass A. *Nonspecific findings.* Includes children with two or more unexplained nonspecific findings that have persisted for more than two months. These findings include fever, failure to thrive or a weight loss of more than 10 percent of baseline, enlarged liver (hepatomegaly), enlarged spleen (splenomegaly), generalized lymphadenopathy (lymph nodes measuring at least 0.5 cm) present in two or more sites, enlarged parotid glands (parotitis), and diarrhea.

Subclass B. *Progressive neurologic disease.* Includes children with one or more of the following findings: (1) loss of developmental milestones or intellectual ability, (2) impaired brain growth (small head size and/or brain atrophy as demonstrated on CT scanning), or (3) progressive bilaterial deficits in motor function as manifested by two or more of these findings: paralysis, abnormal muscle tone, abnormal reflexes, gait disturbance, etc.

Subclass C. *Lymphoid interstitial pneumonitis.* Includes children with confirmed pneumonia that shows lung tissue being infiltrated by lymphocytes on lung biopsy. This pneumonia also may be diagnosed presumptively on the basis of the chest x-ray appearance with positive x-ray findings present for at least two months and which is not responsive to appropriate antibiotic therapy. Other causes of pneumonia in this case should be excluded such as tuberculosis, Pneumocystis carinii, cytomegalovirus (CMV) or other viral or parasitic infections.

Subclass D. *Secondary infectious diseases.* Includes children with the diagnosis of an infectious disease that occurs as a result of immune deficiency caused by infection with HIV.

Category D-1. Includes patients with secondary infectious diseases due to one of the specified infectious diseases listed in the CDC surveillance definition for AIDS: pneumocystis carinii pneumonia; chronic cryptosporidiosis; disseminated toxoplasmosis with onset after one month of age; strongyloidiasis occurring outside the intestine; chronic isosporiasis; candidiasis (esophageal, bronchial, or pulmonary); cryptococcosis occurring outside the lungs; histoplasmosis occurring outside the lungs; mycobacterial infection occurring outside the lungs; cytomegalovirus infection with onset after one month of age; chronic generalized herpes simplex infection involving skin and/or mucous membranes with onset after one month of age; coccidioiodmyosis occurring outside the lungs; nocardia infections; and progressive multifocal leukoencephalopathy.

Category D-2. Includes patients with unexplained recurrent serious bacterial infections (two or more within a two-year period) including bloodstream infection, meningitis, pneumonia, abscess of an internal organ, and bone-joint infections.

Category D-3. Includes patients with other infectious diseases, including Candida infection of the mouth persisting for two months or more, two or more episodes of herpes infection of the mouth within a year, or generalized herpes zoster infection (shingles).

Subclass E. *Secondary cancers.* Includes children with any cancer described below in categories E-1 and E-2.

Category E-1. Includes patients with the diagnosis of one or more kinds of cancer known to be associated with HIV infection as listed in the surveillance definition of AIDS and indicative of a defect in cell-mediated immunity: Kaposi's sarcoma, non-Hodgkin's lymphoma, or primary lyphoma of the brain.

Category E-2. Includes patients with the diagnosis of other malignancies possibly associated with HIV infection.

Subclass F. *Other diseases.* Includes children with other conditions possibly due to HIV infection not listed in the above subclasses, such as hepatitis, heart failure (cardiopathy), kidney failure (nephropathy), hematologic disorders (anemia, thrombocytopenia), and various skin diseases.

Commentary Note

The classification system above is based on present information and understanding of pediatric HIV infection and may need to be revised as new information becomes available.

The definitive diagnosis of HIV infection in infants who have been potentially exposed during pregnancy and children under fifteen months of age can be difficult. At present, close follow-up of these children for physical signs and symptoms indicative of HIV infection and/or persistently positive HIV blood tests is recommended.

The parents of children with HIV infection should be evaluated for HIV infection, particularly the mother. The child is often the first person in such families to become symptomatic. When HIV infection in a child is suspected, a careful history should be taken to elicit possible risk factors for the parents and the child. Appropriate laboratory tests, including HIV antibody testing, should be offered. If the mother is HIV positive, other children should be evaluated regarding their risk of possibly having been infected during pregnancy. The spread of HIV within the family other than transfer during pregnancy or through sexual transmission is extremely unlikely. The identification of other infected family members allows for appropriate medical care and prevention of transmission to sexual partners and future children.

The nonspecific term AIDS related complex (ARC) has been widely used to describe symptomatic HIV-infected children who do not meet the CDC case definition for AIDS. This classification system categorizes these children more specifically under class P-2.

Appendix K
Additional Information on AIDS

A. Telephone Hotlines

The AIDS Information Clearinghouse 1-800-458-5231

Americans for a Sound AIDS Policy 1-900-INF-AIDS

National Sexually Transmitted Disease Hotline/American Social Health Association 1-800-227-8922

Public Health Service AIDS Hotline 1-800-342-AIDS

B. Information Sources

Americans for a Sound AIDS Policy, P. O. Box 17433, Washington DC 20041 (703) 471-7350

Gay Men's Health Crisis, 129 West 20th Street, New York, NY 10011 (212) 807-6655

Local Red Cross or American Red Cross AIDS Education Office, 1730 D Street NW, Washington DC 20006 (202) 737-8300

National AIDS Network, 2033 M Street NW, Suite 800, Washington DC 20036 (202) 293-2437

National Council of Churches/AIDS Taskforce, 475 Riverside Drive, Room 572, New York, NY 10115 (212) 870-2421

San Francisco AIDS Foundation, 333 Valencia Street, 4th Floor, San Francisco, CA 94103 (415) 863-2437

U.S. Public Health Service, Public Affairs Office, Hubert H. Humphrey Building, Room 717-H, 200 Independence Avenue SW, Washington DC 20201 (202) 245-6867

Endnotes

Introduction

1. David Nicholas, *The Medieval West* (Homewood, Ill.: The Dorsey Press, 1973), pp. 219–20.

2. Henri Daniel-Rops, *Cathedral and Crusade,* 2 vols. (Garden City, N.Y.: Image Books, 1963), vol. 2, p. 369.

3. "AIDS Update," *Light* (July/Sept. 1988): 12. Although WHO has subsequently revised the prediction drastically downward, now projecting only five to ten million, the long-range ramifications of the epidemic remain unchanged.

4. Helen Singer Kaplan, *The Real Truth About Women and AIDS* (New York: Simon & Schuster, 1987), p. 146.

5. "Crucial Issues: A.I.D.S." (Nashville: The Christian Life Commission of the Southern Baptist Convention, 1988), p. 7; Leonard J. Martelli, *When Someone You Know Has AIDS: A Practical Guide* (New York: Crown Publishers, n.d.) p. 10.

6. Graham Hancock and Enver Carim, *AIDS: The Deadly Epidemic* (London: Victor Gollancz, Ltd., 1987), p. 51.

7. This slow response is chronicled in Randy Shilts, *And the Band Played On* (New York: St. Martin's Press, 1987). Shilts maintains that the purported movement of the disease to heterosexual men via prostitutes consisted of "more smoke than fire" (p. 513).

8. William M. Hoffman, *As Is* (New York: Vintage Books, 1985), pp. xii–xiii.

9. *Christianity Today,* November 22, 1985, p. 51.

10. A study by the Rand Corporation projected medical costs for AIDS treatment alone to run between $15 billion to a staggering $113 billion for the period 1986–1991. Cited in Richard Merritt and Mona J. Rowe, "Where

the Fight Will Be Fought: AIDS and State and Local Governments," *The Futurist* 22/1 (Jan.–Feb., 1988); p. 21.

11. Earl E. Shelp, Ronald H. Sunderland, and Peter W. A. Mansell, *AIDS* (New York: The Pilgrim Press, 1986), p. 183.

Chapter 1

1. "Pneumocystis Pneumonia in Los Angeles," *MMWR* (1981) 30:250–52. The *MMWR* is prepared by the Centers for Disease Control in Atlanta, Georgia, published in a weekly basis and highlighting interesting or unusual medical cases, infectious disease outbreaks, environmental hazards and other public health problems that are of current interest to public health officials.

2. "Kaposi's Sarcoma and Pneumocystis Pneumonia Among Homosexual Men—New York City and California," *MMWR* (1981) 30:305–8.

3. "Follow up on Kaposi's Sarcoma and Pneumocystis Pneumonia," *MMWR* (1981) 30:409–10.

4. "An Outbreak of Community Acquired Pneumocystis Carinii Pneumonia: Initial Manifestation of Cellular Immune Dysfunction," *New England Journal of Medicine* (1981) 305:431–38.

5. "Persistent Generalized Lymphadenopathy Among Homosexual Males," *MMWR* (1982) 31:249–52.

6. "Update on Kaposi's Sarcoma and Opportunistic Infections in Previously Healthy Persons—United States," *MMWR* (1982) 31:294–301.

7. "Update on Acquired Immune Deficiency Syndrome (AIDS)—United States," *MMWR* (1982) 31:507–14.

8. "Opportunistic Infections and Kaposi's Sarcoma Among Haitians in the United States," *MMWR* (1982) 31:352–61.

9. "Pneumocystis Carinii Pneumonia Among Persons with Hemophilia A," *MMWR* (1982) 31:265–67.

10. "Update on Acquired Immune Deficiency Syndrome (AIDS) Among Patients With Hemophilia A," *MMWR* (1982) 31:644–52.

11. "Unexplained Immunodeficiency in Opportunistic Infections in Infants—New York, New Jersey, California," *MMWR* (1982) 31:665–67.

12. "Acquired Immunodeficiency Syndrome (AIDS)—Europe," *MMWR* (1983) 32:610–11.

13. F. Barre-Sinoussi, J-C Chermann, F. Rey, et al., "Isolation of a T-Lymphotrophic Retrovirus From a Patient at Risk for Acquired Immune Deficiency Syndrome (AIDS)," *Science* (1983) 220:868–71.

14. M. Popovic, M. G. Sarngadharan, E. Read, et al., "Detection, Isolation and Continuous Production of Cytopathic Retroviruses (HTLV-III) from Patients with AIDS and Pre-AIDS," *Science* (1984) 224:497.

15. R. C. Gallo, S. Z. Salahuddin, M. Popovic, et al., "Frequent Detection and Isolation of Cytopathic Retroviruses (HTLV-III) From Patients with AIDS and at Risk for AIDS," *Science* (1984) 224:500–3.

16. "Acquired Immunodeficiency Syndrome (AIDS) Update—United States," *MMWR* (1983) 32:309–11.

17. "Prevention of Acquired Immune Deficiency Syndrome (AIDS): Report of Interagency Recommendations," *MMWR* (1983) 32:101–4.

18. M. G. Sarngadharan, M. Popovic, L. Bruch, et al., "Antibodies Reactive with the Human T-Lymphotrophic Virus (HTLV-III) in the Sera of

Patients with Acquired Immune Deficiency Syndrome," *Science* (1984) 224:506.

19. J. Schupbach, M. Popovic, R. Gilden, et al., "Serologic Analysis of a New Type of Human T-Lymphotrophic Retrovirus (HTLV-III) Associated with AIDS," *Science* (1984) 224:504.

20. B. Safai, M. G. Sarngadharan, J. E. Groopman, et al., "Sero-Epidemiological Studies of HTLV-III in AIDS," *Lancet* (1984) 1:1438.

21. "Antibodies to a Retrovirus Etiologically Associated with Acquired Immunodeficiency Syndrome (AIDS) in Populations with Increased Incidences of the Syndrome," *MMWR* (1984) 33:377–79.

22. "Update: Acquired Immunodeficiency Syndrome (AIDS)—United States," *MMWR* (1984) 33:337–39.

23. J. A. Levy, et al., *Science* (1984) 225:840–42.

24. D. Zagury, J. Bernard, J. Leibowitch, et al., "HTLV-III in Cells Cultured from Semen of Two Patients with AIDS," *Science* (1984) 226:449–51.

25. D. Klatzmann, F. Barre-Sinoussi, M. T. Nugeyre, et al., "Selected Tropism of Lymphadenopathy Associated Virus (LAV) for Helper-Inducer T-Lymphocytes," *Science* (1984) 225:59.

26. G. M. Shaw, B. H. Hahn, S. K. Arya, et al., "Molecular Characterization of Human T-Cell Leukemia (Lymphotrophic) Virus Type III in the Acquired Immune Deficiency Syndrome," *Science* (1984) 226:1165.

27. F. Wong-Staal, G. M. Shaw, B. H. Hahn, et al., "Genomic Diversity of Human T-Lymphotrophic Virus Type III (HTLV-III)," *Science* (1985) 229:759.

28. "Provisional Public Health Service Interagency Recommendations for Screening Donated Blood and Plasma for Antibody to the Virus Causing Acquired Immunodeficiency Syndrome," *MMWR* (1985) 34:1–5.

29. "World Health Organization Workshop: Conclusions and Recommendations on Acquired Immunodeficiency Syndrome," *MMWR* (1985) 34:275-76.

30. "Update: Acquired Immunodeficiency Syndrome—United States," *MMWR* (1985) 34:245-48.

31. "Revision of the Case Definition of Acquired Immunodeficiency Syndrome for National Reporting—United States," *MMWR* (1985) 34:373–75.

32. "Recommendations for Preventing Possible Transmission of Human T-Lymphotrophic Virus Type III/Lymphadenopathy-Associated Virus from Tears," *MMWR* (1985) 34:533–34.

33. J. E. Groopman, S. Z. Salahuddin, M. G. Sarngadharan, et al., "HTLV III in Saliva of People with AIDS-Related Complex and Healthy Homosexual Men at Risk for AIDS," *Science* (1984) 226:477.

34. "Heterosexual Transmission of Human T-Lymphotrophic Virus Type III/Lymphadenopathy-Associated Virus," *MMWR* (1985) 34:561–63.

35. K. G. Castro, M. A. Fischl, S. H. Landesman, et al., "Risk Factors for AIDS Among Haitians in the United States," Atlanta, Georgia, International Conference on AIDS, April 16, 1985.

36. P. Piot, T. C. Quinn, H. Taelman, et al., "Acquired Immunodeficiency Syndrome in a Heterosexual Population in Zaire," *Lancet* (1984) ii:65–69.

37. N. Klomac, P. VandePerre, M. Carael, et al., "Heterosexual Promiscuity Among African Patients with AIDS," letter, *New England Journal of Medicine* (1985) 313:182.

38. "Self Reported Behavioral Change Among Gay and Bisexual Men—San Francisco," *MMWR* (1985) 34:613–15.

39. "Recommendations for Assisting in the Prevention of Perinatal Transmission of Human T-Lymphotrophic Virus Type III/Lymphadenopathy-Associated Virus and Acquired Immunodeficiency Syndrome," *MMWR* (1985) 34:721–26, 731–32.

40. L. Thiry, S. Sprecher-Goldberger, T. Jonckheer, et al., "Isolation of AIDS Virus from Cell Free Breast Milk of Three Healthy Virus Carriers," letter, *Lancet* (1985) ii:291–92.

41. J. B. Ziegler, D. A. Cooper, R. O. Johnson, J. Gold, "Postnatal Transmission of AIDS—Associated Retrovirus From Mother to Infant," *Lancet* (1985) i:196–97.

42. "Apparent Transmission of Human T-Lymphotrophic Virus Type III/Lymphadenopathy-Associated Virus From a Child to a Mother Providing Health Care," *MMWR* (1986) 35:76–79.

43. D. D. Ho, T. R. Rota, R. T. Schooley, et al., "Isolation of HTLV-III from Cerebrospinal Fluid and Neural Tissues of Patients with Neurologic Syndromes Related to the Acquired Immunodeficiency Syndrome," *New England Journal of Medicine* (1985) 313:1493–97.

44. L. Resnick, F. diMarzo-Veronese, J. Schupbach, et al., "Intra-Blood-Brain-Barrier Synthesis of HTLV-III—Specific IGG in Patients with Neurologic Symptoms Associated with AIDS or AIDS-Related Complex," *New England Journal of Medicine* (1985) 313:1498–504.

45. W. D. Schneider, D. M. Simpson, S. Nielsen, J. W. M. Gold, C. E. Metroka, J. B. Posner, "Neurological Complications of Acquired Immune Deficiency Syndrome: Analysis of 50 patients," *Annals of Neurology* (1983) 14:403–18.

46. "Classification System for Human T-Lymphotrophic Virus III/Lymphadenopathy—Associated Virus Infections," *MMWR* (1986) 35:334–39.

47. Public Health Reports (July/August 1986) 101, #4:341–48.

48. F. Clavel, et al., "Isolation of a New Human Retrovirus from West African Patients with AIDS," *Science* 233:343–46.

49. M. A. Fischl, D. D. Richman, M. H. Grieco, et al., "The Efficacy of Azidothymidine (AZT) and the Treatment of Patients with AIDS and the AIDS-Related Complex. A Double-Blind, Placebo Controlled Trial," *New England Journal of Medicine* (1987) 317:185.

50. "Acquired Immunodeficiency Syndrome (AIDS) in Western Palm Beach County, Florida, *MMWR* (1986) 35, #39:609–12.

51. "The Surgeon General's Report on Acquired Immune Deficiency Syndrome," U.S. Department of Health and Human Services, pp. 3–36.

52. "Classification System for Human Immunodeficiency Virus (HIV) Infection in Children Under Thirteen Years of Age," *MMWR* (1987) 36, #15:225–36.

53. "Revision of the CDC Surveillance Case Definition for Acquired Immunodeficiency Syndrome," *MMWR* (1987) 36, #1S:3S–15S.

54. "AIDS Due to HIV-2 Infection—New Jersey," *MMWR* (1988) 37, #3:33–35.

55. F. Brun-Vezinet, M. A. Rey, C. Katlama, et al., "Lymphadenopathy—Associated Virus, Type II in AIDS and AIDS Related Complex: Clinical and Virological Features in Four Patients," *Lancet* (1987) 1:128–32.

56. F. Clavel, K. Mansinho, S. Chamaret, et al., "Human Immunodeficiency Virus Type II Infection Associated with AIDS in West Africa," *New England Journal of Medicine* (1987) 316:1180–85. (See also note #48.)

57. "Report of the Presidential Commission on the Human Immunodeficiency Virus Epidemic," June 24, 1988, U.S. Government Printing Office, pp. 1–201.

58. M. Specter, "450,000 AIDS Cases Seen by '93" (news), *Washington Post,* June 5, 1988, pp. A1, A7.

59. World Health Organization, 525 23nd St. N.W., Washington, D.C. 20037 (202-861-3200).

60. R. J. Blendon, K. Donelan, "Discrimination Against People with AIDS: The Public's Perspective," *New England Journal of Medicine* (October 13, 1988) 319:1022–26.

61. S. Daley, "Two Addicts Seek Needles on First Day" (news), *New York Times,* November 8, 1988, pp. B1, B5.

62. "Early Data Issued on College AIDS Survey" (news), *New York Times,* November 6, 1988, p. 22.

63. Rudy Baum, "Fifth International AIDS Conference Report" (features), *American Society for Microbiology News,* 55, #9 (September 1989):467–71.

64. Gene L. Marx, "New Hope on the AIDS Vaccine Front," *Science* (June 16, 1989) 244:1254–56.

65. Gene L. Marx, "Wider Use of AIDS Drugs Advocated" (news and comment), *Science* (August 25, 1989) 245:8–11.

66. "HIV AIDS Surveillance," Centers for Disease Control, Department of Health and Human Services, September 1989, pp. 5, 12.

67. R. M. Selik, H. W. Haverkos, J. W. Curran, "Acquired Immune Deficiency Syndrome (AIDS) Trends in the United States, 1978-1982," *American Journal of Medicine* (1984) 76:493–500.

68. H. W. Jaffe, D. J. Bregman, R. M. Selik, "Acquired Immune Deficiency Syndrome in the United States: The First 1,000 Cases," *Journal of Infectious Diseases* (1983) 148:339–45.

69. D. Huminer, J. B. Rosenfeld, D. P. Silvio, "AIDS in the Pre-AIDS Era," *Reviews of Infectious Diseases,* 9, #6 (November-December 1987):1102–08.

70. R. F. Gary, M. H. Witte, A. A. Gottlieb, et al., "Documentation of an AIDS Virus Infection in the United States in 1968," *JAMA* (October 14, 1988) 260, #14:2085–87.

71. A. J. Nahmias, J. Weiss, X. Yao, et al., "Evidence for Human Infection with an HTLV-III/LAV-like Virus in Central Africa, 1959," *Lancet* (1986) 1:1279–80.

Chapter 2

1. R. C. Gallo, L. Montagnier, *Nature* (1987) 326:435.

2. J. W. Curran, et al., *Science* (1988) 239:610.

3. T. A. Peterman, R. L. Stoneburner, J. R. Allen, H. W. Jaffe, and J. W. Curran, *JAMA* (1988) 259:55.

4. B. E. Novick, A. Rubinstein, *AIDS* (1987) vol. 1:3. "The Pediatric Perspective."

5. J. W. Ward, et al., *New England Journal of Medicine* (1988) 318:473.

6. W. Blattner, R. C. Gallo, and H. M. Temin, "HIV Causes AIDS," *Science* 241:515.

7. A. T. Haasse, "Pathogenesis of Lente Virus Infections," *Nature* (July 10, 1986) 322:130–36.

8. N. L. Letvin, K. A. Eaton, W. R. Aldricht, et al., "Acquired Immunodeficiency Syndrome in a Colony of Macaque Monkeys," Proceedings of the National Academy of Science, USA (1983) 80:2718.

9. R. V. Henrickson, D. H. Maul, K. G. Osborne, et al., "Epidemic of Acquired Immunodeficiency in Rhesus Monkeys," *Lancet* (1983) I:338.

10. A. J. Nahmias, J. Weiss, X. Yao, et al., "Evidence for Human Infection With HTLV-III/LAV-like Virus in Central Africa, 1959," *Lancet* (1986) 1:1278.

11. V. T. Devita, S. Hellman, S. A. Rosenberg (eds.), "AIDS: Etiology, Diagnosis, Treatment and Prevention," second edition (Philadelphia: J. B. Lippincott, 1988), pp. 3–10.

12. "Pneumocystis Pneumonia in Los Angeles," *MMWR* (1981) 30:250–52.

13. M. E. Gurney, S. P. Heinrich, M. R. Lee, et al., "Molecular Cloning in Expression of Neuroleukin, a Neurotropic Factor for Spinal and Sensory Neurons," *Science* (1986) 234:566.

14. J. D. Roberts, K. Bebenek, T. A. Kunkel, "The Accuracy of Reverse Transcriptase from HIV-1," *Science* 242:1171–73.

15. L. S. Martin, et al., *Journal of Infectious Diseases* (1985) 152:400–3.

16. G. H. Friedland, R. S. Klein, "Transmission of the Human Immunodeficiency Virus," *New England Journal of Medicine* (1987) 317:1125–35.

17. F. Clavel, et al., "Isolation of a New Human Retrovirus from West African Patients with AIDS," *Science* 233:343–46.

18. "AIDS Due to HIV-2 Infection—New Jersey," *MMWR* (1988) 37, #3:33–35.

19. "Update: HIV-2 Infection—U.S.," *MMWR* (1989) 38; #33:572–80.

20. P. D. Markham, S. Z. Salahuddin, M. Popovic, et al., "Advances in the Isolation of HTLV-III from Patients with AIDS and AIDS-related Complex and from Donors at Risk," *Cancer Research* 45 (supplement):4588S-4591S (1985).

21. J. J. Goedert, "Testing for Human Immunodeficiency Virus (editorial)," *Annals of Internal Medicine* (1986) 105:609–10.

22. "Update: Serologic Testing for Antibody to Human Immunodeficiency Virus," *MMWR* (1988) 36:833–40, 845.

23. Devita, Hellman, and Rosenberg, eds., *AIDS* (1988), pp. 423–25.

24. "Interpretation and Use of the Western Blot Assay for Serodiagnosis of Human Immunodeficiency Virus Type 1 Infections," *MMWR* (July 21, 1989) 38, #S-7:1–7.

Chapter 3

1. "Pneumocystis Pneumonia in Los Angeles," *MMWR* (1981) 30:250–52.

2. R. Shilts, *And the Band Played On: Politics, People, and the AIDS Epidemic* (N.Y.: St. Martin's Press, 1987).

3. "Human Immunodeficiency Virus Infection in the United States: A Review of Current Knowledge," *MMWR* (1987) 36, #S-6:2.

4. W. Winkelstein, Jr., D. M. Lyman, N. Padian, et al., "Sexual Practices

and Risk of Infection by the Human Immunodeficiency Virus: The San Francisco Men's Health Study," *JAMA* (1987) 257:321.

5. W. E. Stamm, H. H. Handsfield, A. M. Rompollo, et al., "The Association Between Genital Ulcer Disease and Acquisition of HIV Infection in Homosexual Men," *JAMA* (September 9, 1988) 260, #10:1429–33.

6. "Self-Reported Behavioral Change Among Gay and Bisexual Men—San Francisco," *MMWR* (October 11, 1985) 34:613–15.

7. O. T. Monzon, J. M. B. Capeloan, "Female to Female Transmission of HIV," *Lancet* (1987) 2:40.

8. M. Marmor, D. C. DesJarlais, H. Cohen, et al., "Risk Factors for Infection with Human Immunodeficiency Virus Among Intravenous Drug Abusers in New York City," *AIDS* (1987) I:39.

9. R. A. Han, et al., "Prevalence of HIV Infection Among Intravenous Drug Users in the United States," *JAMA* (May 12, 1989) 261, #18:2677–84.

10. B. Frank, W. Hopkins, D. S. Lipton, "Current Drug Use Trends in New York City, December, 1983," *Trends, Patterns, and Issues of Drug Abuse*, 1983 (Washington, D.C.: National Institute on Drug Abuse, 1984), pp. 7–17.

11. D. C. DesJarlais, S. R. Friedman, "HIV Infection and Intravenous Drug Use: Critical Issues in Transmission Dynamics, Infection Outcomes, and Prevention," *Reviews of Infectious Diseases* 10, #1 (January–February, 1988):151–58.

12. S. H. Weiss, H. M. Ginzburg, J. J. Goedert, R. J. Biggar, B. A. Mohica, W. A. Blattner, "Risk for HTLV-III Exposure and AIDS Among Parenteral Drug Abusers in New Jersey [Abstract #S11, Tuesday, 11:30]," presented at the International Conference on the Acquired Immunodeficiency Syndrome (AIDS), Atlanta, April 14-17, 1985.

13. E. E. Schoenbaum, P. A. Selwyn, R. S. Klein, M. F. Rogers, K. Freeman, G. H. Friedland, "Prevalence of and Risk Factors Associated with HTLV-III/LAV Antibodies Among Intravenous Drug Abusers in Methadone Programs in New York City" [Abstract #198:S34b], presented at the International Conference on AIDS, Paris, June 23-25, 1986.

14. E. E. Schoenbaum, et al., "Risk Factors for Human Immunodeficiency Virus Infection in Intravenous Drug Users," *New England Journal of Medicine* (September 28, 1989) 321:874–79.

15. D. M. Novick, et al., "LAV Among Parenteral Drug Users: Therapeutic, Historical and Ethical Aspects," in L. J. Harris, ed., *Problems of Drug Dependence, 1985*, proceedings of the 47th Annual Scientific Meeting, a committee on problems of drug dependence, inc. NIDA Research Monograph 67. Washington, D.C.: GPO, 1986.

16. J. R. Robertson, A. B. V. Bucknall, T. D. Welsby, J. J. K. Roberts, J. M. Inglas, J. F. Peutherer, R. P. Brettle, "Epidemic of AIDS Related Virus (HTLV-III/LAV) Infection Among Intravenous Drug Users," *British Medical Journal* (1986) 292:527–29.

17. D. C. DesJarlais, E. Wis, S. R. Friedman, R. Stoneburner, S. R. Yancovitz, D. Mildvan, et al., "Intravenous Drug Use and Heterosexual Transmission of the Human Immunodeficiency Virus: Current Trends in New York City," *New York State Journal of Medicine* (1987) 87(5):283–86.

18. M. A. Fischl, G. M. Dickinson, G. B. Scott, N. Klimas, M. A. Fletcher, W. Parks, "Evaluation of Heterosexual Partners, Children, and Household Contacts of Adults with AIDS," *JAMA* (1987) 257:640–44.

19. S. R. Friedman, D. C. DesJarlais, J. L. Sotheran, J. Garber, H. Cohen, D. Smith, "AIDS and Self Organization Among Intravenous Drug Users," *International Journal of The Addictions* (1987) 22:201–19.

20. D. C. DesJarlais, S. R. Friedman, M. Marmor, H. Cohen, D. Mildvan, et al., "Development of AIDS, HIV Seroconversion, and Cofactors for T4 Cell Loss in a Cohort of Intravenous Drug Users," *AIDS: An International Bimonthly* (1987) 1:105-11.

21. M. B. Tucker, "U.S. Ethnic Minorities and Drug Abuse: An Assessment of the Science and Practice," *International Journal of The Addictions* (1985) 20:1021–47. (See also Note #14.)

22. T. R. Kosten, B. J. Rounsaville, H. D. Kleber, "Ethnic and Gender Differences Among Opiate Addicts," *International Journal of The Addictions* (1985) 20:1143–62.

23. S. R. Friedman, J. L. Sotheran, A. Abdul-Quader, et al., "The AIDS Epidemic Among Blacks and Hispanics," *Milbank Q* (1987) 65, suppl. 2:455–99.

24. G. B. Wofsy, J. B. Cohen, L. B. Hauer, et al., "Isolation of AIDS-Associated Retrovirus From Genital Secretions of Women with Antibodies to the Virus," *Lancet* (1986) I:527.

25. M. W. Vogt, D. J. Witt, D. E. Craven, et al., "Isolation of HTLV-III/LAV From Cervical Secretions of Women at Risk for AIDS," *Lancet* (1986) I:525.

26. S. Staszewski, et al., *Lancet* (September 12, 1987) II:628.

27. N. Hearts, S. B. Hulley, "Preventing the Heterosexual Spread of AIDS: Are We Giving Our Patients the Best Advice?" *JAMA* (1988) 259:2428–32.

28. V. Lorian, "AIDS, Anal Sex, and Heterosexuals" [letter], *Lancet* (1988) 2:1111.

29. N. Padian, et al., *JAMA* (1987) 258:788–90.

30. J. M. Jason, et al., *JAMA* (1986) 255:212–15.

31. T. Peterman, et al., Second International Conference on AIDS, Paris, June 23–25, 1986.

32. B. R. Slatzman, et al., Second International Conference on AIDS, Paris, June 23–25, 1986.

33. "Antibody to Human Immunodeficiency Virus in Female Prostitutes," *MMWR* (March 27, 1987) 36, #11:157–61.

34. "Human Immunodeficiency Virus Infection in the United States: A Review of Current Knowledge," *MMWR* (December 18, 1987) 36, #S-6, 4–5.

35. Ibid., pp. 11–12.

36. W. H. Masters, V. E. Johnson, *Masters and Johnson: On Sex and Human Loving* (Boston: Little Brown, 1988).

37. S. Okie, "HIV Infection Found in 1 of 500 College Students" (news), *Washington Post*, May 23, 1989, p. A5.

38. T. J. Dondero, Jr., M. Pappaioanou, J. W. Curran, "Monitoring the Levels and Trends of HIV Infection: The Public Health Services HIV Surveillance Program," Public Health Reports (1988) 103:213–20.

39. "Pneumocystis Carinii Pneumonia Among Persons with Hemophilia A," *MMWR* (July 16, 1982) 31:365–67.

40. "Human Immunodeficiency Virus Infection in the United States: A Review of Current Knowledge," *MMWR* (December 18, 1987) 36, #S-6:3.

41. "Human Immunodeficiency Virus Infection in Transfusion Recipients and Their Family Members," *MMWR* 36, #10, 137–40.

42. J. W. Ward, T. J. Busch, H. A. Perkins, et al., "The Natural History of Transfusion Associated Infection with Human Immunodeficiency Virus: Factors Influencing the Rate of Progression to Disease," *New England Journal of Medicine* (1989) 321:947–52.

43. P. D. Cumming, E. L. Wallace, J. B. Schorr, R. Y. Dodd, "Exposure of Transfused Patients to Human Immunodeficiency Virus to the Transfusion of Blood Components That Test Antibody Negative," *New England Journal of Medicine* (1989) 321:941–46.

44. J. R. Bove, "Transfusion-Associated Hepatitis and AIDS: What Is the Risk?" *New England Journal of Medicine* (1987) 317:242.

45. Centers for Disease Control HIV/AIDS Surveillance, U.S. Department of Health and Human Services, September 1989.

46. "Human Immunodeficiency Virus Infection in the United States: A Review of Current Knowledge," *MMWR* (December 18, 1987) 36, #S-6:4–7.

47. Ibid., pp. 7–8.

48. "Update: Human Immunodeficiency Virus Infections in Health Care Workers Exposed to Blood of Infected Patients," *MMWR* (May 22, 1987) 36, #19:285–89.

49. V. Wahn, H. H. Krammer, T. Voit, et al., "Horizontal Transmission of HIV Infection Between Two Siblings," *Lancet* (1986) II:694.

50. G. H. Friedland, B. R. Saltzman, M. F. Rogers, et al., "Lack of Transmission of HTLV-III/LAV Infection to Household Contacts of Patients with AIDS or AIDS-Related Complex with Oral Candidiasis," *New England Journal of Medicine* (1986) 314:344.

51. K. Martin, B. Z. Katz, G. Miller, "AIDS and Antibodies to Human Immunodeficiency Virus (HIV) in Children and Their Families," *Journal of Infectious Diseases* (1987) 155:54.

52. "Acquired Immunodeficiency Syndrome (AIDS-Europe)," *MMWR* (1983) 32:610–11.

53. "Update: Acquired Immunodeficiency Syndrome—Europe," *MMWR* (January 24, 1986) 35:35–38, 43–46.

54. P. Piot, T. C. Quinn, H. Taelman, "Acquired Immunodeficiency Syndrome in a Heterosexual Population in Zaire," *Lancet* (1984) 2:65.

55. J. M. Mann, H. Francis, T. Quinn, et al., "Surveillance for AIDS in a Central African City: Kinshasa, Zaire," *JAMA* (1986) 255:3255.

56. A. Trebucq, L. Munan, J. P. Louis, "HIV 1 Infection in Males and Females in Central Africa" (letters to the editor), *Lancet* (1989) II:225–6.

57. P. VandePerre, D. Rouvroy, P. Lepage, et al., "Acquired Immunodeficiency Syndrome in Rwanda," *Lancet* (1984) II:62–5.

58. A. J. Nahmias, J. Weiss, X. Yao, et al., "Evidence for Human Infection with a HTLV-III/LAV-like Virus in Central Africa, 1959," *Lancet* (1986) I:1278.

59. E. Serwadda, R. D. Mugewrwa, N. K. Sewankambo, et al., "Slim Disease: A New Disease in Uganda and Its Association with HILV-III Infection," *Lancet* (1985) II:849.

60. P. VandePerre, et al., *Lancet* (1985) II:524.

61. J. K. Kreiss, et al., *New England Journal of Medicine* (1986) 314:414.

62. A. J. Zukerman, "AIDS and Insects," *British Medical Journal* (1986) 292:1094.

63. F. Barin, et al., "Serological Evidence for a Virus Related to Simian T—Lymphotrophic Retrovirus III in Residents of West Africa," *Lancet* (1985) II:1387.

Chapter 4

1. "Pneumocystis Pneumonia—Los Angeles," *MMWR* (1981) 30:250–52.

2. "Kaposi's Sarcoma and Pneumocystis Pneumonia Among Homosexual Men—New York City and California," *MMWR* (1981) 30:305–8.

3. "Update on Kaposi's Sarcoma and Opportunistic Infections in Previously Healthy Persons—United States," *MMWR* (1982) 31:294–301.

4. "Update on Acquired Immune Deficiency Syndrome (AIDS)—United States," *MMWR* (1982) 31:507–14.

5. M. S. Gottlieb, J. E. Groopman, W. M. Weinstein, et al., "The Acquired Immunodeficiency Syndrome," *Annals of Internal Medicine* (1983) 99:208.

6. Classification System for the Human T—Lymphotrophic Virus Type III/Lymphadenopathy—Associated Virus Infections," *MMWR* (1986) 35:334–39.

7. R. R. Redfield, D. C. Wright, E. C. Tramont, "The Walter Reed Staging Classification for HTLV-III/LAV Infection," *New England Journal of Medicine* (1986) 314:131.

8. D. A. Cooper, P. Maclean, R. Finlayson, et al., "Acute AIDS Retrovirus Infection," *Lancet* (1985) I:537.

9. D. D. Ho, M. G. Sarngadharan, L. Resnick, et al., "Primary Human T/Lymphotrophic Virus Type III Infection, *Annals of Internal Medicine* (1985) 103:880.

10. H. A. Kessler, B. Blaauw, J. Spear, et al., "Diagnosis of Human Immunodeficiency Virus Infection in Seronegative Homosexuals Presenting with an Acute Viral Syndrome, *JAMA* (1987) 258:1196.

11. P. Bacchetti, A. R. Moss, "Incubation Period of AIDS in San Francisco," *Nature* (March 16, 1989) 338:251–53.

12. "Persistent, Generalized Lymphadenopathy Among Homosexual Males," *MMWR* (1982) 31:249–52.

13. W. Lang, R. E. Anderson, H. Perkins, et al., "Clinical, Immunologic, and Serologic Findings in Men at Risk for Acquired Immunodeficiency Syndrome," *JAMA* (1987) 257:326.

14. Ibid.

15. R. A. Kaslow, J. P. Phair, H. B. Friedman, et al., "Infection with the Human Immunodeficiency Virus: Clinical Manifestations and Their Relationship to Immune Deficiency," *Annals of Internal Medicine* (1987) 107:474.

16. J. Howard, F. Sattler, R. Mahon, et al., "Clinical Features of 100 Human Immunodeficiency Virus Antibody Positive Individuals From an Alternate Test Site," *Archives of Internal Medicine* (1987) 147:2131.

17. R. S. Klein, C. A. Harris, C. B. Small, et al., "Oral Candidiasis in High Risk Patients as the Initial Manifestation of the Acquired Immunodeficiency Syndrome," *New England Journal of Medicine* (1984) 311:354.

18. J. J. Goedert, R. J. Biggar, S. H. Weiss, et al., "Three Year Incidence of

AIDS in Five Cohorts of HTLV/III Infected Risk Group Members," *Science* (1986) 231:992.

19. M. E. Eyster, M. H. Gail, J. O. Ballard, et al., "Natural History of Human Immunodeficiency Virus Infections in Hemophiliacs: Effects of T-Cell Subsets, Platelet Counts, and Age," *Annals of Internal Medicine* (1987) 107:1.

20. J. J. Goedert, R. J. Biggar, M. Melbye, et al., "Effect of T4 Counts and Cofactors on the Incidents of AIDS in Homosexual Men Infected with the Human Immunodeficiency Virus," *JAMA* (1987) 257:331.

21. Eyster, Gail, Ballard, et al., "Natural History . . . ," p. 1 (see note #19).

22. J. M. A. Lange, D. A. Paul, H. G. Huisman, et al., "Persistent HIV Antigenemia and Decline of HIV Core Antibodies Associated with the Transition to AIDS," *British Medical Journal* (1986) 293:1459.

23. J. P. Allain, Y. Laurian, D. A. Paul, et al., "Long Term Evaluation of HIV Antigen and Antibodies to P24 and GP41 in Patients with Hemophilia," *New England Journal of Medicine* (1987) 317:1114.

24. "Revision of the CDC Surveillance Case Definition for Acquired Immunodeficiency Syndrome," *MMWR* (1987) 36, #1S:1S–15S.

25. "Pneumocystis Pneumonia—Los Angeles," *MMWR* (1981) 30:250–52.

26. T. R. Navin, A. M. Hardy, "Cryptosporidiosis in Patients with AIDS," *Journal of Infectious Diseases* (1987) 155:150.

27. "Update: Acquired Immunodeficiency Syndrome—United States," *MMWR* (1986) 35:542.

28. A. Zuger, E. Louie, R. S. Holzman, et al., "Cryptococcal Disease in Patients with the Acquired Immunodeficiency Syndrome. Diagnostic Features and Outcome of Treatment," *Annals of Internal Medicine* (1986) 104:234.

29. K. Holmberg, R. D. Meier, "Fungal Infections in Patients with AIDS and AIDS Related Complex," *Scandinavian Journal of Infectious Diseases* (1986) 18:179.

30. W. Mandell, D. M. Goldberg, H. C. Neu, "Histoplasmosis in Patients with the Acquired Immunodeficiency Syndrome," *American Journal of Medicine* (1986) 81:974.

31. D. A. Bronnimann, R. D. Adam, J. N. Galgiani, et al., "Coccidioidomycosis in the Acquired Immunodeficiency Syndrome," *Annals of Internal Medicine* (1986) 106:372.

32. G. Sunderam, R. J. McDonald, T. Maniatis, et al., "Tuberculosis as a Manifestation of the Acquired Immunodeficiency Syndrome," *JAMA* (1986) 256:362.

33. "Diagnosis and Management of Mycobacterial Infection and Disease in Persons with Human Immunodeficiency Virus Infection," *Annals of Internal Medicine* (1986) 106:254.

34. C. C. Hawkins, J. W. M. Gold, E. Whimbey, et al., "Mycobacterium Avium Complex Infections in Patients with the Acquired Immunodeficiency Syndrome," *Annals of Internal Medicine* (1986) 105:184.

35. J. L. Jacobs, J. W. M. Gold, M. W. Murray, et al., "Salmonella Infections in Patients with the Acquired Immunodeficiency Syndrome," *Annals of Internal Medicine* (1985) 102:86.

36. G. V. Quinnan, Jr., H. Masur, A. H. Rook, et al., "Herpes Virus Infections in the Acquired Immune Deficiency Syndrome," *JAMA* (1984) 252:72.

37. M. Melbye, R. J. Grossman, J. J. Goedert, et al., "Risk of AIDS after Herpes Zoster," *Lancet* (1987) I:728.

38. "Kaposi's Sarcoma and Pneumocystis Pneumonia Among Homosexual Men—New York City and California," *MMWR* (1981) 30:305–8.

39. "Update on Kaposi's Sarcoma and Opportunistic Infections in Previously Healthy Persons—United States," *MMWR* (1982) 31:294–301.

40. J. L. Ziegler, A. C. Templeton, C. L. Vogel, "Kaposi's Sarcoma: A Comparison of Classical, Endemic and Epidemic Forms," *Seminars in Oncology* (1984) 11:47.

41. "Diffuse Undifferentiated NonHodgkin's Lymphoma Among Homosexual Males—United States," *MMWR* (1982) 31:277–79.

42. "Revision of the Case Definition of Acquired Immunodeficiency Syndrome for National Reporting—United States," *MMWR* (1985) 34:373–75.

43. M. H. Kaplan, M. Susin, S. G. Pahwa, et al., "Neoplastic Complications of HTLV-III Infection: Lymphomas and Solid Tumors," *American Journal of Medicine* (1987) 82:389.

44. D. M. Knowles, G. A. Schamulak, S. Milayna, et al., "Lymphoid Neoplasia Associated with the Acquired Immunodeficiency Syndrome (AIDS," *Annals of Internal Medicine* (1988) 108:744–53.

45. A. A. Gall, P. R. Meier, C. R. Taylor, "Papilloma Virus Antigens in Anorectal Condyloma and Carcinoma in Homosexual Men," *JAMA* (1987) 257:337.

46. K. V. Sitz, M. Keppen, D. F. Johnson, "Metastatic Basal Cell Carcinoma in Acquired Immunodeficiency Syndrome-Related Complex," *JAMA* (1987) 257:340.

47. D. H. Gabuzda, M. S. Hirsch, "Neurologic Manifestations of Infections with Human Immunodeficiency Virus, Clinical Features and Pathogenesis," *Annals of Internal Medicine* (1987) 107:383–91.

48. I. Grant, H. J. Atkinson, J. R. Hesselink, "Evidence for Early Central Nervous System Involvement in the Acquired Immunodeficiency Syndrome (AIDS) and other Human Immunodeficiency Virus (HIV) Infections," *Annals of Internal Medicine* (1987) 107:828–36.

49. B. A. Novia, B. D. Jordan, R. W. Price, "The AIDS Dementia Complex: I. Clinical Features," *Annals of Neurology* (1986) 19:517.

50. B. A. Novia, E. S. Cho, C. K. Petito, et al., "The AIDS Dementia Complex: II. Neuropathology," *Annals of Neurology* (1986) 19:525.

51. B. A. Novia, R. W. Price, "The Acquired Immunodeficiency Syndrome Dementia Complex as the Presenting or Sole Manifestation of Human Immunodeficiency Virus Infection," *Archives of Neurology* (1987) 44:65.

52. R. Yarchoan, G. Berg, P. Brouwers, et al., "Response of Human Immunodeficiency Virus-Associated Neurological Disease to 3′-Azido-3′-Deoxythymidine," *Lancet* (1987) I:132.

53. A. Serwadda, R. D. Mugewrwa, N. K. Sewankambo, et al., "Slim Disease: A New Disease in Uganda and Its Association with HTLV-III Infection," *Lancet* (1985) 2:849.

54. "Unexplained Immunodeficiency and Opportunistic Infections in Infants—New York, New Jersey, California," *MMWR* (1982) 31:665.

55. J. Oleske, A. Minnefor, R. Cooper, et al., "Immune Deficiency Syndrome in Children," *JAMA* (1983) 249:2345.

56. "Update: Acquired Immunodeficiency Syndrome—United States," *MMWR* (1986) 35:757.

57. M. E. Guinan, A. Hardy, "Epidemiology of AIDS in Women in the United States, 1981–1986," *JAMA* (1987) 257:2039.

58. "Acquired Immunodeficiency Syndrome (AIDS) Among Blacks and Hispanics—United States," *MMWR* (1986) 35:655.

59. H. Minkoff, D. Nanda, R. Menaz, et al., "Pregnancies Resulting in Infants with Acquired Immunodeficiency Syndrome or AIDS-Related Complex: Follow-up of Mothers, Children and Subsequently Born Siblings," *Obstetrics and Gynecology* (1987) 69:288.

60. F. Chiodo, E. Ricchi, P. Costigliola, et al., "Vertical Transmission of HTLV-III," *Lancet* (1986) 1:739.

61. A. E. Semprini, A. Vucetich, G. Pardi, et al., "HIV Infection and AIDS in Newborn Babies of Mothers Positive for HIV Antibody," *British Medical Journal* (1987) 294:610.

62. M. F. Rogers, "AIDS in Children: A Review of the Clinical, Epidemiologic and Public Health Aspects," *Pediatric Infectious Diseases* (1985) 4:230.

63. "Update: Acquired Immunodeficiency Syndrome—United States," *MMWR* (1986) 35:757.

64. M. F. Rogers, P. A. Thomas, E. T. Starcher, et al., "Acquired Immunodeficiency Syndrome in Children: Report of the Centers for Disease Control National Surveillance, 1982–1985," *Pediatrics* (1987) 79:1008.

65. L. G. Epstein, L. R. Sharar, J. M. Oleske, et al., "Neurologic Manifestations of Human Immunodeficiency Virus Infection in Children," *Pediatrics* (1986) 78:678.

66. L. J. Burnstein, B. Z. Krieger, B. Novick, et al., "Bacterial Infection in the Acquired Immunodeficiency Syndrome of Children," *Pediatric Infectious Diseases* (1985) 4:472.

67. Rogers, Thomas, Starcher, et al., "Acquired Immunodeficiency Syndrome in Children," p. 1008 (see Note #64).

68. A. Rubenstein, R. Morecki, B. Silverman, et al., "Pulmonary Disease in Children with Acquired Immune Deficiency Syndrome and AIDS-Related Complex," *Journal of Pediatrics* (1986) 108:498.

69. R. W. Marian, A. A. Wiznia, R. G. Hutcheon, et al., "Human T-Cell Lymphotrophic Virus Type III (HTLV-III) Embryopathy. A New Dysmorphic Syndrome Associated with Intrauterine HTLV-III Infection," *American Journal of Diseases of Children* (1986) 140:638.

Chapter 5

1. J. G. Mossinghoff, "Development of AIDS Products: A Twelve Month Review," Update AIDS Products and Development, presented by the Pharmaceutical Manufacturer's Association, 1100 15th St. NW, Washington, D.C. 20005, August 1988.

2. Pharmaceutical Manufacturer's Association, in development: "AIDS Medicines, Drugs and Vaccines," 1100 15th St. NW, Washington, D.C. 20005, Summer 1989.

3. H. Mitsuya, K. J. Weinhold, P. A. Furman, et al., "3′-Azido-3′-

Deoxythymidine (BW A509U): An Antiviral Agent that Inhibits the Infectivity and Cytopathic Effect of Human T-Lymphotrophic Virus Type III/Lymphadenopathy–Associated Virus in Vitro," *proceedings of the National Academy of Sciences* (1985) USA 82:7096.

4. R. Yarchoan, R. W. Klecker, K. J. Weinhold, et al., "Administration of 3′-Azido-3′-Deoxythymidine, An Inhibitor of HTLV-III/LAV Replication, to Patients with AIDS or AIDS Related Complex," *Lancet* (1986) I:575.

5. M. A. Fischl, D. D. Richmond, M. H. Grieco, et al., "The Efficacy of Azidothymidine (AZT) in the Treatment of Patients with AIDS and AIDS-Related Complex. A Double-Blind, Placebo-Controlled Trial," *New England Journal of Medicine* (1987) 317:185.

6. "Results of Controlled Clinical Trials of Zidovudine in Early HIV Infection, AIDS Clinical Trials Alert," (National Institute of Allergy and Infectious Diseases, National Institutes of Health, Bethesda, MD 20892), August 24, 1989.

7. R. Yarchoan, G. Berg, P. Brouwers, et al., "Response of Human Immunodeficiency Virus–Associated Neurological Disease to 3′-Azido-3′-Deoxythymidine," *Lancet* (1987) I:132.

8. F. A. Schmitt, J. W. Bigley, R. McKinnis, "Neuropsychological Outcome of Zidovudine (AZT) Treatment of Patients with AIDS and AIDS-related Complex," *New England Journal of Medicine* (1988) 319:1573.

9. P. A. Pizo et al., "Effective Continuous Intravenous Infusion of Zidovudine (AZT) in Children with Symptomatic HIV Infection," *New England Journal of Medicine* (1988) 319:889.

10. D. D. Richmond, J. Andrews, et al., "Results of Continued Monitoring of Participants in the Placebo-Controlled Trial of Zidovudine for Serous Human Immunodeficiency Virus Infection," *American Journal of Medicine* (August 29, 1988) 85 (supplement 2A):208–13.

11. R. Yarchoan et al., "In Vivo Activity Against HIV and Favorable Toxicity Profile of 2′, 3′–Dideoxyinosine," *Science* (July 28, 1989) 245:412–15.

12. R. Yarchoan et al., "Clinical and Basic Advances in the Antiretroviral Therapy of Human Immunodeficiency Virus Infection" (review), *American Journal of Medicine* (August 1989) 87:191–200.

13. O. S. Wislo et al., "New Soluble-Formazan Assay for HIV-1 Cytopathic Effects: Application to High-Flux Screening of Synthetic and Natural Products for AIDS Anti-viral Activity," *Journal of the National Cancer Institute* (April 18, 1989).

14. R. Baum, "International AIDS Conference in Sweden: A report," *American Society of Microbiology News* (September 1988) 54, #9:486–89.

15. J. L. Marx, "New Hope on the AIDS Vaccine Front" (Research News), *Science* (June 16, 1989) 244:1254–56.

16. M. Murphey-Corb, L. N. Martin, et al., "A Formalin-Inactivated Whole SIV Vaccine Confers Protection in Macaques," *Science* (December 15, 1989) 246:1293–97.

17. W. C. Koff, D. F. Hoth, "Development and Testing of AIDS Vaccines," *Science* (July 22, 1988) 241:426–32.

18. P. J. Fischinger, "Progress in Vaccine Development Against AIDS." *AIDS Updates*, vol. 2, July/August 1989 (from *AIDS: Etiology, Diagnosis, Treatment, and Prevention,*" ed. V. T. Devita, Jr., S. Hellman, S. A. Rosenberg [second edition, Philadelphia: J. D. Lippincott, 1988]).

Chapter 6

1. "Update on Acquired Immunodeficiency Syndrome (AIDS United States)," *MMWR* (1982) 31:507–14.

2. N. Cluemek, J. Sonnet, H. Taelman, et al., "Acquired Immunodeficiency Syndrome in African Patients," *New England Journal of Medicine* (1984) 310:492.

3. P. Piot, T. C. Quinn, H. Taelman, et al., "Acquired Immunodeficiency Syndrome in a Heterosexual Population in Zaire," *Lancet* (1984) II:65–69.

4. R. J. Biggar, "The AIDS Problem in Africa," *Lancet* (1986) I:79–83.

5. A. C. Kinsey, W. B. Pomeroy, C. Martin, *Sexual Behavior in the Human Male* (Philadelphia: W. B. Saunders, 1948).

6. A. C. Kinsey, et al., *Sexual Behavior in the Human Female* (Philadelphia: W. B. Saunders, 1953).

7. M. Hunt, *Sexual Behavior in the 1970s* (Chicago: Playboy Press, 1974).

8. W. W. Darrow, H. W. Jaffe, J. W. Curran, "Passive Anal Intercourse as a Risk Factor for AIDS in Homosexual Men," *Lancet* (1983) II:160.

9. W. Winkelstein, Jr., D. L. Lyman, N. Padian, et al., "Sexual Practices and Risk of Infection by the Human Immunodeficiency Virus: The San Francisco Men's Health Study," *JAMA* (1987) 257:321.

10. K. M. Stone, D. A. Grimes, L. S. Magdar, "Primary Prevention of Sexually Transmitted Diseases: A Primer for Clinicians," *JAMA* (1986) 255:1763.

11. M. Conant, D. Hardie, J. Sernatinger, et al., "Condoms Prevent Transmission of AIDS-Associated Retrovirus," *JAMA* (1986) 255:1706.

12. P. VandePerre, D. Jacobs, S. Sprecher-Goldberger, "The Latex Condom, an Efficient Barrier Against Sexual Transmission of AIDS-Related Viruses," *AIDS* (1987) 1:49.

13. K. M. Stone, D. A. Grimes, L. S. Magder, "Personal Protection Against Sexually Transmitted Diseases," *American Journal of Obstetrics and Gynecology* (1986) 155:180–88.

14. M. A. Fischl, G. M. Dickinson, G. B. Scott, et al., "Evaluation of Heterosexual Partners, Children and Household Contacts of Adults with AIDS," *JAMA* (1987) 257:640–44.

15. J. Mann, T. C. Quinn, P. Piot, et al., "Condom Use in HIV Infection Among Prostitutes in Zaire [letter]," *New England Journal of Medicine* (1987) 316:345.

16. J. L. Martin, "The Impact of AIDS on Gay Male Sexual Behavior Patterns in New York City," *American Journal of Public Health 1987* 77:578–81.

17. Research and Designs Corporation, Communication Technologies, "Designing an Effective AIDS Prevention Campaign Strategy for San Francisco: Results from the Third Probability Sample of an Urban Gay Male Community" (San Francisco: Research and Designs Corporation, Communication Technologies, 1986).

18. "Antibody to Human Immunodeficiency Virus in Female Prostitutes," *MMWR* (1987) 36:157–61.

19. R. Hatcher, *Contraceptive Technology 1986*–1987, thirteenth edition (New York: Irving Publishers, 1987).

20. "Condoms for Prevention of Sexually Transmitted Diseases," *MMWR* (March 11, 1988) 37, #9:133–37.

21. D. R. Hicks, L. S. Martin, J. P. Getchell, et al., "Inactivation of HTLV-III/LAV Infected Cultures of Normal Human Lymphocytes by Nonoxynol-9 In Vitro [letter]," *Lancet* (1985) 2:1422–23.

22. V. T. Devita, S. Hellman, S. A. Rosenberg (eds.), *AIDS: Etiology, Diagnosis, Treatment, and Prevention,* second edition (Philadelphia: J. B. Lippincott, 1988), p. 385.

23. L. S. Brown, D. L. Murphy, B. J. Primm, "Needle Sharing and AIDS in Minorities," *JAMA* (1987) 258:1474–75.

24. M. F. Rogers, W. W. Williams, "AIDS in Blacks and Hispanics: Implications for Prevention," *Issues in Science and Technology* (1987) 3:89–94.

25. J. K. Waters, "Preventing Human Immunodeficiency Virus Contagion Among Intravenous Drug Users: The Impact of Street Based Education on Risk Behavior," *Abstracts of the Third International Conference on AIDS,* Washington, D.C., June 1-5, 1987, p. 60.

26. D. Lofton, "Nations Report on Needle Distribution: WHO Report backed by some experience," *American Medical News,* March 4, 1988:6.

27. C. A. Raymond, "First Needle Exchange Program Approved: Other Cities Await Results," *JAMA* (1988) 259:1289–90.

28. "Provisional Public Health Service Inter-Agency Recommendations for Screening Donated Blood and Plasma for Antibody to the Virus Causing Acquired Immunodeficiency Syndrome," *MMWR* (1985) 34:1–5.

29. Devita, Hellman, and Rosenberg, *AIDS,* p. 376.

30. D. A. Cooper, A. A. Imrie, R. Penny, "Antibody Response to Human Immunodeficiency Virus after Primary Infection," *Journal of Infectious Diseases* (1987) 55:1113.

31. R. C. Horsburgh, Jr., et al, "Duration of Human Immunodeficiency Virus Infections Before Detection of Antibody," *Lancet* (1989) II:637–639.

32. J. R. Bove, "Transfusion-Associated Hepatitis and AIDS: What is the risk?," *New England Journal of Medicine* (1987) 317:242.

33. J. J. Goldert, M. G. Sarngadharan, M. E. Eyster, et al., "Antibodies Reactive with Human T-Cell Leukemia Viruses in the Serum of Hemophiliacs Receiving Factor VIII Concentrate," *Blood* (1985) 65:492.

34. J. Jason, J. S. McDuggle, R. C. Holman, et al., "Human T-Lymphotrophic Retrovirus Type III/Lymphadenopathy–Associated Virus Antibody: Association with Hemophiliac's Immune Status and Blood Component Usage," *JAMA* (1985) 253:3409.

35. "Survey of Non-U.S. Hemophiliac Treatment Centers for HIV Seroconversions Following Therapy with Heat-Treated Factor Concentrates," *MMWR* (1987) 36:121.

36. "Human Immunodeficiency Virus Infection in Transfusion Recipients and Their Family Members," *MMWR* (1987) 36:137.

37. B. J. Turnock, C. J. Kelly, "Mandatory Premarital Testing for Human Immunodeficiency Virus: The Illinois Experience," *JAMA* (1989) 261, #23:3415–18.

38. "Guidelines for Effective School Health Education to Prevent the Spread of AIDS," *MMWR* (supplement, 1988) 37, #SS-2.

39. G. D. Kelen et al., "Human Immunodeficiency Virus Infection in Emergency Department Patients' Epidemiology, Clinical Presentations and Risk to Health Care Workers: The Johns Hopkins Experience," *JAMA* (1989) 262, #4:516–22.

40. Guidelines for Prevention of Transmission of Human Immunodeficiency Virus and Hepatitis B Virus to Health Care and Public Safety Workers," *MMWR* (1989) 38, #S-6.
41. P. Piot, F. A. Plummer, F. S. Mahlu, "AIDS: An International Perspective," *Science* (1988) 239:573.
42. T. C. Quinn, J. M. Mann, J. W. Curran, P. Piot, "AIDS in Africa: An Epidemiological Paradigm," *Science* (1986) 234:955.
43. R. J. Biggar, "The AIDS Problem in Africa," *Lancet* (1986) I:79.

Chapter 7

1. This is not to deny that the church is to practice its God-given task of disciplining its members. Nevertheless, even when church discipline is necessary, reconciliation, not exclusion, is to be the ultimate goal.
2. As cited in William J. Wood, S. J., "Teach the Children Well," *America*, May 16, 1987, p. 400.

Chapter 8

1. New Webster's Dictionary of the English Language, rev. ed. (1981), s.v. "Compassion."
2. Williston Walker, "Compassion," *The International Standard Bible Encyclopedia*, 1st ed. (Grand Rapids: Eerdmans, 1915), II, p. 695.
3. Robert Girdlestone, *Synonyms of the Old Testament*, 2nd ed. (Grand Rapids: Eerdmans, 1897; reprint ed., 1973), p. 108.
4. *Interpreter's Dictionary of the Bible*, 1962 ed., s.v. "Mercy, Merciful; Compassion; Pity," by Elizabeth Achtemeier.
5. Achtemeier thus is incorrect in declaring, "Not once is God's mercy granted to those outside the covenant relationship."
6. Walker, "Compassion," II, p. 695.

Chapter 9

1. Richard L. Shaper, "Pastoral Care for Persons with AIDS and for Their Families," *The Christian Century*, August 12–19, 1987, p. 693.
2. BettyClare Moffatt, *When Someone You Love Has AIDS* (New York: NAL Penguin, 1986), pp. 140–41.
3. James Stulz, "Toward a Spirituality for Victims of AIDS," *America*, June 28, 1986, p. 510. A similar point is made in the context of the euthanasia question by Beth Spring and Ed Larson, *Euthanasia* (Portland, Oregon: Multnomah, 1988), pp. 130–31.

Chapter 10

1. J. Harold Ellens, "AIDS, the Pastor and the Patient Parishioner," *The Journal of Pastoral Care* 6 (1987).
2. Ibid., p. 23.
3. For a response of the Christian counselor to this contemporary situa-

tion, see Paul R. Welter, *Counseling and the Search for Meaning,* in Gary R. Collins, *Resources for Christian Counseling,* vol. 9 (Waco: Word, 1987).

4. Richard A. McCormick, "AIDS: The Shape of the Ethical Challenge," *America* 158/6 (Feb. 13, 1988), p. 154.

5. See, for example, Karl Menninger, *Whatever Became of Sin?* (New York: Hawthorn Books, 1973).

6. Klaus Wendler, R.N., "Ministry to Patients with Acquired Immunodeficiency Syndrome: A Spiritual Challenge," *The Journal of Pastoral Care* XLI, no. 1 (March 1987).

7. M. Pabst Battin, "The Least Worst Death," *Hastings Center Report,* April 1983, p. 15.

8. Elisabeth Kübler-Ross, *On Death and Dying* (New York: Macmillan, 1969).

9. For a brief but helpful description of dealing with persons in each of these stages, see Leonard J. Martelli, *When Someone You Know Has AIDS* (New York: Crown Publishers, 1987), pp. 172–74.

10. Graham Hancock and Enver Carim maintain that such persons ". . . are probably the least infective of all seropositive people. It is difficult for the virus to be cultured from their tissues because they tend no longer to have enough cells to support replication of the virus in their body" (*AIDS: The Deadly Epidemic* [London: Victor Gollancz, Ltd., 1987], p. 84).

11. BettyClare Moffatt, *When Someone You Love Has AIDS* (New York: NAL Penguin, 1986), p. 26.

12. Kittredge Cherry and James Mitulski, "We Are the Church Alive, the Church with AIDS," *The Christian Century,* January 27, 1988, p. 86.

13. Moffatt, esp. pp. 140–41.

14. Earl E. Shelp, Ronald H. Sunderland, and Peter W. A. Mansell, *AIDS, Personal Stories in Pastoral Perspective* (New York: The Pilgrim Press, 1986), p. 33.

Chapter 11

1. For a discussion of these, see Leonard J. Martelli, *When Someone You Know Has AIDS* (New York: Crown Publishers, 1987), pp. 55–59.

2. For a discussion of the grief process from the point of view of the partner, see Martelli, pp. 184–96.

3. Elisabeth Kübler-Ross, *On Death and Dying* (New York: Macmillan, 1969).

4. R. Fulton and G. Owen, "AIDS: Seventh Rank Absolute," in *AIDS: Principles, Practices, & Politics,* ed. Inge B. Coreless and Mary Pittman-Lindeman (New York: Hemisphere Publishing, 1988), 244.

Chapter 12

1. Glenn T. Miller, "Ministerial Ethics and AIDS," *The Christian Ministry,* May 1986, p. 24. For a statement from an Australian perspective, see Graham Hancock and Enver Carim, *AIDS: The Deadly Epidemic* (London: Victor Gollancz, Ltd., 1987), p. 87.

2. Art Ulene, *Safe Sex in a Dangerous World* (New York: Vintage Books, 1987), p. 32.

3. *Argus Leader* (Sioux Falls, S.D.), Sept. 16, 1988.

4. Hancock and Carim, *AIDS: The Deadly Epidemic, p.* 104.

5. "The Surgeon General's Report on Acquired Immune Deficiency Syndrome," U.S. Department of Health and Human Services, p. 16.

6. A recent survey indicates that nearly one of every three hundred college students is already infected with the AIDS virus. *Argus Leader* (November 2, 1988): 8A.

7. The story of a homosexual couple who moved to celibacy as a result of religious convictions is included in Earl E. Shelp, Ronald H. Sutherland, and Peter W. A. Mansell, *AIDS: Personal Stories in Pastoral Perspective* (New York: The Pilgrim Press, 1986), p. 37.

Epilogue

1. For a recent review of the "urgent need for a coherent professional ethic governing the care of human immunodeficiency virus infected persons," see "Physicians, AIDS, and Occupational Risk: Historic Traditions and Ethical Obligations," *JAMA* (October 9, 1987) 254, 14: 1924–28.

2. Unfortunately, the record of the medical profession during major infectious disease epidemics has not always fulfilled the ideal. During the Black Death in Europe, the bubonic plague of London in 1665, and the yellow fever outbreak in Philadelphia in 1793, some physicians deserted their patients. The risks posed to health-care professionals by AIDS, however, are not as great as those posed by these past epidemics.

3. Health and Public Policy Committee, American College of Physicians: and the Infectious Diseases Society of America: Philadelphia, Penn. "The Acquired Immunodeficiency Syndrome (AIDS) and Infection with the Human Immunodeficiency Virus (HIV)," *Journal of Infectious Diseases* (Aug. 1988) 158, 2: 273–85.

Glossary

AIDS (acquired immunodeficiency syndrome) A group of disorders caused by infection with the human immunodeficiency virus (HIV), including a variety of opportunistic infections, cancers, and diseases of the nervous system.

Anemia A below-normal reduction in the number of red blood cells or in the quantity of hemoglobin (the oxygen carrying pigment of red blood cells).

ARC (AIDS-related complex) Stage of HIV infection in those who have developed physical signs and/or symptoms. In general, ARC is considered a stage of HIV infection that preceeds the terminal manifestations of the virus (AIDS).

ARV (AIDS-related virus) An early name for the AIDS virus. ARV was discovered by Dr. J. Levy of San Francisco and has since been dropped in favor of the current designation, HIV.

Condom Sheath or cover for the penis, worn during intercourse to prevent pregnancy or infection.

Dementia Organic mental disorder characterized by loss of intellectual abilities (including memory, judgment, and abstract thinking) and a personality change. Dementia may be caused by many different conditions, including HIV.

DNA (deoxyribonucleic acid) A nucleic acid that constitutes the genetic material of all cellular organisms; as well as the DNA viruses.

ELISA test (enzyme-linked immunosorbent assay) The ELISA test is a method for detecting the presence of antibodies to HIV in the bloodstream. It is currently used as the major screening test for the presence of HIV.

Encephalitis Inflammation of the brain.

Encephalopathy Term used to describe degenerative disease of the brain. Encephalopathy may have a variety of different causes.

Epidemic The sudden appearance of a disease or condition that exceeds normality. It is usually attributed to infectious diseases, but may be applied to any disease, injury, or other health-related events.

Esophagitis Inflammation of the esophagus.

Gamma globulin Blood proteins composed almost entirely of immuno globulins (antibodies). Gamma globulin and immuno globulin are, for the most part, synonymous.

Hemophilia Bleeding disorder related to a deficiency in certain blood-clotting factors. Hemophilia occurs in two main forms: Hemophilia A—classic hemophilia resulting from factor VIII deficiency; and Hemophilia B, also called Christmas disease, which manifests a d ficiency of factor IX.

Hepatitis Inflammation of the liver.

Heterosexuality Sexual attraction toward those of the opposite sex.

HIV (human immunodeficiency virus) The current designated name for the causative agent of AIDS.

HIV-1 Same as HIV.

HIV-2 The second human immunodeficiency virus that has been associated with AIDS. HIV-2 was discovered in 1986 and is mostly limited to West Africa.

Homosexuality Sexual attraction toward those of the same sex.

HTLV-III (human T-cell lymphotropic virus III) An earlier name for the HIV. HTLV-III was discovered by Dr. Robert Gallo of the National Institutes of Health. HTLV-III has been dropped in favor of the designation, HIV.

Immuno globulin Any of the structurally related glycoproteins that function as antibodies.

Incidence The rate at which a certain event occurs (e.g., the number of new AIDS cases occurring during a certain period of time).

KSOI syndrome (Kaposi's sarcoma and opportunistic infection syndrome) KSOI syndrome was one of the descriptive terms given patients with AIDS prior to the actual designation AIDS.

LAV (lymphadenopathy virus) An earlier name for HIV. LAV was discovered by Dr. Luc Montagier of the Pasteur Institute in Paris, France. It has since been dropped in favor of the designation, HIV.

Leukopenia Reduction in the number of leukocytes (white blood cells) in the blood.

Lymphadenopathy Enlargement or proliferation of lymphoid tissue (lymph nodes).

Lymphocyte Particular white blood cell that is found in the blood, lymph, and lymphoid tissues. Lymphocytes are the body's primary participants in making up the immune system. They are divided into two classes, B and T-lymphocytes. One of the T-lymphocytes (T-helper cell) is the target cell infected by HIV, resulting in the immune defect seen with AIDS.

Lymphoma Malignancy of the lymph system.

Meningitis Inflammation of the meninges, which are the three membranes that surround the brain and spinal cord.

Monocyte Particular white blood cell that is normally found in the bloodstream and in many of the body's organ systems. The monocyte plays a crucial role in the body's immune defense system.

Mycobacterium Genus of bacteria that contains many species, including the highly infective organisms that cause tuberculosis (M. tuberculosis). Organisms from this group have been found to cause infections in AIDS patients and include mycobacterium avium-intracellulare and mycobacterium kansasii.

Myelopathy General term denoting functional disturbances and/or pathological changes in the spinal cord.

Neuropathy General term denoting functional disturbances and/or pathological changes in the peripheral nervous system (outside the brain and spinal cord).

Opportunistic infection Infection caused by various viruses, bacteria, fungi, and parasites. These organisms take "opportunity" to cause infection when the immune system has been impaired.

Perinatal Pertaining to that period of time from shortly before to shortly after birth.

Plasma Liquid portion of the blood that contains the microscopically visible elements of the blood (the red blood cells, white blood cells, and platelets).

Prevalence The number of cases of a disease present in a population at one point in time.

Protocol Explicit detailed plan of an experiment.

Replication The process of producing an exact copy. In the case of HIV, it is the process of viral reproduction within human cells (T-helper lymphocyte).

Retrovirus The group of viruses to which HIV belongs. Retroviruses are characterized by the presence of a special enzyme, reverse transcriptase, which enables them to convert from an RNA to a DNA form.

RNA (ribonucleic acid) A nucleic acid found in living cells that is essential to the transfer of genetic information from DNA and is critical to the production of protein within the cell. RNA may be the primary genetic component of a cell (no

DNA present), such as seen in RNA viruses.

Sensitivity The ability of a test (e.g., ELISA screening test) to identify those who are infected with a virus. Also expressed as the probability that a test result will be positive if infection is present.

Seroconversion The change of a serological test from negative to positive, indicating the development of antibodies in response to infection or vaccination.

Serology The study of immune reactions by the measurement of serum antibody levels toward a particular disease (e.g., the serology of HIV describes the measurement of antibody to HIV).

Serum Clear liquid that separates from blood on clotting and contains specialized blood proteins, such as antibodies.

Specificity The ability of a test (e.g., ELISA screening test) to exclude those who are not infected with a virus. Also expressed as the probability that a test result will be negative if infection is not present.

Syndrome Set of symptoms and/or physical signs that describe the entirety of a disorder. In the case of AIDS, it is not just one disease, physical sign, or symptom, but rather a variety of related disorders that together point toward a common defect in the immune system.

Thrombocytopenia Reduction in the number of blood platelets.

Thrush Infection of the mouth secondary to the yeast Candida.

Virus One of a group of minute infectious agents that are characterized by a lack of independent metabolism and by the ability to replicate only within living host cells.

Western Blot Test used to detect the presence of antibodies to HIV. The Western Blot test is currently the major confirmatory test used to "confirm" the presence of HIV when the ELISA test is positive.